A Sense of Place

A Sense of Place

Teaching Children About the Environment with Picture Books

Daniel A. Kriesberg

Illustrated by
Dorothy Frederick

1999
Teacher Ideas Press
A Division of
Libraries Unlimited, Inc.
Englewood, Colorado

TEACHER IDEAS PRESS
A Division of
Libraries Unlimited, Inc.
P.O. Box 6633
Englewood, CO 80155-6633
1-800-237-6124
www.lu.com/tip

Library of Congress Cataloging-in-Publication Data

Kriesberg, Daniel A.
    A sense of place : teaching children about the environment with picture books / Daniel A. Kriesberg ; illustrated by Dorothy Frederick.
    xxvii, 145 p. 22x28 cm.
    Includes bibliographical references and index.
    ISBN 1-56308-565-8 (softbound)
    1. Environmental sciences--Study and teaching (Elementary)
2. Environmental sciences--Study and teaching (Elementary)--Activity programs. I. Title.
GE70.K75 1999
372.3'57044--dc21
                                      98-54378
                                        CIP

Contents

My third-grade teacher, Mrs. MacFarland, assigned research reports. I do not remember the exact assignment. I do remember cutting Ben Burt's weekly bird-watching column from the newspaper and setting up a bird feeder to watch birds. I was the one doing the research. That is where it all began. I am sure many people can look back and remember a pivotal event in their childhood and thank a teacher for it.

From there, all the elements were in place for me to develop a strong connection to the outdoors. My parents were thrilled that I had an interest. They took me on walks to watch birds. There were trips to a zoo any time we traveled. Just a block from my house was Hookway, a small patch of trees, fields, and a muddy stream. Fifty years ago it was a garbage dump. Then the city grew and the dump was closed. Nature has a way of reclaiming the land if given a chance—the trees returned, and it became my place. I knew the trails, kept a list of every bird I saw, and had names for all the landmarks. There were special places all over. I discovered myself in Hookway.

My adventures took me further as I got older. I backpacked all over the Northeast, southern Utah, and the Sierras. In college, I majored in Environmental Policy and Values. After graduating, I became a naturalist at the Greenkill Outdoor Environmental Education Center. Four years later, I moved on to classroom teaching.

Now I live on Long Island, the last place I thought I would ever live. It has a certain irony for someone so interested in being surrounded by nature. As I have yearned for other places with higher mountains, more trees, and fewer cars, I have also discovered how much nature is right in my own back yard, even in the suburbs. Of course, I still go hiking and backpacking whenever I get the chance. That is not enough. Finding my place here has become essential for my happiness.

These lessons have been developed over 10 years of teaching children at outdoor environmental education centers and in a classroom. As a naturalist, I learned very quickly how important it is for children to have fun and explore the outdoors. A hike was a success when I left with children who had never even been to a forest and returned with the 10 dirty, soaking-wet kids who had just slid down a mountain and played in a stream. I wanted them to fall in love with the woods. Later, we learned facts and figures. I saw it work over and over again, whether the children were from inner-city New York or wealthy Long Island suburbs.

As a classroom teacher, I was afraid I would not be able to teach outdoors. It has taken some time, but I have begun to realize the full potential of outdoor education in the classroom. Classroom teaching has allowed me to integrate environmental education into every subject. Having 10 months instead of a few days allows for a great deal of wonderful teaching opportunities—and a much greater opportunity to see the effects of my teaching.

Becoming a parent has also taught me a great deal about how children learn in the outdoors. How does my three-year-old, Zack, learn so much? By taking risks, exploring everything, getting dirty, and using all his senses. He doesn't always take no for an answer. He can spend 15 minutes playing with a single plant. This intensive study turns the commonplace into a magical source of wonder. There is something new each time we go out. If it works for him, it can work for us.

" Exaltation takes practice."

John Hay

" The first law of environmental education: An experience is worth 10,000 pictures."

Noel McInnis

" In the end, we conserve only what we love. We love only what we understand. We understand only what we are taught."

Babr Dioum Dioum, Senegalese Poet

Acknowledgments

Any project of this kind is not the work of one person. I have been fortunate to work with many wonderful educators over the years. With their help, along with the help of my friends and family, this book was possible. I begin my thanks with my wife, Karen, who has put up with late nights and long rambles as I figured out what to write. My parents, Louis and Lois, and my brother, Joe, have been instrumental as editors, critics, and supporters. I would never have found all these picture books without the help of my school librarian, Chris Weil. The librarians at the Bayville Public Library sent in at least 250 interlibrary loan cards so that I could read every book included here, plus all the ones I didn't put in. Vicki Steiner, Lynn Pena, and Stacey Eno, three wonderful teachers, helped with much of the proofreading. I couldn't have developed a program like this without the support of administrators, like Edward Tronolone, Leatice Green, and JoAnn Grim, who gave me the freedom and the support to go outside and try something new. Thanks go to Nancy and Scott Reichert and everyone else at the Greenkill Outdoor Environmental Education Center, who have shared their ideas with me over the years. I learned many of the activities in this book and more about how to teach at Greenkill than anywhere else.

My thanks also go out to the parents of the students I have worked with for understanding that learning is not limited to the world inside four walls. My oldest friend and backpacking partner, Steve, shared his ecology and editing expertise. Joseph Bruchac took time out of his busy schedule to review the activities related to Native Americans. Jennifer Sahn from the Orion Society helped with the introduction. David Sobel's writing and support provided an important inspiration. Suzanne Barchers at Fulcrum Publishing was instrumental in the development of this idea and in sending it along to Teacher Ideas Press. Thanks also go to Stacey Ennis Chisholm, Susan C. Zernial, and Felicity Tucker, my editors at Teacher Ideas Press. Over the years, I have worked with many children. They taught me that education is more than a one-way street. Finally, I would like to thank my sons, Zack and Scott Walden—they have taught me more about having a sense of place than I ever imagined. This is just the first step in a grand adventure.

Becoming a parent has also taught me a great deal about how children learn in the outdoors. How does my three-year-old, Zack, learn so much? By taking risks, exploring everything, getting dirty, and using all his senses. He doesn't always take no for an answer. He can spend 15 minutes playing with a single plant. This intensive study turns the commonplace into a magical source of wonder. There is something new each time we go out. If it works for him, it can work for us.

"Exaltation takes practice."

John Hay

"The first law of environmental education: An experience is worth 10,000 pictures."

Noel McInnis

"In the end, we conserve only what we love. We love only what we understand. We understand only what we are taught."

Babr Dioum Dioum, Senegalese Poet

 # Introduction

Another idea I had for a title of this book was *Creating a Sense of Place with a Sense of Wonder*. To put it simply, a sense of place is the goal, and a sense of wonder is the method. *Sense* is defined in a variety of ways by *The American Heritage College Dictionary*, two of which fit well: "a capacity to appreciate and understand" and "the ability to think or reason soundly." The most useful definition of *place* is "a bounded area." In the *Journal of Environmental Education*, Matt Sanger defines a sense of place as an "experientially-based intimacy with the natural processes, community, and history of one's place." To all this, I add my definition: A sense of place is knowing the stories of the land where you live and feeling a part of those stories. For too many people, this sense is undeveloped; they do not have this relationship with the place where they live.

A Sense of Place

The place is more than simply a name of a location. It is the people who live there; it is the land, the plants and animals, the water, the air, and the soil. It is the history and the stories that connect everything together. The goal of this book is to increase children's knowledge of natural and human history in their community and also to develop an appreciation for their surroundings. This knowledge and appreciation will lead to a connection and a sense of place. Environmental education is best taught in the place where a child lives. The children's own experiences can be a part of their education.

There is a restlessness and a feeling of disconnectedness running through our society. Children want to belong—they yearn to belong, they want to make a difference—but they feel powerless. They want to be part of the story. Children need, want, and can have a sense of place. We can help them, and at the same time, we can help ourselves find our own sense of place. Edith Cobb, author of *The Ecology of Imagination in Childhood*, has described a child's first place as "a place in which to discover a self."

Without a sense of place, we can not only lose ourselves; we can destroy the place. Other animals aside from human beings have a sense of place. They know how to live where they live. They adapt to the place. Too often, people try to adapt the place to themselves. This practice is destructive and wasteful. It is better to know the place and to live with it. Does it make sense to use scarce water to grow green lawns at the Phoenix Airport instead of celebrating the desert? Where I live, in Bayville, New York, houses are built even closer to the Long Island Sound less than a year after a flood covered half the town.

How do we help children find their sense of place when many of us do not feel connected to where we live? Learning together and rediscovering a sense of wonder is the first and most important step in the process.

A Sense of Wonder

Watch any toddler if you want to see a sense of wonder in action. I have learned more about wonder from my son Zack than from anyone else. Watching him on a hike through the woods is a constant reminder of just what a miracle everything is. He is excited to see the same thing over and over again; he is amazed that it is there each time. We have thrown countless stones into streams—each one has a unique splash. We have checked under logs everywhere, and each worm is worth a look. Zack doesn't mind going to the same place twice because he never knows what he is going to see. He asks questions, he uses all his senses, he wants to be lifted up for closer looks, or he squats down to peer intently. His imagination transforms the same stick into a shovel, a dolphin, a fishing pole, and a tail, all within 10 minutes. To have a sense of wonder, one must come to expect wonder. I expect wonder and I am rarely disappointed. Learning to expect wonder makes exploring exciting.

Even when we realize that there are patterns and some predictability, our sense of wonder does not have to die. In his book *Apology for Wonder*, Sam Keen reminds us that "a mature sense of wonder does not need the constant titillation of the sensational to keep it alive. It is most often called forth by a confrontation with the mysterious depth of meaning at the heart of the familiar."

Wonder has two important aspects that make it essential for gaining a sense of place. Wonder leads to a desire to know more, to gain knowledge and understanding. Second, if we wonder about something, we begin to care about it. Empathy can translate into action. These two factors, knowledge and love, inspire connections to place. Edith Cobb describes one more advantage: "The ability of an adult to look upon the world with wonder is thus a technique and an essential instrument in the work of the poet, the artist, or the creative thinker."

What happens to that toddler with a natural sense of place and wonder? Why does Zack ask me a hundred questions a day? A young child keeps asking and looking because he or she is not sure the same thing will happen twice. As we get older, we think we know it all. Gaining a sense of wonder is admitting to not knowing. As the Zen parable goes, we learn better when we have an empty cup. We need to open our minds as well as our senses and let wonder back in. In her book *The Having of Wonderful Ideas*, Eleanor Duckworth puts it this way: "Knowing the right answer requires no decisions, carries no risks, and makes no demands. It is automatic. It is thoughtless." Too often children want the quick, easy answer. They learn one fact and believe they know it all. There is power in not knowing. It leads to a willingness to learn, to wonder.

Rachel Carson wrote a beautiful book entitled *A Sense of Wonder*. In it, she explains just why this sense is so valuable: "Those who dwell, as scientists or laymen, among the beauties and mysteries of the earth are never alone or weary of life. Whatever the vexations or concerns of their personal lives, their thoughts can find paths that lead to inner contentment and to renewed excitement in living. Those who contemplate the beauty of the earth find reserves of strength that will endure as long as life lasts."

Her wish is my wish: "If I had influence with the good fairy who is supposed to preside over the christening of all children I should ask that her gift to each child in the world be a sense of wonder so indestructible that it would last throughout life, as an unfailing antidote against the boredom and disenchantments of later years."

Contact with Nature

To make Rachel Carson's wish come true, children need direct contact with nature. They need to be outside. They need to explore, get dirty, find stuff—they need to have fun. They need to catch animals and let them go. Sometimes they may even cause a bit of environmental damage. When I worked at Greenkill, I used to take children straight down the Ridge. It was a loose shale slope, and each time down we caused our share of erosion. Yet the kids loved the adventure of sliding and climbing up and down a mountain. The Ridge gave more than a memory, and if anything happened to the Ridge, they would care. I am not advocating cruelty to animals or purposeful environmental destruction, but children need to experience nature hands-on. In his memoir *Thunder Tree: Lessons from an Urban Wildland*, Robert Michael Pyle puts it this way: "There needs to be places that are not kid-proofed." Children need to be able to hold nature in their hands whether it is a rock, flower, or salamander.

The problem is children do not have these opportunities. Kids today average four hours a day in front of the television. Seven out of 10 children say that television is their number one source of information about the environment. About half of these children feel they learn "only a little/practically nothing" in school about the environment. Unless they watch the local news often, they are not learning about the place where they live. Children don't need National Parks; they need empty lots, forgotten woods, patches of trees, and backyards where they can explore and find special places. The problem is that small bits of wild places where kids can explore are disappearing quickly. Houses are squeezed into empty lots. Fences are put up, and malls are built. Every time I see a for sale sign on a patch of woods, my heart breaks. The places are harder to find, and fewer adults are interested or have the desire and knowledge to take children to the wild places and let them dive in. Time is another issue. Children today have much less time. A child's schedule can be packed with this lesson and that lesson. Even playtime is organized. Children do not have a chance to play on their own. Robert Michael Pyle calls this the "extinction of experience," the loss of contact with nature in nature. As the wild places and the time to go visit them become rarer and rarer, children lose experiences that are rightfully theirs. I would add to Rachel Carson's wish one extra thought: All children should have a wild place they can get to on their own. Habitat loss and loss of time are the major causes of the "extinction of experience." When these neighborhood wild areas disappear, an extinction of childhood follows. What can teachers do? We can reintroduce children to their home ground. Two-thirds of the children surveyed reported that they would be interested in working with others to benefit the environment. When these children were presented with a list of 15 activities that might increase interest in environmental issues, the most popular activity by far was "going camping or hiking, or spending time closer to nature." I'll bet your own experience working with children would support these findings. The children are ready for us.

Begin by celebrating the local area. It is close by. It has meaning. The kids already know something about it, and there is much to do and learn nearby. The place where we grow up has a permanent impression on us, both consciously and unconsciously. It is the benchmark that we use to compare to everywhere else, the place that holds memories. It is "native ground," as Scott Russell Sanders calls it. As teachers, we can help; we can give children a gift. The gift we can give is a connection to a place. It is truly a gift worth giving and receiving.

Giving children this chance is simple. The goal of this book is to combine the idea of giving children total freedom to explore the wild with the demands of the curriculum. We need to "re-mystify the city," as Randy Haluza-DeLay wrote in *Green Teacher Magazine*. Nature is not something that exists only out there, someplace else. There is plenty to see and do in any outdoor setting. In order to care about the natural world, we must learn that it is everywhere. The best time to do this is during the elementary school years.

Research has shown that the human brain develops in such a way that there are a variety of skills best learned at certain stages of development. Miss that stage, and it gets much more difficult to learn the skills. Learning a foreign language is a classic example. A young child can learn a second language much easier than an adolescent can. Of course, in most schools, we wait until they are adolescents to teach foreign languages. We are making the same mistake when it comes to environmental education.

The years between seven and 12 are the wonder years for children. These are the years to bond with the environment. Think back; for many of us, those were years of first friendships and a time to play and to develop interests and passions. These years are a window of opportunity when children move out of the family circle and bond with the Earth, before adolescence and all the distractions kick in. Paul Shepard says it beautifully: "A decade, from the beginning of speech to the onset of puberty, is all we have to load the ark." A friend put it another way when referring to his sixth-grade daughter: "I have only a few more months to teach her everything."

Children in the middle grades are old enough to have the skills needed to explore their world and are young enough to have a joy for learning and an enthusiasm for the process. Fantasy is still a powerful teaching tool. It is at this age that a child's "way of knowing is by becoming," to borrow a phrase from Edith Cobb. Or, as Walt Whitman wrote, "A child went forth every day. And the first object he look'd upon, that object he became." Just as children this age have strengths that lend themselves to developing a sense of place, they have limits on their abilities that force us to reconsider how and what we teach.

Remember Jean Piaget and all those educational psychologists we studied as undergraduates? It is worth reminding ourselves of the difficulty children have with abstract thinking. They need to experience more of what they learn. When we move beyond the neighborhood, the learning can become too abstract. Learning must begin with the concrete and then move to the abstract. We cut children off from the most important place in their lives and devalue it by emphasizing other places. They need to build their learning on what they know. We can't teach children about rain forests before they know about oak trees. We can't teach them about holes in the ozone layer before they understand the carbon cycle. This approach does not mean "dumbing down" the content. It means putting the content in a local context before going out further. This does not mean children in the middle grades are not thinkers. A reading of Robert Coles's *The Spiritual Life of Children* will give a glimpse into the serious thought children of all backgrounds give to their spiritual life, nature, and their role in the world.

Teaching About Environmental Issues

Environmental issues are complex. If there were simple answers, there wouldn't be as many problems. There are shades of gray, not black and white. Young children can't be expected to grasp all of the many sides of the argument. It takes a while in everyone's moral development to be able to put oneself in another's shoes and to make decisions based on society interest, not self-interest, and on some other basis of reality.

Focusing on environmental tragedies can scare children, giving them a sense of powerlessness and cutting them off from the natural world. The response to overwhelming problems often is to ask oneself, Why bother doing anything? rather than dedicating efforts to solve the problem. We care for something by learning to love it, not by fearing it. *Beyond Ecophobia: Reclaiming the Heart of Nature Education*, David Sobel writes, "no tragedies until fourth grade." Even then, keep the focus on what Lucy Sprauge Mitchell calls "the here and now." There are plenty of local issues on which to work.

Childhood experiences with nature matter. Edith Cobb studied the lives of 300 geniuses to find common patterns in their lives. Their genius began in "the little-understood prepubertal halcyon, middle age of childhood, approximately from five or six to eleven or twelve . . . when the natural world is experienced in some highly evocative way, producing in the child a sense of some profound continuity with natural processes." In his book *Ecological Identity*, Mitchell Thomashow finds a similar pattern among the environmental activists he has interviewed all over the world. They all remember special childhood places where they were able to bond with the land as key influences in their work as adults.

In a review of the research on environmental sensitivity between 1980 and 1995, Leesa Sward and Tom Marcinkowsi found that childhood experiences do lead to environmentally responsible citizens. They also report that environmental education efforts should focus on local areas and impacts. This doesn't mean everyone will or should become an activist. Being connected to the place can translate into many roles. Some of the experience of developing environmental sensitivity may be outside the scope of a school, but there are ways schools can have an influence by providing knowledge, experience, and exposure to role models.

As teachers, we still have an influence on children of this age. Research supports the fact that children learn from role models with whom they have a warm relationship and who have power in their lives. When there is the perception that the role model gains from the behavior they are trying to instill, there is more of an effect on children. Your pleasure and enthusiasm for learning about the place rubs off. When you get excited about a discovery, the children get excited. When you learn from a mistake, the children learn an important lesson as well. When you respond to a question with "I don't know" and then go and find the answer, they learn more than the fact you dug up. I am asked at least one question per hike that I can't answer.

We are role models whether we like it or not. I ride my bike to school every day. Once I forgot my helmet. At least five students saw me and commented. They pay better attention than we think. Our actions model to children our values. We must practice what we preach.

Participating yourself shows them that you're willing to learn and that learning never stops. It is a powerful statement when children see adults consider the work so important that they do it themselves. It makes the work relevant, real, and practical. You don't have to be an expert naturalist. Identifying every bird and plant is not the goal. You don't even have to love bugs. You do have to be willing to take risks, try something new, and learn together with your students. There is absolutely no problem with saying "I don't know."

Environmental educators are beginning to recognize the power of place in a child's environmental education. In their thought-provoking collection of essays, *The Geography of Childhood: Why Children Need Wild Places*, Gary Paul Nabhan and Stephen Trimble suggest three principles of a place-based program: "Intimate involvement with plants and animals, direct exposure to a variety of wild animals carrying out their routine behaviors in natural habitats, and teaching by community elders (indigenous or otherwise) about their knowledge of local biota."

I would also add Mitchell Thomashow's three principles from his book *Ecological Identity*: highlight the importance of the learner's experience; establish open, cooperative learning spaces; and provide a conceptual vision to a well-rounded, integrated program. These guidelines can help you design a program for your children where you teach.

The problem is that a great deal of the environmental education being done in our schools is not helping children connect to the place where they live. In fact, some of it may be doing more harm than good. Survey your own school. Are children spending more time studying the rain forest and other faraway places? It is easier to study rain forests; there are plenty of prepackaged lesson plans, and no one has to go outside and get dirty. Children can study rain forests at their desks.

Too much of the environmental education in elementary school is spent on learning about the problems in the environment. Although these issues are important, we can't teach them first. Are children learning more about pollution and other environmental issues before they even care about the place where they live? If nature is seen as a place full of problems, poisons, and garbage, why would you want to go out and enjoy it?

This isn't the only problem. Most of the information children learn about the environment comes from television. They are not learning from their teachers or other adults, and they're not learning for themselves from direct contact. I am not saying all television is bad. I credit Mutual of Omaha's *Wild Kingdom* with Marlin Perkins as a major influence on my love for animals. According to a survey by the National Environmental Education and Training Foundation titled "Environmental Attitudes and Behaviors of American Youth," when 71 percent of the children say television is their major source of information, we have to change things.

Science textbooks are written for the mass market. They are general in focus and are geared to the widest possible audience. At the age of the students we are teaching, environmental education should be local in order to be meaningful. Materials should help children connect to their own unique place. Even the photographs in these texts emphasize animals that most children are unlikely to see. Thomas Nelson, in his article "Paradigms and Paradox: Belief Structures in Environmental Education," cites a study by K. S. Wade that reports that professional development in environmental education is dominated by activity-based, nationally produced curricula, which is primarily science-oriented rather than interdisciplinary and is concerned with environmental content rather than educational context.

When it is taught, environmental education is separated from everything else. It is done by specialists on field trips, in special places, or maybe it consists of a few lessons for Earth Day in the spring. This approach sends children a message: Environmental education is only for a chosen few with some sort of special, mysterious talent, when in fact it is for everyone; it must be for everyone.

The other issue is the teachers. Of course, there are many wonderful teachers who are not teaching very much environmental education. Just because a teacher doesn't take children outdoors doesn't make him or her a poor teacher. There are many barriers that prevent teachers from integrating environmental education into their curriculum. They don't have the expertise, they feel there is no place to teach it, there is no time, or they simply do not know what to do. All these barriers are legitimate.

Despite all this, children need to go outdoors to learn about the place where they live. How can one teach children about flowers or insects without going out and looking at some? A teacher in one of my recent environmental education courses told me that she started taking her second graders out each day for a few minutes to write in their weather journals. She had been teaching weather for years and had never taken the children out before. I wondered how many other children learn about weather in school without even being told to look out the window.

This book addresses these concerns and, I hope, will provide some answers. No one has ever said to me, "Dan, take this out of your curriculum." I have only been told to add more of this or more of that. I am not suggesting that place-based environmental education be another subject to squeeze in right after math and before current events. Instead, I suggest place-based environmental education as a way of teaching other subjects. It can be a theme that runs throughout the school year, whether it is reading, writing, science, math, or social studies.

John Elder was only half joking when he suggested that environmental education should be called simply education, "in contrast to the disciplinary compartmentalization and abstraction that often characterize conventional curricula." He goes on to compare interdisciplinary environmental education with an ecotone. An *ecotone* is the ecologist's word for a place where two habitats meet. Because of the diversity of habitat, the diversity of species increases. The connection between two or more subjects will increase the diversity of learning.

Integrating Environmental Education Thoughout the Curriculum

By integrating subjects, children see that learning cannot be classified into neat 45-minute packages of math, science, social studies, or writing. By integrating environmental education into the entire curriculum, you can find the time to teach these activities. It is not another subject; it is another way of teaching each subject. Children will see that learning one subject will help them do better in another. A year-long study teaches children that learning takes time. Patience and hard work are required. Once children are excited about learning, it will carry over to other areas. A nonreader who wants to learn more about pond life will want to read.

Integration not only provides the time; it means the curriculum can have greater depth rather than breadth. To borrow a metaphor from Eleanor Duckworth: When building towers, we do not just put one block on top of another; a tower with a wider base can go higher. Children need time to develop a clear understanding of what they are being taught. Too often, children are exposed to a rapid succession of topics in a race to get through the curriculum. Duckworth explains further, "Exploring ideas can only be good, even if it takes time. Wrong ideas, moreover, can be productive. A lesson learned from a mistake is stronger than the lesson learned without the mistake." A simple example makes the reason for depth clear. If we measure the temperature of two glasses of water that are 100 degrees each and mix them together, the temperature should be 200 degrees if we base our answer on other measuring experiences. Children often make this mistake. They know how to measure but do not know why, when, or whether. The same is true about many other experiences.

David Orr suggests that one cause of our environmental problems is the problem of specialization in one subject. The engineer may be expert enough to solve the engineering problems but does not know enough to understand the consequences of the solution on the environment. We need to begin early so that children see the world as an interrelated web of cause and effect. It can be a little upsetting to learn of the consequences of our action, but it is the only way to eventually solve problems.

Currently, my social studies textbook allows for two lessons on Native Americans, one lesson on the geology of Long Island, and nothing about its natural history in its rush to cover 15,000 years of history. No matter what we are going to teach, we have to select some content and leave out other areas of information. We may as well teach what we select in depth. We need to teach children a love for learning and to give them the skills to learn more in addition to the content. As teachers, it is important to raise questions and to push the limits. Only by going in depth can this be done.

This habit of learning a little bit about many things means that children do not have the experience of learning deeply about a certain topic. They do not have the chance to be experts, which is what we do as adults, or at least hope that we do. A habit of superficial learning leads to an attitude of false knowledge. Children who think they know all the answers have more trouble understanding than children who allow for the possibility that there is more to learn. Children can become knowledgeable; look at all those eight-year-old dinosaur experts.

Integration helps solve the ever-present time problem. A lesson on perimeter and area can be taught outdoors. Mapping the school yard is no longer an isolated lesson but part of a long-term project to learn about the place where students live. Writing can be done with a place-based focus. Even social studies has its place in the outdoors. Keep your eyes open; there are many ways to weave place-based environmental education into what you are already doing. Take a chance and make a change in your teaching practices.

Addressing Diverse Learning Styles and Needs

Much interesting work has been done on how people learn. As we learn more about learning, it is clear that environmental education has a great deal to offer. Many environmental education techniques can be applied to teaching other subjects. The Proster Theory, developed by Leslie Hart, proposes that the brain aggressively tries to make sense of the world. By making learning situations compatible with the brain, more can be learned. The following guidelines are suggested:

More learning takes place in the absence of threat. In threatening situations, older brain functions take over that are not effective for learning.

Encourage basic skills of communication such as oral and written.

Learners need the freedom to manipulate materials in a hands-on manner.

Expose students to reality.

Assess learning through performance, not by answering questions.

Place-based environmental education cannot be integrated only through a curriculum; it also addresses the variety of students in any given population. Children learn in a variety of ways. Each child is unique. Bernice McCarthy's work describes four general types of learners:

Those who learn best by relating to other people.

Those who learn best by watching and listening.

Those who learn best through intellectual understanding.

Those who learn best by doing.

Another approach to the fact that children do not all learn in the same way is Howard Gardner's theory of multiple intelligences. He has defined intelligence as "the human ability to solve problems or to make something that is valued in one or more cultures." The ability must meet other criteria: Is there a particular representation in the brain for the ability? Are there populations that are especially good or especially impaired in an intelligence? Can an evolutionary history of the intelligence be seen in animals other than human beings? Originally, seven intelligences were defined: linguistic, logical-mathematic, spatial, kinesthetic, musical, interpersonal, and intrapersonal. Recently, an eighth intelligence was defined: naturalist. *Naturalist intelligence* refers to the ability to discriminate among living things as well as sensitivity to other features of the natural world. Personally, I'm glad to know that my strength is being recognized.

There is a genetic basis for intelligences, and different people have different strengths. The diversity of place-based education can help children use their strengths as well as develop new ones.

Not every activity covers every learning style or intelligence, but doing a variety of activities gives each learning style a chance and gives children a chance to strengthen other learning styles. The variety of activities in this book makes it possible to reach more students. Keeping that idea in mind will help you reach more of your students.

There are other advantages for our diverse populations. Children with learning issues have the chance to shine in new ways. Skills that are not always used in the traditional classroom setting take on a new importance when exploring the outdoors. There are new ways to achieve success. Reading and writing are not the sole areas of succeeding in class. Finding the coolest-looking insect can do surprising things for self-esteem. Information is not just gathered from reading or listening. In many of the activities, group work allows children with learning issues to contribute.

Sometimes, the achievement is something so subtle it is easy to miss. I once had a student who spent several hours a week with an occupational therapist, getting special help for body control. One day we took a trip to a nearby beach. I was taking groups of children out on a dock to catch glass shrimp. The tide was out, so the ramp angled down at a steep decline. We headed out. I turned to check on the student and saw him hesitate, almost call out for help, then go carefully, watching each step. He did this all by himself. He thought no one was watching. When he got on the dock, I saw a smile that made my day.

Enrichment is another challenge. Place-based environmental education offers a variety of ways to help challenge children in new areas. Opportunities for more in-depth research crop up all the time. An in-depth project is particularly good for high-achieving students who are used to running quickly through their work. They will realize that they do not know it all and that the more one learns, the more there is to learn. Many of the activities can be extended easily into new areas, or motivated children can find their own projects. Many of the projects are open-ended, giving children a chance to go much further if they can.

Because gender issues are less distracting during the middle years, this is an opportunity to expose children to experiences that help break down some of the traditional beliefs about girls and boys. Place-based environmental education appeals to girls who may not always be encouraged to show an interest in science. This approach is an opportunity to encourage girls to get involved in science and bring their perspectives to the experiences. Boys see girls interested in enjoying science. Boys and girls see each other in a fresh light and can be put in groups easily when the activity overshadows the fact that two boys and two girls may actually be in the same group. Indoors, it is easy to rely on the old rules; going outside changes things. It is easy to assume all girls hate bugs until a boy sees a girl pick one out of pond muck. Other girls learn that it is acceptable to be interested. An important note: Girls mature faster; all too quickly their bodies and thoughts change. The window of opportunity for bonding is smaller and needs to be addressed.

Feeling part of the place and being part of something builds self-esteem in a natural and honest way. "One of our first relationships and one of the most sustaining, can be a relationship with the earth one built on trust and understanding, learning to comfort," writes Stephen Trimble.

Becoming an expert, overcoming challenges, learning new skills—these experiences build self-esteem much more than many of the cookie-cutter self-esteem activities ready-made for teachers. The elementary school setting lends itself to place-based environmental education because of its naturally nurturing climate. In a self-contained classroom, teachers have the opportunity for more flexibility and innovation. We are not limited by 45-minute blocks of time, although sometimes we self-impose these limits. For the first time this year, I set up my schedule to have a weekly, two-and-a-half-hour block of science instead of three 45-minute classes. I did the same for social studies. Clean-up time was cut down, transitions were easier, and we spent less time reviewing. We went from one activity to another so easily that I spent much more time on each task. I couldn't believe it took so long to make the change in scheduling. Lessons that are working can go longer; lessons that are not can be ended.

"Our children are losing the land. It doesn't go to work on them anymore. They don't know the stories about what happened at these places. That is why some get into trouble" (said by Ronnis Lupe, 42 White Mountain Apache Tribe). The previous quote could be applied to many groups, not just to the Apaches. What she means is that in the Apache culture and in other indigenous cultures, stories play a key role in educating the child. This comes from Keith H. Basso's work with the Apaches in the village of Cibecue on the Fort Apache Indian Reservation in east-central Arizona. One of his observations was that place-names were very common in the stories. Each name was a sentence unto itself. These place-names were an important part of the stories. Locations all through the reservation are reminders of stories that happened there. These stories teach important lessons, and every time a child passes the spot, it serves as a reminder of the lesson learned. The land reminds children of the stories, and the stories are guides on how to behave. Perhaps we can learn something from these ideas. Instead of storytellers, we have picture books.

Using Children's Books

Picture books are like bringing a storyteller to the class to act as a guide for the experience. Stories have always been the most powerful way to teach children about the natural and human history of the place where they live. For thousands of years, the knowledge of the place was continued orally, through stories. The best teachers were the best storytellers. There are stories that have the power to teach and to connect children to their place.

These books give a voice to the land. We can use them to put into words what we have trouble expressing. Oftentimes, it is easier to read someone else's words than our own when discussing an emotional topic. I am always amazed at the power of reading out loud—at the attention children give to a good story and the way they notice the smallest details in the illustrations.

Many times it is enough to simply read the book and say nothing. I like to trust the book to be strong enough on its own and trust the children to get the point. A great hike would encompass picking five or six books, taking a walk, and simply stopping to read each one and never say another word.

Picture books are powerful at any age because of the themes with which many of them deal. Issues and concepts raised by these books apply to children of all ages. Different children will gain different things from the stories. Even the simplest picture book can have meaning for a sixth grader or even an adult. There is no age limit for picture books. The stories are powerful for adults as well. Many of these books have been published only recently; older children may have missed them the first time around.

These books are too good to miss. The writing can serve as a model for the children's own writing. The best way to learn to write in a certain genre is to read books in that genre. Picture books allow children to read a wider selection, thereby exposing them to more possibilities for that particular genre.

Most of these books can be read in a short amount of time. They are not meant to replace the activity, but they can replace some of the time a teacher spends lecturing or introducing a concept. They can either introduce an activity or be used to wrap it up. Even if the book is set in a different place than your own, the books can serve as models for writing, inspiration, and knowledge. A collection of books can be kept on hand for children to read on their own. I have a special shelf set aside in the classroom for the children to enjoy.

I discovered these books in a number of places: bibliographies, such as science books of the year published by the National Science Teacher's Association; The Orion Society; and *E for the Environment*. I read many back issues of *Booklist* and *School Library Journal*, and most importantly, I simply explored the children's sections of every library close to my house and any bookstore in which I happened to be. I looked for books that told stories that enhanced and complemented the activities. The books selected are written in language that stood out, and I looked for illustrations that could capture and hold a child's attention. There are many books that could have been added. Wonderful new ones keep coming out. Keep your eyes open. I am sure I missed a few good ones. Feel free to make substitutions. I am also sure new ways to use the books will be discovered.

Even if the book is set in a different region of the country than your own, it may still be valuable to read. The book can serve as a model for a writing project or as a guide for investigating your local area. By seeing different places, the children can highlight what makes their own place special and unique as well as see what they have in common.

Many of the authors have several titles listed in the bibliographies. Byrd Baylor has written many books that demonstrate her sense of connection to the Southwest. Joanne Ryder has many wonderful books that bring children into animals' lives. Thomas Locker's paintings would make a wonderful illustrator study. Check the other work of the authors you like. As you discover authors whose work you enjoy, and the children respond by finding more of their books, you can conduct an author study.

This all sounds great, but you may still be wondering, Does it work? Does place-based environmental education make a difference? The answer is yes. Children are motivated, and their parents can see it. The parents are happy when their child is happy and interested in school. As teachers, we must believe that we make a difference. Otherwise, why else would we be doing this? Our effect cannot be measured in a single year. Twenty years later, an adult acts on something he or she learned in elementary school. We need faith and a belief in our method of teaching. Perhaps animals will still become extinct, and oil will still spill, but we can change the lives that will change the world.

Research in Environmental Education

I want to go beyond all the anecdotes and even the common-sense belief that children need to bond with where they live before going out to care for other places. I want to share some of the research. One of the significant changes in many school districts is the growing influence and involvement of parents. On the whole, this is a step in the right direction. As parents begin to question what we do, we have to be prepared. We need to have the confidence in what we are doing; we need to be able to articulate what we are doing and why we do it. We need to educate the parents. Having a rationale and being backed by research to support the way one teaches are instrumental in getting support for the work. Knowing the research and being able to articulate the philosophy behind the way one teaches send a strong message about the kind of educator you are.

Stewart Cohen, in his essay "Children's Environmental Knowledge," cites a number of studies that demonstrate the link between real involvement in nature as an important component in fostering children's ecological understandings. Another important aspect that the research supports is that active participation facilitates scientific- and ecological-based learning.

For children to gain the most out of place-based environmental education, they must go outdoors. Teachers will have to extend their classroom outside of the four walls. This truth is also the biggest stumbling block. It is not that teachers are against teaching about nature; they just may not be comfortable taking children out of the classroom. Going outdoors doesn't have to be scary.

Outdoor Activities—Safety Equipment and Supervision

Safety has to be the number-one issue. Common sense is the best warning system—listen to it. It is also important to impress upon the children that safety is your number-one concern and that the rules you have are in place for that reason. To avoid problems, pre-visit any new area you will be taking the class to. Scout out good places for the group to do activities and learn where the poison ivy, muddy spots, and other hazards are. Be aware of the unique hazards in your local area.

Not all children are comfortable sitting on the ground at first. Pick a spot with places to sit or even bring a piece of cardboard. This will become less and less of an issue as the children become more comfortable. Encourage the children to wear clothes that can get dirty. Warm clothes make a trip much more comfortable; it is worth reminding them.

It is a good idea to check with the nurse before taking everyone out in case there are any medical problems you should know about. Bring a first aid kit. There is nothing worse than a tiny cut becoming a major issue because you do not have a Band-Aid. Take the time to check your supplies because you will not be able to go back and get something left in the classroom. Remind the children to go to the restroom before heading out.

On trips off the school grounds and even on school grounds, bring along another adult or two. Teaching outdoors means giving up some control and being flexible. You may have the perfect lesson planned, but then it pours all day, or no one can find enough leaves. Nature is not always cooperative or predictable, which is a good lesson to learn.

When selecting places for activities or when using the school grounds, watch for distractions such as children playing at recess, sunlight in the children's eyes, or too many acorns on the ground. Make it very clear what your expectations are for each activity. There should be clear boundaries regarding where the children can go and what they can pick up and do. These places are part of the classroom, so expect the same behavior. I usually have to bring my class in early a few times before they get the idea. Of course, there will be more distractions—things happen. A hawk flies over in the middle of your explanation of the water cycle. A spider crawls over someone's leg the moment they get quiet. If you can, use these distractions as teachable moments. Be flexible. It is easy to overplan for any of these outings. Things take longer when the children find something worth looking at that was not on the agenda.

Most of these activities require very few materials and can be done in almost any outdoor setting. Of course, there is field equipment that is useful if it is available: binoculars, nets, field guides, hand lenses, sketch pads, and watercolors. Supplies can be obtained from the children, parent council, school budget, or grants. Ask around—you may be surprised at what you can get. Don't be afraid to ask for buses, equipment, or any other help. The worst they can do is say no.

I encourage parents to join me whenever possible. I want them to see what we are doing. I also take advantage of open house to explain the philosophy and rationale behind the program. I want the parents to understand clearly the academic benefits of place-based environmental education. They always learn something new themselves and spread the word about the value of these experiences. Parents are a great source of support. I can honestly say I have never had a problem with parents about the work we do outside. Through my own experience, parents are thrilled to have their children come home happy and excited about school. They are glad to see children learning and having fun. A Roper survey printed in the July/August 1997 issue of *Environmental Communicator* reports that 96 percent of parents approve of environmental education. That number indicates a good base of support. At open house, I explain the philosophy and plans for the year. The parents offer an opportunity for support and help on trips and expertise. Take the time to explain the plans and to involve the parents. Environmental education is not a gimmick to use instead of teaching basic skills. It puts the skills in context and motivates children to learn. Parents can become your biggest supporters. It is the same with administrators: Keep them informed not only on your trips but on what else you are doing.

How to Use This Book

There are a variety of ways to use this book. It can be used as a bibliography for picture books or for an occasional activity, or it can be the basis of an elementary program that builds upon new experiences and activities in each year. Most likely, the book will be used for something between these two extremes. The book is made to be adapted to each teacher's goals and objectives. No one is going to do everything. It will be important to learn something about your local place.

Each chapter begins with a brief introduction, followed by an annotated bibliography of picture books. Read the book summaries. As you look through them, pick out the ones that will help you strengthen the activities you are doing with your group. The picture books are a great way to introduce a concept or to reinforce the concept. They can be the center of the lesson or an added support.

The third section consists of the activities. The activities vary in length from just a few minutes to major units that take more time. Each chapter includes a variety of activities in addition to having a language arts project, as well as other activities to integrate math and art.

As you design your program, be careful to make sure the hands-on activities have educational merit. Consider what you want the children to know and experience and use an activity that will help to achieve this objective.

Evaluation is important and can take many forms. The content can be evaluated by teacher-made tests. Use a hands-on project so that other aspects can be evaluated by teacher observations. I highly recommend keeping a class journal. Spending five or 10 minutes a day recording some of the goings-on can help you to remember the children's comments and reactions. Many of the activities can also be used as ways to evaluate the children's understanding of the content. In planning your evaluation, think about how you are teaching, and gear the evaluation tools to that. If you are learning to identify plants, give the children an unknown leaf and a guide and create a hands-on test. If they are learning to conduct experiments, evaluate their progress by having them conduct an experiment.

Don't forget to evaluate yourself and the program. Get feedback from the children and parents. Keep a reflective journal. Watch yourself on videotape. Try some pre- and post-activities that show the effect of the activities. A possibility could be a map of the community drawn before and after the lessons. Compare the answers to questions about the community before and after the lessons.

Place-based environmental education is not just tree-hugging fun and games. It can be an integral part of a school curriculum. Place-based environmental education can easily be used to meet many of the national standards being developed for each subject area. Here in New York, all New York State Math, Science, and Technology standards can be addressed from activities in this book, as well as many of the social studies standards being developed.

The number-one rule is to have fun and explore. Children need a chance to find themselves in the outdoors, to explore, and to discover for themselves. Today's children may know a great deal about the environment, but that knowledge comes from television. Children need time to play in wild places. Children must go out and learn directly. It is possible for them to make their own discoveries. Sometimes lectures and rote memorization are the best method, but when it comes to environmental education, learning by self-discovery is the most effective.

Just go: The children cannot *not* get something out of it being outdoors. Helping children find their own sense of place will help you to find yours. In 1949, Aldo Leopold wrote a book entitled *A Sand County Almanac*. It is perhaps the most important book ever written about the environment. His thinking was way ahead of his time. Leopold wrote about the need for a new ethic, one that included the land: "The problems we face are the extension of the social conscience of people to the land." Over the centuries, our ideas of what is protected by our ethics have expanded. He writes, "It is inconceivable to me that an ethical relationship to the land can exist without love, respect, and admiration." Later, in his essay "Conservation Ethic," he notes, "The most serious obstacle is the fact that our education and economic system is headed away from rather than toward an intense consciousness for land." We have to reach a state of harmony between land and human beings. When this harmony is reached, people will care in ways that translate into action.

References

The American Heritage College Dictionary. Boston: Houghton Mifflin, 1993. ISBN 0-395-66917-0.

Basso, Keith H. "Stalking with Stories: Names, Places, and Moral Narratives Among the Western Apache." In *On Nature: Nature, Landscape, and Natural History*, edited by Daniel Halpern, pp. 95-116. San Francisco: North Point, 1986. ISBN 0-86547-283-1.
> Keith Basso's essay is part of a collection of essays from a wide variety of writers. The suggested readings at the back of the book are a great place to extend your own thoughts.

Carson, Rachel. *A Sense of Wonder.* Photographs by William Neill. Berkeley, CA: The Nature Company, 1990.
> If you are only going to read one book from this list, this title is the one. Rachel Carson's immense writing talents work to portray a powerful statement about our sense of wonder. Through her experiences with her nephew Roger, she shares ideas about the importance of a sense of wonder and the magical possibilities of sharing these opportunities with a child.

Checkley, Kathy. "The First Seven and the Eighth." *Educational Leadership* 55 (September 1997): 8.
> The entire issue is devoted to Howard Gardner's theory of multiple intelligences, with a focus on the newly explained naturalist intelligence.

Cobb, Edith. *The Ecology of Imagination in Childhood.* Dallas, TX: Spring Publications, 1977. ISBN 0-88214-360-3.
> An interesting book describing the importance of wonder and a sense of place for developing creativity and genius.

Cohen, Stewart. "Children's Environmental Knowledge." In *Environmental Education at the Early Childhood Level*, edited by Ruth A. Wilson, pp. 19-22. Troy, OH: North American Association for Environmental Education, 1994. ISBN 1-884-008-14-3.
> A collection of essays that covers both the philosophical and research perspective to suggestions for program ideas and activities. For young children.

Coles, Robert. *The Spiritual Life of Children.* Boston: Houghton Mifflin, 1990. ISBN 0-395-55999-5.
> Interviews with children all over the world about their beliefs on God, nature, and their own roles in the world.

Duckworth, Eleanor. *"The Having of Wonderful Ideas" and Other Essays on Teaching and Learning.* New York: Teachers College Press, 1987. ISBN 0-8077-2876-4.
A collection of essays with a strong focus on what is developmentally appropriate for teachers to teach. A strong argument for teaching children in depth about their world.

Environmental Attitudes and Behaviors of American Youth, with an Emphasis on Youth from Disadvantaged Areas. National Environmental Education and Training Foundation. December 1994. http://www.nceet.snre.umich.edu/:801ROPER/TOC.html. (Accessed February 28, 1998.)

Hay, John. "Teaching at the Edge." *Orion Afield* (Winter 1997/1998): 42-43.

Keen, Sam. *Apology to Wonder.* New York: Harper & Row, 1969.
An interesting book about the wonder of wonders.

Knudson, Douglas M., Ted T. Cable, and Larry Beck. *Interpretation of Cultural and Natural Resources.* State College, PA: Venture Publishing, 1995. ISBN 0-910251-70-3.

LaChapelle, Dolores. *Sacred Land, Sacred Sex Rapture of the Deep. Concerning Deep Ecology and Celebrating Life.* Silverton, CO: Finn Hill Arts, 1988. ISBN 0-917270-05-3.
A wide-ranging book that will help with a further understanding of deep ecology.

Leopold, Aldo. *A Sand County Almanac.* New York: Ballantine Books, 1968.
One of the most important and beautiful books about nature. Aldo Leopold was truly ahead of his time (the book was first written in 1949). The first half is a year-long diary of the world around his farm in Wisconsin. It is a tribute to the wonder of the natural world that surrounds us all. The second set of essays explain his view of a new land ethic. Reading this book will change the way you look at the place in which you live and the land on which you live. If only this was required reading for every elected official!

Minuchin, Patricia P. *The Middle Years of Childhood.* Monterey, CA: Brooks/Cole, 1977. ISBN 0-8185-0136-3.
A good reference on child development.

Mitchell, Lucy Sprauge. *Young Geographers.* New York: Bank Street College of Education, 1990.
A short but powerful reminder of how important it is to teach geography based on the local area.

Nabhan, Gary Paul, and Stephen Trimble. *The Geography of Childhood: Why Children Need Wild Places.* Boston: Beacon Press, 1994. ISBN 0-8070-8254-3.
A collection of thought-provoking and wonderful essays by two of our country's better writers/naturalists. The essays cover a range of issues regarding children and nature, from gender bias to the kinds of places they need. The research, anecdotes, and examples they share will motivate your own work and provide you with important background information. It is a true pleasure to read.

National Science Standards. Washington, DC: National Academy Press, 1996.

Nelson, Thomas G. "Paradigms and Paradox: Belief Structures in Environmental Education." In *Environmental Education for the Next Generation. Selected Papers from the Twenty-fifth Annual Conference of the North American Association for Environmental Education*, edited by Robert Abrams, pp. 257-260. Troy, OH: North American Association for Environmental Education, 1996.

Orr, David W. *Ecological Literacy.* Albany, NY: State University of New York Press, 1992. ISBN 0-7914-0874-4.
> An interesting discussion of what we need to know about the environment and how to teach people about it.

Pyle, Robert Michael. *Thunder Tree: Lessons from an Urban Wildland.* Boston: Houghton Mifflin, 1993.
> Robert Michael Pyle writes about his childhood and shows just how important it is for children to have places to explore.

"Roper Survey" *Environmental Communicator* July/August 1997: 9.

Sanders, Scott Russell. *Staying Put: Making a Home in a Restless World.* Boston: Beacon Press, 1993. ISBN 0-8070-6341-X.
> A collection of essays on home and place. Scott Russell Sanders's childhood experiences show their influence throughout his writing.

Sanger, Matt. "Sense of Place and Education." *Journal of Environmental Education* 29 (1997): 4.

Shepard, Paul. *Traces of an Omnivore.* Washington, DC: Island Press, 1996. ISBN 1-55963-431-6.
> The essays "Ark of the Mind" and "Place in American Culture" are important reading for anyone interested in studying place-based environmental education in depth.

Sobel, David. *Beyond Ecophobia: Reclaiming the Heart of Nature Education.* Great Barrington, MA: Orion Society, 1996. ISBN 0-913098-50-7.
> In less than 50 pages, David Sobel writes a compelling argument for a new focus in teaching children about nature. This wonderful little book explains not only the problems with environmental education based on environmental problems but also offers ideas for an alternative. David Sobel's book will provide you with background and an explanation of why environmental education for young children should be focused on the here and now.

Standards for the English Language Arts. Urbana, IL: International Reading Association and National Council of Teachers of English, 1996.

Sward, Leesa, and Tom Marcinkowski. "Environmental Education for the Next Generation." Selected papers from the Twenty-Fifth Annual Conference of the North American Association for Environmental Education, p. 310. Edited by Robert Abrams. Troy, OH: North American Association for Environmental Education, 1997.

Thomashow, Mitchell. *Ecological Identity: Becoming a Reflective Environmentalist.* Cambridge, MA: MIT Press, 1996. ISBN 0-262-70063-8.
> A book guaranteed to make you think about one's work in environmental education. Mitchell Thomashow touches on issues both professionally and personally that will make one be more connected and a better educator.

Winkler, Robert. "Wildlife Participation Is Holding Steady." *The New York Times* 8 (February 1998).

Young, Bill. "Children's Literature in Middle and Secondary Classrooms." Dakota Writing Project, 1997. http://www.usd.edu/engl/young97ar1.html. (Accessed February 28, 1998.)

Chapter One
The Wonder of the Place

"Stay together. Learn the flowers. Go light."

Gary Snyder

"Wonder is the beginning of wisdom."

Greek Proverb

"My parents taught me this—to gasp, and feel lucky. They gave me the gift of making mountains out of nature's exquisite molehills."

Barbara Kingsolver

"Come forth into the light of things, Let Nature be your Teacher."

William Wordsworth

"Talk of mysteries! Think of our life in nature, rocks, trees, wind on our cheeks! the solid earth! the actual world! the common sense! Contact! Contact!"

Henry David Thoreau

"We always enter the story of a place through the narrative of our individual lives."

John Elder

"Knowledge becomes understanding when it is coupled with feeling."

Alexander Lowen

"To see a world in a grain of sand And a heaven in a whole flower. Hold infinity in the palm of your hand. An eternity in an hour."

William Blake

"The beauty of this place is becoming part of me."

Everett Ruess

"Beauty before me I walk
Beauty behind me I walk
Beauty above me I walk
Beauty below me I walk
Beauty all about me I walk
In beauty all is made whole
In beauty all is restored."

Traditional Navaho Prayer

"That the sky is brighter than the earth means little unless the earth itself is appreciated and enjoyed."

Helen Keller

"This was the gift I really wanted to give my children, for what good are straight teeth and trumpet lessons to a person who cannot see the grandeur that the world is charged with."

Katherine Patterson

"Our job is to act like magnifying glasses, to enlarge what is too small for others to see, and bring into focus those things that are too large."

Barbara LaCorte

"The objective is to teach the student to see the land, to understand what he sees, and enjoy what he understands."

Aldo Leopold

"The lasting pleasures of contact with the natural world are not preserved for scientists but are available to anyone who will place himself under the influence of earth, sea, and sky and their amazing life."

Rachel Carson

"You learn that if you sit in the woods and wait, something happens."

Henry David Thoreau

These people say it better then I ever could. Our connection to the natural world must begin where we live. These activities serve as an introduction to place. They are a way to get things started. Choosing some of the lessons will help your students begin to find their place and sense of wonder. They will also help you find yours.

Books to Use

Asch, Frank. *The Earth and I*. San Diego, CA: Harcourt Brace Jovanovich, 1994. ISBN 0-15-200443-2. Inspired by children around the country who completed the phrase: "The Earth and I . . ." Frank Asch's book tells the story of the special relationship a child can have with the Earth. The paintings playfully and beautifully illustrate how a child can dance, sing, and play with the Earth. Asch shows how the Earth and the child both benefit by listening to each other, helping each other, and playing with each other. This book is a great way to help students begin to think about their relationship with the Earth.

Baylor, Byrd. *The Best Town in the World*. Illustrated by Ronald Himler. New York: Charles Scribner's Sons, 1982. ISBN 0-684-18035-9. A child shares the wonders of the town in which his father grew up. The flowers were more beautiful, the people were nicer, the swimming was better: Everything that was important was the best.

Baylor, Byrd. *The Desert Is Theirs*. Illustrated by Peter Parnall. New York: Charles Scribner's Sons, 1975. This Caldecott Honor Book shows us that even places with harsh environments are places in which people live and are places people love. In the desert, people know the beauty in lonely canyons, cactus, and lizards. They learn from the animals how to make a home in the desert. Byrd Baylor captures their love in this book. This book celebrates the desert and is a wonderful model for a class book. Try rewriting the words of the book to fit the place you live.

Baylor, Byrd. *I'm in Charge of Celebrations*. Illustrated by Peter Parnall. New York: Charles Scribner's Sons, 1986. ISBN 0-684-18579-2. In the desert, a girl describes some of the amazing things she has seen through her explorations. She does not limit her celebrations to the traditional holidays. She remembers these events by celebrating them each year. One of her celebrations is Green Cloud Day, when she saw a green cloud that looked like a parrot. Dust Devil Day celebrates when she saw bunches of dust devils from the back of the truck. By recording these events in her journal, she makes them special. Children can start to record their own celebrations.

Baylor, Byrd. *Your Own Best Secret Place*. Illustrated by Peter Parnall. New York: Charles Scribner's Sons, 1979. ISBN 0-684-16111-7. In an old cottonwood tree, a girl finds the secret hiding place of William Cottonwood. The discovery reminds her of other secret places she has found. The suggestions at the end for finding secret places will help inspire children to find their own.

Borden, Louise. *The Watching Game*. Illustrated by Teri Weidner. New York: Scholastic, 1991. ISBN 0-590-43600-7. The narrator of this story tells us about her Nana's house and what happens when all the cousins visit. Through all the seasons they come and sled, catch fireflies, and carve pumpkins. Through it all the fox watches them and they watch the fox; it is the watching game.

Bouchard, David. *If You're Not from the Prairie . . . .* Illustrated by Henry Ripplinger. New York: Atheneum Books for Young Readers, 1995. ISBN 0-689-80103-3. An absolutely stunning book with powerful words and lush paintings. Each page begins with "If you're not from the prairie you don't know." The book goes on to describe prairie sun, cold, wind, snow, and more. The end tells it all. "If you're not from the prairie, you don't know me. You just can't know me." The book tells of a place and makes a perfect model for children to write their own versions.

Buchanan, Ken. *This House Is Made of Mud*. Illustrated by Libba Tracy. Flagstaff, AZ: Northland, 1991. ISBN 0-87358-518-6. The story of one family's adobe house in the Southwestern desert. Built of mud and straw, the family shares the house with birds, lizards, and other animals. The words show how a house can be part of a larger place. The narrator reminds us that all of our surroundings is our home. "The house has a yard. It is round too. We call it the desert." Libba Tracy's watercolors bring alive all the visitors to the house.

Bunting, Eve. *Secret Place*. Illustrated by Ted Rand. New York: Clarion Books, 1996. ISBN 0-395-64367-8. Even in a city, there can be secret places where nature can be seen. A young boy discovers a place where birds live and ducks have ducklings. He shares this place with his father and just a few other people. He even gets to go there at night. Just one of many Eve Bunting books that reminds us that wonder is everywhere.

Burns, Marilyn. *The Greedy Triangle*. Illustrated by Gordon Silveria. New York: Scholastic, 1994. ISBN 0-590-48992-5. At first, the triangle is very happy with all that it can do. Yet after a while it wants more sides. As a square there are new ways to keep busy, but then he wants five sides, then six, and so on. With each additional side, the triangle can do more and be more. Things get a little out of control before he goes back to being a triangle. A great way to get kids to look for shapes all around them.

Chall, Marsha Wilson. *Up North at the Cabin*. Illustrated by Steven Johnson. New York: Lothrop, Lee & Shepard, 1992. ISBN 0-688-09732-4. A young girl describes all the wonderful things she does in the summer at her family's cabin. Her account is not simply a list of each activity. It shows her personal connection to the place. A reminder that we can have special places all over.

Cherry, Lynne. *The Armadillo from Amarillo*. San Diego, CA: Harcourt Brace Jovanovich, 1994. ISBN 0-15-200359-2. Aside from having a great title, *The Armadillo from Amarillo* is a wonderful book to use for helping inspire children's curiosity about the place where they live. An armadillo named Sasparillo decides to see what is out there. Off he goes across Texas, encountering a variety of habitats and historical places. Eventually, Sasparillo joins with an eagle and a space shuttle to go further and see how his place fits in with the world. All along, he sends postcards to his cousin Brillo in the Philadelphia Zoo. The illustrations by the author are full of detail and possibilities for discussion.

Clifton, Lucille. *The Boy Who Didn't Believe in Spring*. Illustrated by Brinton Turkle. New York: E. P. Dutton, 1973. ISBN 0-525-27145-7. Tony and King Shabazz live in the city. Winter is over, but there is no sign of spring. It takes a while, but they find flowers and bird nests even in the city.

Couture, Christin. *A Walk in the Woods*. New York: Farrar, Straus & Giroux, 1993. Nine children go off on a walk through the woods. They see plenty of interesting plants and animals. Even though the illustrations are filled with much more than one would see on a hike, they are matched with a field guide in the back. Children can try to find as many of the animals and plants as they can in the illustrations.

Cunningham, David. *Nightfall, Country Lake*. Morton Grove, IL: Albert Whitman, 1995. ISBN 0-8075-5624-6. Elegant pastels illustrate this short book about a boy sitting on a country lake at sunset. It is a wonderful inspiration for a silent sit.

Devall, Bill, and George Sessions. *Deep Ecology: Living As If Nature Mattered*. Salt Lake City, UT: Gibbs Smith, 1985. ISBN 0-87905-247-3.

Fanelli, Sara. *My Map Book*. New York: HarperCollins, 1995. ISBN 0-06-0264-55-1. *My Map Book* takes the idea of maps a step further. There is a map of the author's family, a map of her favorite foods, a map of her day, and a map of her bedroom, among others. Each map is brightly colored and labeled with the highlights of each place. These maps will help children look at their world in a different way and give them ideas for their own maps.

Feldman, Judy. *The Alphabet in Nature*. Chicago: Childrens Press, 1991. ISBN 0-516-05102-4. Photographs of various natural objects that spell out the letters of the alphabet. There is a tree for N and a hummingbird for F, among others.

Feldman, Judy. *Shapes in Nature*. Chicago: Childrens Press, 1991. ISBN 0-516-05102-4. A collection of photographs of natural objects in a variety of shapes. There is a mountain in the shape of a triangle and a heart-shaped sponge, among many others.

Fleming, Virginia. *Be Good to Eddie Lee*. Illustrated by Floyd Copper. New York: Philomel, 1993. ISBN 0-399-21993-5. An absolutely beautiful book about the relationship between Eddie Lee, a young boy with Down's syndrome, and a girl named Christy. When Christy and another neighborhood boy run off to try to get rid of Eddie Lee, he follows them anyway. Eddie Lee ends up being the only one who can find what they are looking for. He shows Christy his secret place with waterlilies and frogs. Later, while looking at reflections in the water, he teaches Christy what really counts. A special book for the beginning of the year or anytime.

Florian, Douglas. *Nature Walk*. New York: Greenwillow Books, 1989. ISBN 0-688-08266-1. The perfect introduction to a walk in the woods. *Nature Walk* will prime a child's observation skills and prepare him or her for an adventure. The crayon drawings will inspire a child's artwork, and the simple text will provide ideas of what to look for on a hike.

Garland, Trudi Hammel. *Fascinating Fibonaccis: Mystery and Magic in Numbers*. Palo Alto, CA: Dale Seymour Publications, 1987. ISBN 0-86651-343-4. An comprehensible explanation of the Fibonacci pattern. There is a whole chapter on finding the pattern in natural objects.

George, Jean Craighead. *To Climb a Waterfall*. Illustrated by Thomas Locker. New York: Philomel, 1995. ISBN 0-399-22673-7. Jean Craighead George's book combines her talents for nature writing with Thomas Locker's stunning painting to tell the story of a young girl's climb to the top of the waterfall. We learn just how to climb a waterfall and what we learn along the way. The text refers to stream animal adaptations and to an artist and writer she sees along the way. In the end, the experience becomes a part of you.

Goffstein, M. B. *A Writer*. New York: Harper & Row, 1984. ISBN 0-06-22142-9. This small but elegant book beautifully describes what it means to be a writer. Comparing a writer to a gardener, the book explains how one must plant, grow, and nurture a seed or an idea, "for a writer always studies, looks and listens." Soft watercolors add beauty to this simple but powerful book.

Hartman, Gail. *As the Crow Flies: A First Book of Maps*. Illustrated by Harvey Stevenson. New York: Bradbury Press, 1991. An eagle, a rabbit, a crow, a horse, and a seagull travel a wide range in the course of the day. This book of maps follows each animal's adventures through mountains, farms, cities, and the ocean. Children will enjoy seeing the maps of the animals' lives and will get ideas for creating their own maps.

Hartman, Gail. *As the Roadrunner Runs: A First Book of Maps*. Illustrated by Cathy Bobak. New York: Bradbury Press, 1994. ISBN 0-02-743092-8. Using the Southwest as a setting, Gail Hartman describes the movements of a variety of desert animals. Each animal has its own map of its place. There is even a map of where the wind goes.

Hauk, Charlotte. *Secret Places*. Illustrated by Lindsay Barrett George. New York: Greenwillow Books, 1993. ISBN 0-88-11669-8. This book is a series of poems about secret places in children's lives. The secret places can be bedrooms, blankets on a porch, or hideouts in a tree. The variety of poems and places will help children find their own secret places.

Henderson, Kathy. *A Year in the City*. Illustrated by Paul Howard. Cambridge, MA: Candlewick Press, 1996. ISBN 1-56402-872-0. Each month has its own poem that wonderfully describes the season. Not all the images are of natural scenes, but the book is a great model for a nature calendar and is a reminder that even in the city the natural cycle of the year is very much evident.

Hines, Anna Grossnickle. *Sky All Around*. New York: Clarion Books, 1989. ISBN 0-89919-801-5. The wonders of nature do not end when the sun goes down. A father and daughter climb to the top of a nearby hill and watch the stars come out. They find their own shapes in the sky and make up stories about the constellations.

Hines, Anna Grossnickle. *What Joe Saw*. New York: Greenwillow Books, 1994. ISBN 0-688-13123-9. It is time for a nature walk to a park at Joe's preschool. Always at the end of the line, slower than everybody else, Joe ends up seeing much more than anyone else. The other children tease him until they realize how much they are missing.

Johnson, Steven. *Alphabet City*. New York: Viking, 1995. ISBN 0-670-85631-2. This book is a winner of the Caldecott Honor Book for illustrations. A wordless ABC book, it contains paintings of objects in the city that look like a letter in the alphabet. There is an introduction explaining the criteria for counting an object as a letter. A good model for an alphabet scavenger hunt.

Jonas, Ann. *The Trek*. New York: Greenwillow Books, 1985. A young girl is old enough to walk to school on her own. Along the way she sees all sorts of wild animals in the trees, buildings, stairs, and stores. The animals are not all native to the United States, but it is a fun book that reminds children to use their imagination and to pay attention. Some of the animals are quite a challenge to find in the illustrations.

Krudop, Walter Lyon. *Blue Claws*. New York: Atheneum, 1993. ISBN 0-689-31787-5. During his first trip alone with his grandpa, a boy goes fishing for blue crabs. The book isn't as simple as that. It is a wonderful example of a child and an adult together in the outdoors. After catching and eating the crabs, they sit down to watch the rain and listen to the bulrushes in the salt marsh. This is also a good book for introducing the idea of an elder.

Krupinski, Loretta. *A New England Scrapbook: A Journey Through Poetry, Prose, and Pictures*. New York: HarperCollins, 1994. ISBN 0-06-022950-0. This book is a wonderful and unique account of New England. It also is a great model for a way for children to write a class book about the place where they live. Each page begins with a statement about what New England is. For example, "New England is Fog." Krupinski includes a poem about fog, one of her beautiful paintings, and some background on New England fog. Children could come up with their own list of what their place is and combine it with their illustration and poetry they find about the place or write their own.

Lasky, Kathleen. *Pond Year*. Illustrated by Mike Bostock. Cambridge, MA: Candlewick Press, 1995. ISBN 1-56402-187-4. Two girls share a pond and their adventures through the year. This book is a perfect example of the wonder children enjoy when given the opportunity to play in a natural setting. The girls play in the muck, catch crayfish, and wait for the mysterious muskrat.

Lionni, Leo. *On My Beach There Are Many Pebbles*. New York: Mulberry Books, 1961. A great way to start an exploration of a place with many rocks. With detailed black-and-white drawings, Lionni reminds us that pebbles, like clouds, can have all sorts of shapes and patterns that look like animals, letters, people, and more.

LoManaco, Palmyra. *Night Letters*. Illustrated by Normand Chartier. New York: Dutton Children's Books, 1996. ISBN 0-525-45387-3. An absolutely wonderful book for introducing journal writing. Every evening Lily takes a walk with her notebook to write down what the plants and animals in her backyard tell her about their day. She reads the ant tracks that tell her "Dear Lily, my children and I picnicked on bread crumbs and sesame seeds that you dropped from your lunch. Thank you. Very truly yours, the Ant Family." The old sycamore tree tells her the most. This book will inspire journal entries.

MacLachlan, Patricia. *All the Places to Love*. Illustrated by Mike Wimmer. New York: HarperCollins, 1994. ISBN 0-06-021098-2. The connection to place of a young boy named Eli is lovingly described in a story of his family farm. Each member of the family has a special place on the farm. They pass their love on to Eli. Eli shares with the reader his family's favorite places and the beauty that surrounds them. When his sister is born, he carries on the family tradition of sharing all the places to love. Mike Wimmer's illustrations recreate the beauty of farm life.

Magnus, Erica. *My Secret Place*. New York: Lothrop, Lee & Shepard, 1994. ISBN 0-688- 11859-3. Magnus reminds us that every child should have his or her own secret place to let the imagination run wild. With his bear and his imagination, a boy grows to a giant size and shrinks to the size of tiny ants. Even rain doesn't ruin his adventure.

Mason, Jane B. *River Day*. Illustrated by Henri Sorensen. New York: Macmillan, 1994. ISBN 0-02-762869-8. Alex goes on a special canoe trip with her grandfather. Last time they didn't see the eagle, but this time Grandpa feels the time is right. Along the way they see so much else that no matter what, they have captured the magic of a day on the river. Just as they turn to leave, an eagle dives down and snatches a fish.

McFarlane, Sheryl. *Jessie's Island*. Illustrated by Sheena Lott. Custer, WA: Orca Books, 1992. ISBN 0-920501-76-1. Jessie gets a letter from her cousin who can't understand how she can have any fun on an island in the middle of nowhere. Jessie writes back explaining all the wonders of the place where she spends her summers. The letter format is a good model for the children to use as a journal entry or an actual letter to a friend or relative about the place in which they live.

McMillan, Bruce. Counting Wildflowers. New York: Lothrop, Lee & Shepard, 1986. ISBN 0-688-02859-4. McMillan uses his photographs to create a picture book of flowers that counts the numbers 1-20. A good inspiration for a variety of counting books.

Moss, Marissa. *Amelia's Notebook*. New York: Scholastic, 1995. ISBN 0-590-10794-1. Amelia's journal is filled with her life and all its aspects as she moves to a new house and a new school. The journal is filled with all the possibility a journal has for art, pasting gin souvenirs, complaining, and recording life. This is a good book to show children and to make available for the ones who may need some ideas. It is part of a continuing series.

Murphy, Jim. *Into the Deep Forest with Henry David Thoreau*. Illustrated by Kate Kiesler. New York: Clarion Books, 1995. ISBN 0-395-60522-9. Combining elegant illustration and plenty of quotes, Jim Murphy's biography of Thoreau focuses on his three trips to Maine. The opening chapter provides some background on Thoreau's life. By focusing on one area of his life, the author provides the reader with a much better sense of the type of person he was and his philosophy of life. The journal excerpts are wonderful models.

Owens, Mary Beth. *A Caribou Alphabet*. Brunswick, ME: Dog Ear Press, 1988. ISBN 0-937966-25-8. Written in conjunction with the Maine Caribou Transplant Project, this ABC book focuses on one animal. Each letter is represented by a fact about the caribou's life.

Parnall, Peter. *Quiet*. New York: Morrow Junior Books, 1989. A boy lays down to rest quietly on the grass in the forest. In the quiet, he is visited by chickadees, ravens, and chipmunks. He listens to the sounds of the animals, wind, and water. Sitting quietly, he becomes part of the place. Parnall's unique illustration style will capture any child's attention.

Powell, Consie. *A Bold Carnivore: An Alphabet of Predators*. Niwot, CO: Roberts Rinehart, 1995. ISBN 1-57098-023-3. An ABC book focused on predators. Each animal shown is described with a short poem that tells the reader about the animal.

Radin, Ruth Yaffe. *High in the Mountains*. Illustrated by Ed Young. New York: Macmillan, 1989. ISBN 0-02-775650-5. A young girl tells the story of her grandfather's home in the mountains. The words are beautiful, and the illustrations are unique. A great book to read before using watercolors on a walk.

Ray, Mary Lyn. *A Rumbly Tumbly Glittery Gritty Place*. Illustrated by Douglas Florian. San Diego, CA: Harcourt Brace Jovanovich, 1993. ISBN 0-15-292861-8. Only a child could see the wonders in a gravel pit, but that is what this story is about. This child can even see past the gravel pit to a time when deer come back again. A truly wonderful book.

Ryder, Joanne. *The Goodbye Walk*. Illustrated by Deborah Haeffele. New York: Lodestar, 1993. ISBN 0-525-67405-5. At the end of her summer vacation, a girl takes a "Goodbye Walk" through her special places. Readers learn directly from the text that a goodbye walk means capturing memories, seeing new wonders, and making connections. Ryder writes some wonderful and unique phrases to describe what the young girl sees that are good examples for children to read.

Ryder, Joanne. *My Father's Hands*. Illustrated by Mark Graham. New York: Morrow Junior Books, 1994. ISBN 0-688-09189-X. There are more wonders than a young girl imagines in her father's hands. In their garden he shows her worms, snails, and beautiful insects. She makes friends with a praying mantis before giving it back to the garden. Mark Graham's paintings capture the wonder in a child's eye.

Ryder, Joanne. *Step into the Night*. Illustrated by Dennis Nolan. New York: Four Winds Press, 1988. ISBN 0-02-777951-3. This book captures the wonder and mystery of a night walk. Ryder shows us that if we blend in quietly with the night and become part of a tree, part of the night, we can become the creatures of the night. The reader becomes a bullfrog, a lightning bug, a mole, a spider, and other creatures of the night. There are special sounds and sights if we go out after dark.

Shannon, George. *Climbing Kansas Mountains*. Illustrated by Thomas B. Allen. New York: Bradbury Press, 1993. ISBN 0-02-782181-1. It is hot out in Kansas, really hot. Even the illustrations in this book feel hot, hazy, and humid. Sam is bored until his father tells him to get ready to climb a Kansas mountain. Sam is confused until he learns the plan. His father is going to take him to the top of a grain silo: a "Kansas mountain." There he can see all across the land. There is another tie-in. Sam observes a pattern between the land and his kitchen table, a reminder to be on the lookout for patterns everywhere.

Skofield, James. *All Wet! All Wet!* Illustrated by Diane Stanley. New York: Harper & Row, 1984. A rainy day is no reason to stay inside. With boots and an umbrella, a young boy starts off on a walk around a pond. He sees all sorts of animals and plants. The book portrays that there is a special sound and feel to being out in the rain. There is wonder to experience in all weather.

Soya, Kiyoshi. *A House of Leaves*. Illustrated by Akiko Hayashi. New York: Philomel, 1986. ISBN 0-399-21422-4. Sarah is out playing in her yard when rain begins to fall. She finds a hiding spot in the bushes. When she sits very still, a variety of insects join her in the hiding place.

Stevens, Carla. *A Book of Your Own: Keeping a Diary or Journal*. New York: Clarion Books, 1993. ISBN 0-89919-256-4. This book can provide you with background information on journal writing to share with the children. It also has excerpts from a variety of journals written by children and adults—some famous and others not. The excerpts are helpful examples to show what a journal is all about.

Sweeney, Joan. *Me on the Map*. Illustrated by Annette Cable. New York: Crown, 1996. ISBN 0-517-70095-6. A simple book that begins with a map of a young girl's bedroom. The map expands to cover her house, street, town, state, and onward to the world and back again. It is a good introduction to the important but basic idea of where one lives as a part of a larger place.

Thaxter, Celia. *Celia's Island Journal*. Adapted and illustrated by Loretta Krupinski. Boston: Little, Brown, 1992. ISBN 0-316-83921-3. On September 5, 1839, Celia Thaxter went to live on an isolated island off the coast of New Hampshire. She was only five. Over the years she kept a remarkable journal of the experience. Loretta Krupinksi has adapted her journal for children. The book is not only a great example of journal writing but a demonstration of finding the wonders of nature.

Thoreau, Henry David. *Walden*. Text selected by Steve Lowe. Illustrated by Robert Sabuda. New York: Philomel, 1990. ISBN 0-399-22153-0. Anyone interested in developing a sense of place should read Thoreau. For adults, the essay "Walking" is a good place to start. For children, this book is perfect. The book includes some biographical information and selections from his most important work. His words lead us down the right trail.

Voce, Louise. *Over in the Meadow*. Cambridge, MA: Candlewick Press, 1994. ISBN 1-56402-428-8. A traditional counting rhyme matched with fun-loving watercolors. "Over in the meadow," there are many animals to count and meet.

Wright, Virginia Frierson. *A Desert Scrapbook*. New York: Simon & Schuster, 1996. ISBN 0-689-80678-7. A loving description of the Sonoran Desert in the form of a field journal. There are field notes, sketches, and pictures of items pasted in. This is a great model for journal writing as a wonderful way to learn about a habitat.

Yolen, Jane. *All in the Woodland Early*. Illustrated by Jane Breskin Zalben. Cleveland, OH: Collins, 1979. ISBN 0-529-05508-2. A story and song about a walk through the woods and seeing all the animals from A to Z.

Ziefert, Harriet. *Sarah's Questions*. Illustrated by Susan Bonners. New York: Lothrop, Lee & Shepard, 1984. Another good book for inspiring journal entries. Sarah and her mother take a walk through their neighborhood playing "I Spy" (a good game to play on a hike). On the way home, Sarah is full of questions about the animals and other things they see. A whole walk can be patterned after this book.

Activities

Taking a Nature Walk

Simply taking a walk outdoors is a way to introduce children to the place in which they live. Many of the activities in this book can be done simply by walking out the classroom door and on to the schoolyard. Yet there is even more opportunity if you simply take children for a walk in the outdoors off the school grounds. Expert knowledge is not the most important requirement. Children are very good at finding things. A nature walk can be used to teach a variety of concepts or simply as a free exploration. The walk can include a combination of activities and occasional stops to point out items of interest.

The best way to influence your students is by being a model. It is not what you say, it is what you do. If a picture speaks a thousand words, then an action speaks a million. If you get excited, children will follow suit. If you model love, wonder, and concern for nature, children will notice. Children learn a lot when you sit quietly and watch a bird or even when you say, "Wow, look at that."

The walk can be through the school yard, down the street, to a local park, in an empty lot or local preserve, or even in a cemetery. A nature walk is simple. All you have to do is take a walk with your class, stop every once in a while, and show them something of interest. What you show them depends on your objectives. Optimally, you will be able to take regular walks and make outdoor experiences a ritual.

Take the following steps to plan your hike. Pick a route and remember children walk slowly with the few exceptions who always want to run ahead. Do not be overambitious the first time. Walk the route and pick out five to 10 spots that demonstrate an aspect of nature and the outdoors that you want to teach your class. Be flexible enough to allow for "teachable moments." You never know what the group will find or see that will provide you with a chance to teach.

On the hike there are a couple things to keep in mind. Be sure to gather your class around so that everyone can hear you and see what you are showing them. Avoid places with distractions. Position the children so the sun is not shining in their eyes. Stand in the middle of the group so everyone can hear you. Be very clear about your expectations. It is good to have another adult bring up the rear while you stay in front. Try to keep the group together; think safety.

This is a sample of a typical walk I go on in the beginning of the year. Other walks may have a more specific theme, such as using our senses or animal adaptations. On some walks, I simply read stories along the way or do activities. Usually I include some stops to explain something interesting about local plants, animals, or natural features and time to write in journals, sketch, and observe. Each walk includes one or more activities. We play a game to learn a concept or conduct an investigation to learn more about the place. Here are 10 stops that can be adapted to your place. Start with some of these, but do not be afraid to try others. Use the knowledge you have or do a little research. Nonfiction children's books are the best source.

Plant Adaptations. For example, bright flowers attract insects for pollination. Trees have a thick bark for protection from insects and disease. Many plants have thorns for protection. Pine needles have a tough covering to survive the winter. Poison ivy uses chemical protection.

Squirrels. Squirrels are rodents. That means their teeth never stop growing. This is an important adaptation because the teeth wear down gnawing through hard shells. The bushy tail helps the squirrel keep its balance when jumping from branch to branch. The squirrel's coloring provides protection as well. From below, their white belly blends in with the sky. From above, their fur blends in with tree branches. Squirrels are one of the few animals that can climb down a tree head first. By burying acorns, they help oak trees spread their seeds.

Seed Dispersion. Because plants cannot move, their seeds have to move; otherwise, overcrowding would result. Seeds are dispersed by wind, water, and animals. They can cling to animal fur, get buried, and even get spread through animals' droppings. Find seeds in the fall, and the students can guess how they are dispersed. Plants must produce many extra seeds because most of them end up in places they cannot grow.

Introduced Species. Many common animals in the United States were introduced from other countries. Starlings, pigeons (rock doves), and house sparrows all originally lived in Europe. In many cases, introduced species cause ecological problems and displace native species. They overpopulate the habitat due to the lack of competition.

Erosion. Erosion is the act of soil wearing away. It can be caused by water, wind, ice, and humans. Find examples of each type of erosion on the walk. Erosion is an important factor in creating landforms. It takes a long time for soil to form.

Local Wildlife. Even if the class doesn't see any wildlife, you can discuss suburban wildlife. Searching for animal signs, a footprint, a half-eaten acorn, a bird's song: all are clues that animals share our place. Raccoons, foxes, rabbits, and chipmunks are some of the animals that have adapted to life with people. Even coyotes are living in the suburbs of New York City. This can also lead to a discussion of the animals that used to live in the area and are now extinct.

Tree History. Stand the class next to the largest tree along the walk. Estimate the age of the tree. Discuss what the tree saw in the local history of the community standing there for all those years.

Food Chains. Find a leaf that has been chewed on by an insect. Use this to begin a discussion of the parts of a food chain. Along the hike see if they can find any other parts of a food chain.

Worms. Dig up a little bit of soil and show everyone a worm. Worms are incredibly important to our soil. They help decompose plant material and create tunnels that allow water and air into soil. There can be thousands of worms in a cubic foot of soil. Worms breathe through their skin and have hairs on their bodies that help them move and sense vibrations in the ground. They may be slimy, but our world wouldn't be the same without worms.

Stand Silently. Have your class stand silently for one minute. What sounds of nature can they hear?

Nature Walk Game. As you lead the hike, pick up an item of interest and pass it to a person with instructions to continue passing it back one person at a time. You can also send information back through the line asking each person to point out the object of interest to the next person as they walk by.

Walking. While walking, challenge the children to find something that begins with each letter of the alphabet.

Just Explore

This is a simple but important activity. One of the most important aspects of place-based environmental education is the opportunity for children to discover for themselves. In a safe place with clear boundaries, give the children time to learn something about the place where they are. That is all you say. Go, learn something, come back, and teach me and the rest of the group. Some of them will wander aimlessly, and others will make wonderful discoveries. Depending on the situation, the children can use journals, hand lenses, field guides, and other equipment.

Nature Art

Another way to introduce children to exploring their place is art. Allow them time to collect natural objects from the schoolyard, their backyard, or local places they visit. Avoid collecting living plants except for single leaves or flowers. Remind them not to pull plants from the roots. Using natural items they collect, children can create a work of art. The project can be abstract or representational. It can be flat or three dimensional. It can be a sculpture or a mobile. It can combine drawing and painting. With rocks, leaves, sticks, rocks, feathers, and seeds, it is amazing what children can create. Use glue, tape, a hammer, nails, and string to hold items together. Ask the children to create a piece of art that symbolizes their place, their role in the place, or another living thing's role in the place.

Alphabet Books and Counting Books

Writing alphabet and counting books is a great way to get children started thinking about the place in which they live.

No matter what type of writing children are doing, it is helpful to show them models. Picture books can be used to model all genres of writing. This is a good way to introduce them to the idea that as writers they read for enjoyment, for information, and for ideas. Read some counting and alphabet books to your class to give them some ideas for their own books. In the library, let the children find their own books to study. They can use the books for ideas on illustrations, layout, letter style, and design.

Next, brainstorm all the possible animals, plants, and other natural features of your area on a huge list. From the list, children can create their own books complete with artwork. This project can be done with any elementary age child. Older children can make books for younger children. Make class books, group books, or individual books depending on the students, time available, and objectives.

Another suggestion is to make a nature calendar. Each month can be illustrated with the children's artwork. The calendar can include special events observed by the children; it can be a record of bird migration, a first snowfall, flower blooms, and many other natural events.

Running Lists

One way to keep children aware of their natural surroundings all year is to keep running lists throughout the year. There is a variety of lists the children can keep. Simply make a large chart in the room to keep track of each animal the class sees in the school yard or on nature walks. Personal lists can be kept in students' journals. There could be another list of plants they are able to identify. In the spring, keep track of the arrival of migrating birds and record the dates. Each year, the new class can compare the arrival dates to previous classes. This could also be done with first blooms of local wildflowers. Celebrate each addition to the chart, and children will search harder for new finds. There can be lists for amazing sounds, special moments, incredible beauty, best questions, and the like. A running list is a good reminder that the study of a place is an ongoing project.

Place Maps

Maps

Find as many maps as you can that include the place where the children live: local maps, county maps, state maps, regional maps, maps of the United States. Try to find a variety of types of maps: topographical, road, physical, political, and so forth. Have the children find their community on each map. Make them aware of their geographic location and what points of interest, cities, and major natural features are near their place. It is also an opportunity to introduce or review map scale and other mapping skills.

Where Are We?

Another way to help children understand where they live in relation to other places is a signpost. Using travel charts or map scales, children can calculate the distance from their area to other major cities, national parks, and other places around the country. Make a poster recording their results.

Area Maps

The maps children draw give us an insight into what they know, pay attention to, and care about. Drawing maps is an practical way to evaluate the effect these activities will have on their sense of place. Maps drawn in the beginning of the lessons can be compared to maps drawn in later in the program. They are a visual pre- and post-test.

Make the instructions simple. Ask the children to draw a map of the area in which they live. Do not give them any other instructions. The purpose of this activity is simply to see what to include in their maps. They will ask for clarification, but do not give them any. It is interesting to see what they include in their area. At the end of the year, repeat the activity. Compare the maps to see what they have changed. Try not to lead them to think you have a specific expectation. Simply tell them to draw a map. Leave it at that, and see what they create. Deliberately keep your directions vague. Let the child be creative. This will give you a better sense of what is important to the child, not what is important to the adult. As the children learn more about the place where they live, important features, places, plants, and animals will end up on their maps. Children can also make maps of their backyards, favorite places, or their community.

Trip Maps

After any trip, have the students draw a map of the trip. See how the maps change as they go on a number of trips.

Other Maps

Children can make maps of animal signs, trees, where children play, or just about anything else.

Giving Directions

Ask the children to draw and write a map that gives directions to their house and describes some of the highlights along the way. When they are done, ask for volunteers, read their directions out loud, and use a local street map to show were you would end up. You can evaluate them by trying out some of the directions and seeing if you get to the right house.

Create a Walk

Children can also design a walk and draw a map that guides someone past the more interesting natural features and points of interest near the school. The map and description should help you find out what the children consider interesting. For homework, they can lead their parents on the walk they design.

How Much Do You Know?

Ask the children a series of questions about the place where they live. Ask yourself. The answers are the basic information we all should know about the places in which we live. If no one knows the answer, the class has the perfect opportunity to do some investigating.

- What is the nearest body of water?
- Describe the climate.
- What are 10 native plants and animals?
- Describe the soil.
- What is the closest wild area to the school?
- Where does the water your community drinks come from?
- What Native American tribes lived in your area before the explorers arrived?
- Name five native plants, trees, mammals, and birds that live in your area.
- What animals used to live in your place?
- Where does your garbage go?
- What did the place look like 50 years ago?

- 100 years ago?
- A million years ago?
- Which way is north from where you are now?
- What was the last natural disaster to effect your area?
- What crops are grown in your area?
- What are the most pressing environmental problems in your area?
- Why is your town where it is?
- How does the local geography effect your area?
- What geologic event helped to create the landscape in your area? (Questions adapted from *Deep Ecology* by Bill Devall and George Sessions, p. 22.)

Secret Places/Favorite Places/Special Places

Think back to your childhood. Did you have a special place or a secret spot somewhere outside? Ask your friends. Almost everyone had one. It is a universal practice for children to make hideouts and forts, to find secret places and to have favorite places. Secret places may be at summer homes or a fort built in the backyard. It may be a park down the street or a lake from their summer vacation. It may be a favorite tree or a clump of bushes. These places provide independence and foster exploring. These are places children create themselves, places for their imagination to run wild. In these places, children first connect to the Earth on their own. Children have to make their own secret places, but teachers can have a role in fostering the concept and validating the worth. By seriously thinking about why these places are special and sharing the place with others, the connection grows even stronger.

Start the children off by asking them to draw a map of their special places. They do not have to reveal the exact location if they do not want to. If a child does not have a special place, ask them to draw one they would like to have.

Children can also create collages to share these places. A collage can be made from photographs of their place, natural objects from the place, and drawings of the place. Encourage students to use anything that represents some aspect of their special place. The collage will tell a story of the place. As the children share their collages, ask them to think about why these places are special. What makes them their favorite places? For more information on secret places, see David Sobel's book *Children's Special Places: Exploring the Role of Forts, Dens, and Bush Houses in Middle Childhood.*

Scavenger Hunts

Scavenger hunts are a great way to get the children to explore. There are any number of scavenger hunts on which to send your class. They allow freedom to search with a focus to keep them on task, the task being: pay attention to their world, explore, and wonder. There is a type of scavenger hunt to fit almost any objective. They can search for shapes, colors, textures, sizes, animal signs, plants, and stones, among other things. Depending on the local environment, your list will vary.

There are also a number of ways to organize a scavenger hunt. Children can be given a list of items to find and then sent out to find them. The items can be presented in the form of a riddle for more of a challenge. If you like, the various items can be given a point value depending on the difficulty of finding them. The winner is the team with the most points. Another technique is to gather the group together and tell them what to search for one item at a time. After someone finds an item, the groups gather together for the next challenge. Challenges can be placed in envelopes and distributed for added suspense. Instead of a list, make a Tic Tac Toe chart with the challenges in 4-by-4 inch array of boxes. Children have to find enough items to get four in a row. Scavenger hunts can also be an opportunity for group cooperation. Children can work as individuals, in pairs, or the entire group can work together to find the items on the list.

Here are some suggestions for making the scavenger hunt a success. Explain the rules carefully: Make the boundaries clear, and respect the natural environment when collecting items. If they are collecting insects and other small creatures, they should treat them with care and respect. They should be released right away. Children can always bring you over to show you what they find if they can't bring it to you.

You may want to provide the children with a plastic bag for collecting and a hand lens for viewing. Don't be surprised if someone comes back with an item not on the list but interesting just the same. Use this opportunity as a teachable moment. When the time is up, sit down with the group and discuss the findings, answer questions, and record unanswered questions for research. Use the time to reinforce the objectives you have for the lesson.

Scavenger hunts will be used in other chapters of the book to teach other concepts. The ideas listed here help foster basic exploring and introduce children to their place.

A feather.

The most dangerous animal (humans).

An animal track.

A decaying leaf.

A leaf chewed on by an animal.

Three different plants.

A nut chewed on by a squirrel.

A piece of litter.

An animal tunnel.

A red, gray, and white rock.

A bird nest.

Moss.

An actual animal sighting.

A mushroom or fungus.

Animal scat.

A stick that looks like a letter (besides "l" or "I") .

A bird song.

Something about which you have a question.

Animal bones.

A seed.

A spiral-shaped object.

A seed spread by wind or animal.

Two stones that fit together.

Natural objects to make music.

Something unimportant to the forest (there isn't anything).

Something you think is interesting.

Depending on the site and the number and age of participants of the scavenger hunt, you may have to adjust the items. This is a list to pick and chose from; ten items can be plenty. It is okay to have a few that are difficult to find. A fun homework assignment is a take-home scavenger hunt.

Start a Collection

Children love to collect things. Students can make a collection of rocks, leaves, insects, sticks, or whatever else they can find. Collections help the student practice organizing and classifying. They can make a collection of bones, bird nests, feathers, track casts, and other animal signs Other collections could be made of rocks, photographs, leaves, seeds, or even sticks. The children can write labels for the items they collect and display.

A classroom nature museum can be created. Finding a feather can lead to a variety of questions. Each item can be the subject of further research. Research does not always have to end with a written report. Information can be reported orally, on video, on a cassette tape, or even as a comic book. Give children a chance to explore the library and find as many facts as possible about the animals and other natural features that exist in their community. Children should have opportunities to use the library simply to answer a single question instead of always having to take notes and write a bibliography and a report. Sometimes it is good enough just to find the short answer. Children can write a few interesting facts on a 3-by–5 inch card and display it with the item. The collections can inspire a list of amazing facts about local plants and animals. Displays and charts of amazing facts will help inspire more explorations. Hold an "amazing fact" contest.

Math

A geometry scavenger hunt is a good way to help tie in math to your study of place, as well as to encourage close observation and the search for patterns. Make a list of geometric shapes with which the children are familiar. Send them out to find the shapes in nature. The students make a check for each shape they find and, if possible, collect the rock, leaf, or branch that shows the shape.

Measuring

The outdoors is the place for a variety of measuring activities. Use the schoolyard to practice taking temperatures. Challenge the children to find the warmest place on the playground. Record the results; next they can try to find the coldest. The difference can be striking.

Children can measure the length of anything between a leaf and the entire playground. Practice finding perimeter and area with shapes on the playground. Measure the area and make a rough map to scale. Use coordinate geometry to place trees and other features on the maps.

Patterns

Finding patterns is an important problem-solving skill. Ask students to search for patterns. They will have to look closely at seeds, flowers, and other items. They may notice patterns in the weather, in flowers, in the behavior of their pets, or in the branches of a tree. Seeing patterns helps children understand what is going on. Scientists use an understanding of patterns to make predictions. The addition of a hand lens opens a whole new world of patterns for those who look carefully.

For older children, these two patterns will give them something for which to look. Approximately 800 years ago, Leonardo of Pisa wrote a book describing the Fibonacci number pattern. The pattern is "1,1,2,3,5,8,13,21,34 . . . ." The pattern is made by adding the two previous numbers to get the next number. A Fibonacci ratio is made by dividing any Fibonacci number by another. These numbers and ratios can be found in places. The children can search for plants with leaves, petals, or stems growing in groups of Fibonacci numbers. Pine cones have a Fibonacci number in the pattern of their bracts. For more information, read Trudi Hammel Garland's *Fascinating Fibonaccis: Mystery and Magic in Numbers*. There are Fibonaccis in art, architecture, music, and technology.

Geographic Features

The geography of a place has a major impact on the natural and human history of the place. Mountains, lakes, and oceans all have an effect on climate, habitats, and the life in the area. Learning the features of the place is an important part of understanding how the place works and the environment's effect on people and their culture.

Use maps of the local area to identify the geographic features in the area. Using maps of other places, observe more examples of the geographic features children should know. Make a list and generate definitions for the geographic features. The list may include island, peninsula, bay, sound, valley, canyon, river, stream, pond, isthmus, hill, archipelago, mountains, plateau, estuary, and so on.

If possible, take a trip to a place to view some of these features directly. Even a nearby pond may have small bays and peninsulas that help children see for themselves about what they are learning. Water runoff can create a miniature canyon or valley. A pile of dirt can show children what a plateau looks like. Research the names of the features in your areas. Why is each place called what it is? The town clerk, local historians, and the library are all sources of information.

To reinforce and evaluate their knowledge of geographic features, children can draw imaginary islands and include a number of the geographic features they have studied. Each feature should be labeled and named by the student.

Our Climate

The climate is the average weather of the place. Understanding the climate of the place will help children see how it affects the animals and plants and their adaptations as well as its effect on human history in the area. You can easily explain some of the basic factors effecting climate.

Distance from the equator: The further from the equator, the cooler the climate. Spinning on an axis, the Northern Hemisphere is sometimes tilted toward the sun, and sometimes it is not, thus creating four seasons. Look at temperature maps in an atlas and temperatures across the world. Give the children a chance to find the pattern before explaining it to them.

The moderating effects of the ocean: Water is slower to absorb and release heat. This moderates the temperature on land near water. Once heated up, water takes longer to cool off than land; water also take longer to heat up than land. To demonstrate, fill a tray with water and another with soil. Put a lamp over both trays and record the temperature every ten minutes. After a couple hours, turn off the lamp and continue recording the temperature. Graph the results for the children to see how the moderating affects of water. A city in North Dakota has much wider temperature swings than a city on the East Coast at the same latitude.

Rain shadows from mountains: When moisture is blown toward a mountain, it rises, cools down, and falls to Earth on one side of the mountain range. The other side is usually much drier. Look at physical maps of the United States to see the effect of the Sierras or Rocky Mountains. Point out the amount of rain found on the eastern sides of these mountains.

Discuss which of these factors affect the place you live the most. There may be local factors that also create the local climate.

Nature Survey

Children can conduct a survey to find out what other children think about the place in which they live. The survey can cover questions about knowledge of the place. Other questions can relate to attitudes. For example: Would you rather play indoors or outdoors? How often do you play in a natural area? Where do you learn about the outdoors? On a scale of 1-10, how much do you know about nature? What are your favorite things to do or favorite places to go?

Discuss survey techniques with the class before they gather the data. There are two basic types of questions. Fixed response are questions where the person must choose a response from several possible answers given by the poll taker. These answers are easier to tabulate and compare. Open-ended questions allow the person to give an answer in his or her own words. They give a better sense of what the person thinks but are difficult to tabulate. For this poll, it is best to use both types of questions. It is important to pretest the survey in order to evaluate the effectiveness of the questions.

After gathering and compiling the information, students can discuss the results and the implications. How can this knowledge help educators teach children about the environment? Math skills can be used to graph the results and present the information using fractions, decimals, and percentages.

One Square Plot

Stake out a one-meter-square area on the school lawn or other natural area that the children can visit often. This one square can be the site of an intense study. One square meter can provide much learning. There are activities from a every chapter that could be conducted and related to the square. Students could do sketching and journal writing, conduct populations studies, identify plants, and watch succession. Combine these with a variety activities from other chapters. Pick one activity to do every two weeks or every month, record the results, and keep track all year.

Mystery Photos

Take some pictures around the community of both natural and human-made features. Post them and see if the children can guess where the picture was taken.

Top 10

The children can make a list of the top 10 reasons to live in their place. The list could also be of the 10 best features of the place.

Nature Journals

Writers keep journals. Introducing children to journal writing is truly beneficial for young writers. One way to introduce journal writing is through the natural world. Virtually all of our most famous and influential naturalists kept journals. Henry David Thoreau, John Muir, Aldo Leopold, and Rachel Carson all used journals, and for the same reason children should keep journals.

Journal writing is a way to live life over again; to recapture the past, to preserve it, and to better understand our lives. Journals preserve the moment and make it special. Journal writing is a chance to reflect, question, wonder, scream, and yell. It is a place to be sad or happy. Journals listen to whatever we write. They are places without editors. Children can experiment, take chances, and be honest. Our role is to encourage, inspire, prompt, provide opportunity, help, and guide.

Journals can make the everyday magic. A random thought or an interesting observation take on an importance when recorded in a journal. Journals help children realize that their thoughts matter; they are worth recording. They do not have to have something "important" to say. What may seem unimportant now doesn't always end up that way. The entries in the journals will be the ingredients for poetry, stories, essays, and reports.

Good writers lead wide-awake lives. Keeping a nature journal is also a wonderful way to help young writers pay better attention to the world around them. It helps children walk with their eyes open to the world and to their feelings. A nature journal becomes the history of the place and of the person. The journal is first-hand research. It is also a gift for the future. As adults, a journal from our childhood is a window to our past.

The beginning of the year is the time to start a nature journal. The skills the children learn will be important all year. There are many ways to set up a journal writing program in your class. It can be daily, weekly, monthly, or saved for trips to local natural areas. It is important to make it a habit. Regular journal writing becomes a ritual that demonstrates its importance. There can even be a class journal with different entries each week by different students. The focus here is on a nature journal, but it will be inevitable for some children to expand their scope on their own or under your guidance. The nature journal can be part of writer's notebook or can be used as a way to introduce journal writing to children.

One hopes some of the students will become true journal writers and will carry their journals everywhere. The writing should be done in the outdoors as much as possible. Direct contact with the outdoors makes the writing vivid. A great deal is lost with distance from the source of inspiration. Encourage children to write with detail and reflection. A journal entry is more than an account of the day's events. Journals are not limited to words. The journal should be a child's place to put down thoughts; questions; story ideas; memories; and images they see, smell, hear, and taste in the outdoors. They can be places in which to sketch and to paste in pictures, photographs, feathers, pressed flowers, and other items that have meaning to the child.

Model the way you keep a journal by sharing some of your entries and the thought process you go through when writing in your journal. Entries should be dated, and nothing should be thrown out. One line can be just as important as 20 lines. Read passages from other writer's journals. Collect good journal entries from students to serve as a benchmarks, in order for children to have a better idea of the standards you expect and the level they can achieve.

A journal is not simply a record of the day's events. It is reflection and reaction to life's experiences. Continue to model and share journal entries throughout the year to maintain a high quality. Give the children the respect and privacy a journal deserves. I leave it up to the students to decide if they want to share a reading with the class or with me. Throughout the year, remind the children to refer to their journals for their poetry, fiction, and even nonfiction writing.

Of course, each child needs a journal. There are a wide variety of journals from which to choose. Because much of your journal writing time will be outside, durability is essential. Spiral notebooks usually don't last. Other than that, the choice is wide open. It should be a personal decision. Personally, I like the black-and-white marbled composition notebooks. You may want to make your own journals with the students.

I divide the journal entries into three categories: free entries, suggested entries, and required entries. Over the year, the students experience a mix of these.

Free Writing

Free writing is exactly that, free writing. I give the children time to write whatever they want.

Suggested Entries

I use these when I want a little more focus from the students. Sometimes I may give them a choice of various prompts. Sometimes there is an opportunity for free writing with suggestions. The main thing is to get them to write. Some children prefer to have suggestions and may even need them. In the beginning, children may need prompts more than later in the year. Depending on your objectives and the place in which you are working, your suggestions will vary. This is a list of prompts, in no particular order of importance:

Take someone on a walk through the place. What would you show them?

How is your mood affected by the place?
Imagine being in the place a whole year.

Imagine you have just seen the whole history of the place in five minutes.

If a friend said, "It's a _____ day," what kind day would it be?

Pretend you are blind. How would you describe the place?

What is the opposite of the place?

In what weather is the place most itself?

What are the rhythms and patterns of the place?

How does this place compare to a place that you hate?

Is this the kind of place you like?

What kind of places do you like?

What animals would you like to be in the place?

What questions would you ask the place?

What questions do you have about . . . ?

What to you know about . . . ?

What did you learn in this activity?

What did you see today?

What has changed since last time?

Pick one thing to write about every time you see it.

Record regular entries on the changing seasons.

Respond to books and quotes read on nature.

Assigned Entries

Any of these suggestions can become assigned questions. Assigning journal entries is a good way to do a quick evaluation of an activity or find out what the class is thinking. It is also helpful if everyone has been given the same question or some thought for class discussion. If you decide to have a system for reading these entries, you will have the chance to write back and have more interaction with the children. You can ask the children to mark the page to be read so their privacy is ensured.

I lean toward the freedom side rather than the structured side when giving journal writing time. My overall goal is to help my students become life-long journal writers. This is in a child's control. It has to be their choice, their place to write without worry. An occasional required assignment is fine. Some children will not produce much when given the freedom. Others will use it to the fullest, and it allows them to shine more than if you required everyone to do the same thing.

Keep journal writing going all year.

Chapter Two

Sensing Our Place

"You learn that if you sit in the woods and wait, something happens."

Henry David Thoreau

" It would provide us a more serene and confident future if at the start of our sixth century of residence in America we began to listen to the land, and hear what it says and know what it can and cannot do."

Wallace Stegner

"Living in outer nature keeps the senses keen."

Henry Beston

"Poetry is as necessary to comprehension as science. It is impossible to live without reverence as it is without joy."

Henry Beston

"The invariable mark of wisdom is to see the miraculous in the common."

Ralph Waldo Emerson

Introduction

To connect to the natural world, children must know what is there. Too often children look but don't really see. Children need to use more than their eyes. Using all their senses helps them make more observations, see changes, and learn patterns. Using all their senses helps them learn more and remember more. If a child knows what a white pine tree looks like and how the bark feels, he or she will know more and remember more. Children who only use their sense of sight limit the wonders they can find. The memory of a garter snake will last longer if it is touched and smelled.

Whatever teachers do the first days of school sets a tone for the rest of the year. The children learn what we value and what will be important for the year. A key part of the first days of school in my class are a series of sensory awareness activities. I start the year with these because they emphasize one of the most important goals of my classroom: to be aware and to appreciate the world around them. Being better observers makes them better scientists and writers. Good scientists notice the world around them. The more they see, the more information they have, the better they can understand what is happening. Good writers pay attention to details and lead wide-awake lives. They can create a picture with words that uses all the senses.

Some of these activities require blindfolds. Homemade blindfolds can be made from cloth strips or even T-shirts. An added benefit is that many of the activities help build trust and cooperation between children, an important part of community building. Safety is an important consideration for any blindfold activity. Be sure the children understand that there is no room for goofing around. The guide has a responsibility to keep the blindfolded person safe. The one sense that is left out in this chapter is the sense of taste.

Paying close attention and using all our senses helps us find the incredible in the everyday. Show the children you are paying attention by using your senses. Point out the things you hear. Comment on how something feels. Stop and smell a flower as you walk by.

Books to Use

Adams, Adrienne, ed. *Poetry of the Earth.* New York: Charles Scribner's Sons, 1972. ISBN 0-684-13012-2. This collection of poems from a variety of well-known poets, including Emily Dickinson and Robert Frost, is a good introduction for students. The examples demonstrate the variety of topics poems can cover and an assortment of styles.

Adoff, Arnold. *In for Winter, Out for Spring.* Illustrated by Jerry Pinkney. San Diego, CA: Harcourt Brace Jovanovich, 1991. ISBN 0-15-238637-8. A collection of poems told by a young girl describes her life outdoors through all seasons. There are poems about the games she plays, the life that surrounds her, and her relationship with her family. The arrangement of the words in the poems serves as a model for children to consider how they will arrange their own poems.

Arnosky, Jim. *Drawing from Nature.* New York: Lothrop, Lee & Shepard, 1987. ISBN 0-688-01295-7. Divided into four sections—water, land, plants, and animals—Arnosky has shared some of his specific techniques for drawing from nature. This book would most likely be used for a child that is particularly interested in nature drawing or as a guide for a specific drawing project.

Arnosky, Jim. *Sketching Outdoors in Summer.* New York: Lothrop, Lee & Shepard, 1988. ISBN 0-688-06286-5. This addition to Jim Arnosky's drawing books is more like a visit to his sketch pad. Each page shows the reader a sketch, suggestions for sketching, and an account of how and why the picture was drawn. Sharing some of the pages will help children understand the thoughts behind a drawing. The series includes books for each season.

Barasch, Lynne. *A Winter Walk.* New York: Ticknor and Fields, 1993. On a dreary winter day, Sophie complains of being bored. Her mom suggests a walk: "We'll find the color of winter." Sophie and her mother find all sorts of colors—red, rust, yellow, green, brown, and more—as they walk through fields and forests around their house. Beautiful watercolor illustrations remind us that no matter the season, all we have to do is look, and there are many colors to see.

Baylor, Byrd. *The Other Way to Listen.* Illustrated by Peter Parnall. New York: Atheneum Books, 1978. ISBN 0-684-16017-X. Baylor tells us there is another way to listen, a way to listen beyond hearing the song of a bird or wind in the trees. In this story, an old man teaches a girl that by knowing a place, *really* knowing a place, you can hear what the rocks are saying, what stars sound like, or even when the hills answer back to your hello. To do this, one must go out into a place, sit, and listen. A good book to read in conjunction with *Matthew's Meadow*.

Bliss, Corinne D. *Matthew's Meadow*. Illustrated by Ted Lewin. San Diego, CA: Harcourt Brace Jovanovich, 1992. ISBN 0-15-200759-8. A very memorable book that will inspire a new way of looking at the world. Each year from the age of nine, Matthew goes up to the meadow. A hawk speaks to him and teaches him something new about using his senses to understand the world. As Matthew grows up, he continues to learn more from the hawk and himself. The hawk tells Matthew his grandmother is speaking to him, but it is not until the end that Matthew figures out how to speak to her.

Bouchard, David. *Voices from the Wild: An Animal Sensagoria*. Illustrated by Ron Parker. San Francisco: Chronicle Books, 1996. ISBN 0-8118-1462-9. A unique book of poetry from the point of view of several animals. Each animal explains how its senses help it to survive and the amazing things it can do.

Brenner, Barbara, ed. *The Earth Is Painted Green: A Garden of Poems About Our Planet*. Illustrated by S. D. Schindler. New York: Scholastic, 1994. ISBN 0-590-45134-0. A large collection of poems related to the Earth from a variety of authors.

Carlstrom, Nancy White. *What Does the Rain Say?* Illustrated by Henri Sorensen. New York: Macmillan, 1993. ISBN 0-02-717273-2. What does the rain say? A young boy goes out into the rain and finds the answer, along with much more. A beautiful reminder to pay attention to the everyday when we are outdoors. The writing models wonderful uses of language to describe a feeling of nature in words. Carlstrom's book *How Does the Wind Walk?* is also a good addition.

Collins, Pat Lowery. *I Am an Artist*. Illustrated by Robin Brickman. Millbrook, CT: Millbrook Press, 1992. ISBN 1-56294-7028. A great book for inspiring children's artwork. The text and illustrations show the reader that to be an artist, one has to see the natural beauty around him or her using all the senses. Each image begins with the phrase, "I am an artist when"; for example, "I am an artist when I crunch through winter snow and stop to gather winter's hush around me."

Edwards, Betty. *Drawing on the Right Side of the Brain*. Los Angles: J. P. Tarcher, 1979. ISBN 0-87477-088-2. A series of exercises that will improve your drawing, but only if you take the time to practice.

Esbensen, Barbara Juster. *Echoes for the Eye: Poems That Celebrate Patterns in Nature*. Illustrated by Helen K. Davie. New York: HarperCollins, 1996. ISBN 0-06-024398-8. A book of poetry about patterns in nature. The poems highlight a new way to look at everyday things. A variety of shapes are examined. The title alone is worth sharing with children.

Ferra, Lorraine. *A Crow Doesn't Need a Shadow*. Illustrated by Diane Boardman. Salt Lake City, UT: Gibbs Smith, 1994. ISBN 0-87905-600-2. A great book that is focused on how to write nature poetry. It is filled with samples of poetry written by children that are very helpful for discussing various poetry writing techniques. The book also includes ideas and exercises to use with children.

Frank, Josette, ed. *Snow Toward Evening: A Year in a Valley*. Illustrated by Thomas Locker. New York: Dial Books, 1990. ISBN 0-8037-0810-6. This collection of poems from a variety of poets tells the story of one place through the seasons. Locker's incredible paintings add a special beauty to this collection.

Heard, Georgia. *For the Good of the Earth and Sun: Teaching Poetry*. Portsmouth, NH: Heineman Educational Books, 1989. ISBN 0-435-08495-X. This book alone can be your guide for poetry writing. Each chapter takes you step-by-step through the process of writing poems with children, from generating ideas to revising and editing.

Higginson, William. *Wind in the Long Grass*. Illustrated by Sandra Speidel. New York: Simon & Schuster, 1991. ISBN 0-671-67978-3. A collection of haikus arranged by the seasons. This collection not only explains how to write haiku but provides beautiful poems showing the power of just a few well-chosen words.

Hughes, Shirley. *Out and About*. New York: Lothrop, Lee & Shepard, 1988. ISBN 0-688- 07690-4. A collection of poems about two young children and their adventures going out and about. Not all the poems are directly related to nature, but it is still a fun collection for young children.

Jenkins, Steve. *Looking Down*. New York: Houghton Mifflin, 1995. ISBN 0-395-72665-4. This wordless picture book begins in outer space. With each page, the reader moves closer and closer to a child looking at a ladybug. The cut paper collages are particularly eye-catching. The book manages to convey the message without words that it all depends on one's point of view.

Kroll, Virginia. *Naomi Knows It's Springtime*. Illustrated by Jill Kastner. Honesdale, PA: Boyd Mills Press, 1993. ISBN 1-56397-006-6. An incredibly beautiful and simple book. Naomi can tell it is spring by the way it feels, sounds, and tastes. It is only at the end of the story and in a subtle way do we learn that Naomi is blind.

Larrick, Nancy, ed. *Room for Me and a Mountain Lion: Poetry of Open Space*. New York: M. Evans, 1974. ISBN 0-87131-124-0. A good collection from a variety of poets. A wide range of topics related to nature and open spaces. A handy book to have around.

Leslie, Clare Walker. *The Art of Field Sketching*. Dubuque, IA: Kendall/Hunt, 1995. ISBN 0-7872-0579-6. This book is a helpful guide for learning and improving sketching. There are sketching exercises and many example of the author's own work. She covers material related to keeping a nature journal. There is also information on sketching in a variety of habitats from urban to forest.

Levy, Constance. *A Tree Place and Other Poems*. Illustrated by Robert Sabuda. New York: Margaret K. McElderry, 1994. ISBN 0-689-50599-X. A collection of 40 short poems covering a range of topics in the natural world. Many of the poems are about common, everyday animals, plants, and natural events.

Major, Beverly. *Over Back*. Illustrated by Thomas B. Allen. New York: HarperCollins, 1993. ISBN 0-06-020286-6. Behind the farmhouse, behind the fields, over the wall is "over back." It is a place to explore and to find wonderful things. There is wintergreen to taste, arbutus to smell, and frog eggs that feel like Jell-O. Once the young girl is home on the farm, all she can think about is going "over back."

Martin, Bill, Jr., and John Archambault. *Listen to the Rain*. Illustrated by James Endicott. New York: Henry Holt, 1988. ISBN 0-08050-0682-6. The authors put the sound of rain into words and create a song. They describe the sounds of the rain from the beginning of the storm, to a thunderstorm crashing through the sky, and down to the last raindrop falling.

Miranda, Anne. *Night Songs*. New York: Bradbury Press, 1993. ISBN 0-02-767250-6. A mother tells her baby all about the songs of the night while putting her down to sleep. They hear songs from a variety of places. The songs of desert, pond, city, and more are beautifully described. The childlike illustrations are a good reminder to children that all drawing does not have to be perfectly realistic to be interesting.

Rotner, Shelly, and Ken Kreisler. *Nature Spy*. Photographs by Shelley Rotner. New York: Macmillan, 1992. ISBN 0-02-777885-1. Brilliant photographs and words of advice from the little girl in the book remind us to look closely at what we see and we will see more. The leaves, a rock, a spider web, and a flower are reason enough to get down on our hands and knees and become a nature spy.

Rylant, Cynthia. *All I See*. Illustrated by Peter Catalanotto. New York: Orchard, 1988. ISBN 0-531-05777-1. Gregory paints everyday on the lakeshore. When he is not painting, he floats on a canoe staring at the sky. Every day, Charlie watches hidden in the trees until he sneaks down and looks at what Gregory is painting. Each painting is of a whale. The two meet, and Gregory teaches Charlie how to paint. When Charlie asks Gregory why he only paints whales, Gregory replies, "That's all I see." Charlie looks out over the lake and knows there will be something for him, something that will inspire him, and he will paint.

Showers, Paul. *Listening Walk*. Illustrated by Aliki. New York: HarperCollins, 1991. ISBN 0-06-021637-9. Taking a walk without talking is a "Listening Walk." With her father and dog, Major, a young girls, hears the sounds of the city. In a park, the sounds of trees, birds, and other animals fill her ears. Like the girl in the book, readers of can have fun imitating the sounds they hear on their own listening walks.

Singer, Marilyn. *Turtle in July*. Illustrated by Jerry Pickney. New York: Macmillan, 1989. ISBN 0-02-782881-6. A collection of poems about a variety of animals throughout the seasons. A great example of how to write poems from an animal's point of view.

Thornhill, Jan. *Before and After: A Book of Nature Timescapes*. Washington, DC: National Geographic Society, 1997. A unique book that will get the observation skills going in whomever reads it. The book is made up of a series of detailed picture of various habitats. The second picture in each set shows the view sometime later. The times range from a few minutes to a few hours to more. The idea is to look close enough to see what changed over the given amount of time.

Yolen, Jane. *Water Music*. Photographs by Jason Stemple. Honesdale, PA: Boyd Mills Press, 1995. ISBN 1-56397-336-7. Inspired by Stemple's photographs, Yolen's poems are all centered around the theme of water. These poems are wonderful examples of finding the magic in the everyday.

Activities

## General Observation Activities

Solo Silent Sit

This activity is best done in a forest, field, or other natural area but can be done anywhere. It is one of the most important experiences described in this book. Tell the children to spread out and find a place to sit in silence and listen. To insure the children spread out, it may be helpful to assign spots along the trail. Tell them to sit so quietly and be so still that the place goes on as if they were not there. If they can sit still, there will be so much to see and hear. Maintain strict rules. Anyone who makes noise makes it harder for everyone else to concentrate. Five minutes of silence is a good start. Participate yourself and be a model for their sake and your own. Be patient; it will take a little while for everyone to settle down. Although some will think it is the longest five minutes of their lives, others will be upset when you end it. If possible, "Silent Sit" in different habitats and compare experiences. Eventually, children can sit for quite a while. It is great if you can return to the same place over and over again so children can pick one special place.

Longest List

Challenge the children to make the longest list of everything they can see in a given amount of time. The first items on the list are easy, but by the end they will really have to look to come up with something new. Children can work individually, in pairs, or in groups.

Framing Pictures

When we focus on a small area, we see more. Children can use a coat hanger, a paper towel tube, or a 4-by-4-inch square piece of cardboard. Hold the frame against the ground, trees, sky, or other subject and focus on what is inside. They can write, draw, or discuss what they see. Challenge them to write the longest list possible of what they see in their frame.

Object Memory

These activities test how well children pay attention. Put a number of natural items under a blanket or sheet of paper. Lift the cover and give the children two minutes or less to memorize what is there. When time is up, cover the items and ask the children to list them. Children can work as individuals or in a group. In the second version, collect pairs of natural objects that look nearly the same. One child arranges the objects in a pattern and gives the rest of the group two minutes to observe. The next step is to give the group a chance to match the two designs.

What Is Different?

As the leader, change something about your appearance. For example, switch your ring to another finger, unbutton one button, change hairstyles. Stand in front of the class and see if they notice. Try changing something in the room.

What Doesn't Belong?

Lay out some items on the trail that do not belong and challenge the children to find them.

Are You Paying Attention?

Cover a child with a blanket or send him or her out of the room. Ask the class what color shirt, pants, or shoes the child is wearing. Try this one: Ask questions about the school and see if anyone ever noticed enough to answer the questions. How many swings are on the playground? What color is the hallway? How many classrooms are on the first floor? What color are the steps? What number is on the cornerstone? Take a walk through your schoolyard to come up with other ideas.

What Is It?

This game can be played in groups of two or three. One person secretly picks an object in the forest. The child then gives sensory clues to his or her partner. For example, "it is brown, it is smooth, it is thin and has ridges" (fallen leaf).

What Is the Food?

Blindfold the child or use one child as a model. Give the child a bag of potato chips. When a child is blindfolded, a bag of potato chips can be confused with other bags of snack food. First, test his or her sense of hearing. Can he or she tell what it is when you shake the bag? Open the bag. Can he or she identify it by smelling? Let someone put his or her hand in; can he or she tell what it is using his or her sense of touch? Give him or her a chance to taste it. Now does he or she know? Other possible foods to try that require more then a sense of sight are various fruits or different packages of cookies.

Color Walk

Make a list of colors. While exploring a place, the children search and find natural objects that match the colors on the list.

Point of View

Sometimes we notice more if we look at it from a different point of view. Have the children lie on their backs and look up. Children can look at a tree while standing on their heads. Ask them to try walking backwards though the woods. Stand on a rock or log and look around. Crawl on the ground and look at things from an ant's point of view.

Sensory Scavenger Hunt

Make up a scavenger hunt that requires your children to use all their senses. These are some suggestions for the list: something soft, something fuzzy, something rough, something hard, something square, something thin, something beautiful, something flat, something smelly, something that bends, something cold, something square, something colorful, something slimy, something yellow, something ugly.

The items they return with will be the basis for an interesting discussion. The results are subjective in many cases. This can lead to a healthy discussion on understanding differences and tolerating a variety of points of view. If you want a little competition, challenge them to find the roughest, smoothest, reddest, or squarest items.

Leaf Observation

Each child picks two or three leaves from the same tree. Ask all the children to look at them closely and notice the subtle differences.

Where Is It?

This activity is best done on a field, in school yards, or at some other open area. Children put a stake in the ground as a marker, then pull it up. After walking about 50 feet away, they turn around and try to find the spot where they put the stake. Afterwards discuss what landmarks they used to find their spot.

Where Did I Get This?

Gather some natural objects together, such as a pine cone, a flower petal, or a tree leaf. Show the objects to the group. They have to search for the place in which you found the object.

One Sense

The children describe an object or place using only one sense. The challenge will be to provide enough information.

Mystery Box

Not only is this a wonderful sensory activity, it can also be used to teach children important ideas about how science works and about how theories are developed and discoveries are made. This activity can either be teacher-led or each child can work on his or her own mystery box. The boxes are simple to make. Put an object in a box and tape it shut so no one can see what is inside. Hold the box up and shake it gently. The first step is to record all the observations one can have about what is in the box without looking inside. They should not try to guess what is inside. After the observations have been made, give the box to a single student to hold. The rest of the group can ask a few questions about the object inside and add these to their list of observations. At this point, the children should record their guesses. These guesses should be considered a theory. Next allow the children to stick a pencil in the box and see if they can observe any more useful information. They can revise their guess or note if the new information confirms the first guess. Allow them to ask three questions about the object but not ask what it is exactly. Now, with this added information, the children can make a new theory or reinforce the original idea. Finally, after all three guesses are recorded, open the box.

The children can bring in their own mystery box, and each child can go through each step his or herself. Discuss how this activity is a model of how science works. We make theory based on the available evidence. Science can be advanced when there are new tools to help us gain more information. The activity also shows children how scientists learn about things they cannot even see. A wrong answer based on the lack of information may seem ridiculous now, but in the past that is all scientists knew. Someday people are going to look back on this time and wonder about what we currently think is true.

Touch Activities

Trust Walks

Working in pairs, one child guides another child on a tour of the playground, forest, classroom, or whatever place is being studied. One child will be blindfolded, and the other will be a guide. The guide leads his or her partner around the place. As they explore, the guide will hand the blindfolded child objects or put his or her hand on a tree, a rock, or something else. It is a good idea to make worms and other living creatures off-limits. The blindfolded child tries to guess the name of each object at each stop. Try to get the children to think about what each item feels like instead of just guessing what it is. Part of the activity can be for the blindfolded person to say out loud or even dictate what the objects feel like. At your signal, the children switch roles.

Rope Walk

Tie a rope between several trees, connecting them together. A child starts at one end of the rope with a blindfold on. He or she slowly walks along, holding the rope. Put a knot or some other marker on the rope a foot in front of each tree so the child knows he or she is approaching a tree. At each tree, the child can use his or her senses to form a mental picture of the tree. There can be other stops on the rope walk to touch, listen, hear, or even taste. A tape recorder can be set up to play mystery sounds. At another stop, a child can hand the walker something to touch. Another station can test the sense of smell. Use old film containers with various scents for the children to sniff and guess. Another variation is to explain a challenge that each child will try at a certain stop. For example: Stop Two—find something on the ground that is smooth; Stop Four—remember five sounds you hear.

Feeling Box

Put a natural object in a box. Cut out a hole large enough for a hand to fit in. Old socks with the ends cut out can be used to prevent peeking. Staple one end of the sock around the hole. The children put their hands in and try to guess the object in the box. Use natural objects, such as a leaf, a pine cone, a stone, or a shell. Children can bring in their own boxes, their own surprises. Paper bags can also be used.

Pass the Twig

Put the children in groups of six or seven. Each child comes to the group with a small twig. The group should feel the twig and get to know it by their sense of touch. Take the twigs from the children and mix them up. The object of the game is for each child to end up with his or her original twig without looking. Hand out the twigs while they sit in a circle. With their eyes closed, they pass the twig to their neighbor, pausing to feel the twig and mixing up all the twigs. On your signal, the children pass the twigs again and again until they find their twig. Once a child finds the right twig, he or she should hang on to it and simply pass other twigs that come through. When everyone thinks that he or she has his or her original twig, the children open their eyes and see if they found the right one.

A variation of this game is for each child to place a rock, a stick, or a twig in a bag. Shake the bag and let each child have chance to reach in, feel the objects, and pull out the one they think is his or hers.

Belly Touch

Compare the sense of touch of different parts of a body. How does an object feel when the child touches it with an arm, a palm, a cheek, or a belly? Can the child identify the object by touch without using his or her fingers?

Listening Activities

Sound Scavenger Hike

Give the children a list of sounds to listen for on an outing through the school neighborhood or on any field trip. Depending on the place you are visiting, the list may include certain bird songs, insect songs, leaves rustling, or a horn honking.

Stalking

To begin, the children stand in a large circle around a blindfolded child. The game can also be played along a hiking trail. The leader picks a few of the children at a time to approach the child. When the blindfolded child hears someone sneaking up, they point at that person. If correct, that person is caught and is out of the game. The blindfolded child can't just randomly point anywhere. As the leader, you will have to be a judge. The rest of the class must remain silent. This game can serve as a lesson on predator-prey relationships and adaptations for survival.

Who Did That?

One person stands in front of the group with his or her back facing the children. The other children line up about 15 feet away. Silently point to a child in line. That child makes some sort of sound. The listener turns around and has two chances to figure out who made the sound.

Mystery Tape

Make a tape recording of sounds heard in a forest or even around the house. Some sounds to record are leaves blowing in the wind, rocks hitting each other, bird songs, water running, or squirrels chattering. The child can try to guess what the sounds are. On their own, children can make their own tapes and challenge their friends. Bring a tape recorder on a nature walk and record some of the sounds that are heard.

Sound List

The class can keep a list of all the interesting natural sounds they hear throughout the year.

Deer Ears

We can improve our senses by taking ideas from other animals. One method is to simply cup our hands around our ears like a deer. To dramatize the difference, tell your children to rub their feet on the ground. On your signal, they put up their "deer ears" and keep rubbing the ground. Tell them to listen for the difference. We can learn a lot about animals by watching their sensory techniques.

Smelling Activities

Smell Walk

Before the class arrives, mark a number of trees in the schoolyard by rubbing onion on the bark. The class walks around smelling the trees, trying to figure out which ones were marked. A more elaborate smell walk can be made by marking the trees in a path that leads to a prize. Challenge the children to find the trail and follow the path.

Smell and Guess

Put various strong smelling materials in black film canisters. Some possible materials are perfume, garlic powder, orange juice, lemon juice, and mustard. The children smell the film canister and guess what is inside.

Sketching

Field sketching is a great way to become more aware of natural surroundings. It is not reserved for artists. The goal of a field sketch book is not museum artwork. The goal is to help children become more aware of their surroundings and record what they see. It is a way to have fun. Art is for everyone, not reserved for a chosen few. All too quickly, we are divided at a young age into two groups: those who can draw, and those who cannot. In Betty Edwards's book, *Drawing on the Right Side of the*

Brain, she explains what happens. As we grow up, we develop a set of symbols for what we see. Trees are puffy balls on top of two lines for a trunk. The sun is a circle with triangles around it. Instead of drawing what we see, we draw these symbols.

Learning to draw means learning to see instead of drawing from generic symbols our brain has memorized. This means a change in how we look; to really see each individual tree, leaf, bird, or flower. Every child can draw. We need to give them the place to draw without the pressure of a perfect cat or tree. In sketching, they are their only audience. The sketching can be part of the child's journal or kept in a separate sketchpad. Just as we never throw away pages of our journal, we do not throw away sketches. Just as we date journal pages, we date sketches. Just like journals, you need to provide sketching time on a regular basis throughout the year. It should be a ritual. Here are some sketching activities to introduce the children to field sketching. You do not have to be a great artist to use these activities. These exercises are based on ideas from Edwards's book and *The Art of Field Sketching* by Clare Walker Leslie.

These sketching techniques help us break the habit of drawing symbols instead of what is there. By changing the way we look, we see more. We draw what we actually see.

Upside Down Drawing

Take a stick, flower or whatever the subject is and turn it upside down. Draw the object upside down. This technique is effective because it makes the subject less recognizable. It is harder for our brain to classify what we are looking at, which forces us to look at the subject as unique.

Framing

Use a coat hanger, toilet paper roll, or a piece of cardboard with a square cut out of the middle to frame a small area—a couple of leaves, a part of a rock. The child focuses on that area and draws only what is in the frame. Another way to use frames is to help focus on the negative space. Instead of drawing what is there, draw the lines that show what is not there. By drawing the negative space, the subject will appear.

Partner Sketching

One child holds a leaf, a rock, or another object from nature and describes everything he or she can about the object, using as much detail as possible. The partner draws the object based on the description given.

Still Life

The children collect natural objects and set up a still life arrangement. Without looking at their paper, the children do quick sketches of the arrangement. They should follow the outline of the subject with their eyes and draw it, keeping their eyes on the arrangement. Then they can try drawing the still life again looking at the arrangement. They can compare drawings and see which one they like better.

Magnifying Drawings

Holding a hand lens in one hand, children fill up the paper with a giant-size drawing of what they see through the hand lens.

Memory Sketches

Either back in the classroom or in another place on the walk, the children can draw quick sketches from memory.

Free Sketch

Sketching should not always be exercises. Give children a chance to draw whatever they want outdoors. Discuss how the outdoor setting influences their work. Help them think about how they think.

The sketch pad can also be used to draw pictures of things about which the children are learning. The children can draw different tree leaves, tracks, or pictures that will help them remember or even study for a test.

A few last reminders. Practice. It will take time. Watch how their sketches change over time. This is not a one-time activity. Do not draw large scenes or landscapes; focus on the small wonders. Children should draw with their eyes on the subject, not on the paper. When a child asks the inevitable question, "Is this good?" use it as an opportunity to teach. A casual "That's good," will not help. Point out the detail you like. Explain why you like it. Ask the child to explain what they drew. Help them to see, not to draw. When they see better, they will draw better.

Poetry

Poetry can be a part of any of the chapters in this book, but good poets use all their senses, so what better place than here to discuss the possibilities. Early on, we want to help children think like poets, not only to make them better observers, but also to help them be better writers in any genre. Two great books on writing nature poetry are *A Crow Doesn't Need a Shadow* by Lorraine Ferra and *For the Good of the Earth and Sun* by Georgia Heard. I am not going to try to duplicate these works. I have just added a few ideas and words of encouragement.

The natural world is a great subject for poetry. Children are natural poets. Listen to toddlers talk as they learn new words and concepts. They are walking poets, filled with metaphors for the world. A boat is not moving on top of the water, it is "swimming"; a life jacket is a "boat sweater"; a rock with black stripes is a "Zebra rock." In order to understand new ideas and observations, toddlers organize them with what they already know. We can help children get back to that creative thought.

Read poems to them as much as you can and provide opportunities for children to read poetry themselves, especially to read poems out loud. The emphasis may be on nature, but do not limit yourself. Use a variety of poems to show the range of topics, styles, and techniques they can use. Poems do not have to rhyme. Knowing this frees children from a limited vocabulary. Too often, words are chosen only because they rhyme, not because they add meaning to the poem. Poems can be about anything, and you can even break the rules of writing as long as you have a reason that helps make the poem better.

As the children read poems and picture books, they can mark lines they like in the books with yellow stickies. Favorite lines can be copied in their journals, simply read to the class, or posted on a special bulletin board. The better writing they read, the better writing they will produce.

The first step, as always, is to have ideas. Ideas for the poems come from their journals and outdoor experiences. Even if you can't take a walk through a natural area, go out, sit under a tree in the schoolyard, and have your class write. Details and feelings will be much stronger when the poem is based on direct experience. Children should brainstorm many ideas from which to chose; it is not always the first idea that is the best.

I encourage my students to write as much as they can on the idea and cut out later the parts that don't work. As they cut out the extra words, the poem takes shape. The white spaces in the poem are just as important as the words that are written. Pick a short poem and rearrange the line breaks. Show both versions of the poem to the children and discuss the need to consider carefully when each line ends and how the words are arranged.

Rarely does a child get from idea to poem in one step. Much of our work is done by revising. It takes time, modeling, encouragement, and effort to get children to revise. The results are worth the effort. Once the children have accumulated a body of work, they evaluate their own poems and pick the ones they like the best for a personal book of poetry that they will self-publish.

Some ideas for getting them started: Free form—just having time to write is enough for many children. Their heads are full of ideas and words. Let them go. Acrostics, haiku, and other forms of poetry with set structures can limit the possibilities for some children. Others need the structure, especially in the beginning. They can be a helpful option for some children. Sometimes it makes sense to give them an assigned topic for a poem.

To focus and to organize ideas, children can make charts to plan their poems—Observations/Reflections, Sightings/Descriptions, Places/Feelings, Animals/Questions. Make lists of metaphors and similes based on what the children see on an outing from the classroom. Make lists of adjectives and adverbs that are interesting, specific, and not overused. Make lists of favorite words, sounds, an names in nature. Like a sketch, poems can be done quickly. Try writing short, quick poems while on a nature walk. Some of the lines may find their way into poems back in the classroom. Like a sketch, a poem can be focused on a single leaf, flower, or feather. Bring in items to show children to prompt quick poems or journal entries that may become poems. Review journal entries that can become poems. Look at photographs of animals, plants, and natural areas in magazines for ideas or reminders of detail. Research the animal, plant, or place. Facts can be a part of poetry. A thesaurus is a must for a poet. It can be a lot of fun and a great way to find just the right word.

Can they answer the following question about their poems? What are you trying to say? Make a list of adjectives to avoid: pretty, nice, beautiful, or clichés, such as: the clouds are pillows in the sky. Provide time and place and the audience for poetry to be shared.

Being able to think of a metaphor that explains ecological principles shows creativity and understanding. Begin by thinking of human inventions or ideas and compare them to life in the natural world.

These forms of poetry can be used if more direction is desired:

Haiku: Three lines of five, seven, five syllables. For example:

> Rain falls from the sky
> Wet, Washing, Flowing, Going
> Trees grow in the sun

Cinquain: This form is a five-lined poem based on syllables or words. The title is two words or syllables, the second line is a description of the title in four syllables or words, the third line is a description of action in six syllables or words, the fourth line is a description of feeling in eight syllables, and the fifth line is another word for the title in two syllables or words. For example:

> The Bear
> big, brown, black, hairy
> rumble, ramble, climb, dig, splash, scary,
> cuddly, friendly, furry, funny
> The King

Diamante: These poems are shaped in the form of a diamond. Words can be related through shades of meaning, from one extreme to another. The poem follows a pattern of parts of speech.

> noun
> adjective adjective
> participle, participle, participle
> noun, noun, noun, noun,
> participle, participle, participle
> adjective adjective
> noun

For example:

Desert
Hot, Hotter
Walking, Wandering, Journeying
Cactus, Snake, Lizard, Sand
Changing, Moving, Finding
Green, Moist
Forest

Chapter Three

Adapting to the Place

"The true impact of the landscape upon the beholder is not the present scene alone. Rather understanding lies in knowledge of the many forces—climate, vegetation, soil, geologic change—that have molded the scene."

Peter Farb

"Billions of extraordinary and exquisitely evolved creatures share our planet with us."

Warren D. Thomas and Daniel Kaufam

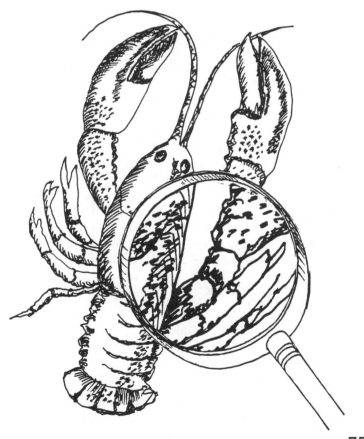

Introduction

Every living thing needs a place to live, including us. The place where a plant, animal, or any other living thing lives is called a *habitat*. Every habitat is made of two main parts: the *abiotic*, or the non-living part, and the *biotic*, the living part. The abiotic parts of a habitat are the sun, soil, air, and water. They are the physical factors that influence each habitat. These factors never were alive, never will be alive, but are still important. The biotic part is the plants, animals, and other organisms living in the habitat. Each habitat is made up of an interrelationship of all these parts. What makes each habitat different is the variability of each abiotic factor. One place has more water than another; another has colder temperatures.

Each community has a variety of habitats, forests, fields, ponds, deserts, streams, and mountains. Each habitat must provide plants and animals with their basic needs for survival. For animals, this means food, water, and shelter; and for plants, enough sun, soil, air, and water.

To survive in their habitats, living organisms have adaptations. An *adaptation* is a trait a living organism has that helps it live in its habitat. In other words, an adaptation is something an animal does or has that helps it survive. It may be a behavior, such as the opossum's habit of playing dead in the face of danger, or a physical characteristic, such as the bird's hollow bones for flying. The same adaptation that helps animals survive also limits where they can live. The dolphin's flippers are great for swimming in the ocean, but they would not do very well in a forest.

All animals need adaptations to find food, to find water, to provide shelter, to reproduce, and to protect themselves from other animals and the physical conditions of their habitat. Plants also need protection and need to reproduce. In addition, plants need adaptations for finding sun, soil, air, and water.

Because each habitat is different, there are a variety of living things. Some animals are adapted to very specific habitats, and others can survive in a variety of places. Kirtland's warbler can only live in jack pine forests that are burned periodically. The Norway rat can live just about anywhere. The danger for animals adapted to specific places is that if those habitats are destroyed, the animal cannot simply switch habitats. The greatest cause of extinction is habitat destruction.

For children, knowledge of their habitats leads to an understanding of their own place. A forest is not just trees. It is the deer, ferns, mice, and all the other living and nonliving parts. Like the deer living in a forest, a child is also part of the place where they live. From learning about the adaptations of animals and other living organisms, children become witnesses to some of the amazing things animals and plants can do. A sense of wonder is created by just knowing the amazing things animals and plants can do. Children also learn a critical lesson: We all have a habitat, we all need a habitat, we all need to learn to live with our habitat, and the only way to do this is to know your habitat.

By learning about the habitats in the place they live, children see first hand the connection animals and plants have with their habitat. It is the same connection they have with their place.

The chapter begins with several activities that help introduce the concept of a habitat. The investigations help children study habitats and the factors that shape them in more detail. The second half of the chapter makes the connection between habitat and adaptation by playing active games and then by studying adaptations in the local area. The entire concept of habitat and adaptation can be evaluated by the invent-an-animal project and the folktale project.

Books to Use

Amsel, Sheri. *A Wetland Walk*. Brookfield, CT: Millbrook Press, 1993. ISBN 1-56294-213-1. Ospreys, dragonflies, spring peepers, and spiders are just a few of the creatures a young boy sees on his walk through the wetlands. The book reminds us that animals big and small are worth our notice. The final page of the book provides additional information in a question-and-answer format on wetlands.

Arnosky, Jim. *Crinkleroot's Guide to Knowing Animal Habitats*. New York: Simon & Schuster Books for Young Readers, 1997. ISBN 0-689-80583-7. Arnosky's nature expert, Crinkleroot, is the subject of many books. In this one, Crinkleroot gives the reader a lesson on what a habitat actually is and takes us to wetlands, forests, fields, and prairies. There are also Crinkleroot guides to common birds, fish, and mammals as well as guides on walking in wild places and tracking. Arnosky would a great subject for an author study.

Arnosky, Jim. *I See Animals Hiding.* New York: Scholastic, 1995. ISBN 0-590-48143-6. Animals are hiding throughout Arnosky's pictures. Children will learn about the adaptations animals have for hiding while they search the pictures.

Arnosky, Jim. *In the Forest: A Portfolio of Paintings.* New York: Lothrop, Lee & Shepard Books, 1989. ISBN 0-688-08162-2. In this book of paintings, Arnosky shows the reader that a forest is made up of a variety of different places. For each painting of each place, he has written a short essay explaining the painting, including some natural history and his personal experiences creating the scene. The book is a trip to the forest on paper.

Aruego, Jose. *Symbiosis: A Book of Unusual Friendships.* New York: Charles Scribner's Sons, 1970. Each page introduces the reader to another pair of animals living in a symbiotic relationship. Cartoon-like illustrations are a nice change of pace. The reader will meet ants that herd caterpillars, a plover that picks the insects from an alligator's mouth, and many others.

Brenner, Barbara, and Bernice Chardiet. *Where's That Insect?* Illustrated by Carol Schwartz. New York: Scholastic, 1993. ISBN 0-590-45210-X. Each illustration, painted realistically, is accompanied by a text that shares a fascinating fact, a short poem, and a hint for what to look for in the painting.

Caduto, Michael, and Joseph Bruchac. *Keepers of the Earth.* Illustrated by John Kahionhes Fadden and Carol Wood. Golden, CO: Fulcrum, 1988. ISBN 1-55591-027-0. This collection of folk tales is organized for using the stories to teach a variety of ecological concepts. Each folk tale is accompanied by background information and environmental education activities. The books in this series are incredible sources for stories and activities. The other books in the series are *Keepers of the Animals*, 1991; *Keepers of the Plants*, 1994; and *Keepers of the Night*, 1994.

Cannon, Janell. *Stellaluna.* San Diego, CA: Harcourt Brace Jovanovich, 1993. ISBN 0-15-280217-7. A tender story of a fruit bat named Stellaluna. Separated from his mother, Stellaluna is raised by birds. He tries to fit his adaptations to a bird's life. Eventually, he finds his way back to his mother and his life as a bat. It is a story of adaptations and a story of friendship. Cannon's illustrations are amazing.

Carle, Eric. *The Mixed-Up Chameleon.* New York: Thomas Crowell, 1975. When a certain a chameleon finds a zoo and sees what other animals can do, he starts making wishes. Soon he is such a mixed-up animal with parts from different animals, he can't catch a fly. So he wishes himself back to his original state. The chameleon learns that every animal has its own adaptations. As usual, Carle's illustrations are eye-catching, and the book design is unique.

Carrick, Carol, and Donald Carrick. *Swamp Spring.* New York: Macmillan, 1969. Carol and Donald Carrick describe life in a swamp as winter melts into spring. This book captures life in a wetland habitat as well as seasonal change.

Cole, Sheila. *When the Tide Is Low.* Illustrated by Virginia Wright-Frierson. New York: Lothrop, Lee & Shepard, 1985. ISBN 0-688-04067-7. Impatient, a young girl repetitively asks her mother to take her to the beach. Her mother patiently replies, "When the tide is low." While pushing the girl on the swing set, the mother explains the difference between high tide and low tide. They talk about all the animals she will see when finally the "tide is low." The last two pages are an illustrated glossary that describes all the animals they see.

Cristini, Ermanno, and Luigi Puricelli. *In the Pond.* Salzburg: Neugebauer Press, 1984. 0-907-234-43-7. This wordless picture book, along with others in the series—*In the Woods* and *In the Garden*—are stunningly illustrated. The pages go together in a panorama of each habitat. There are plenty of animals to find on each page as well as plants that grow in each habitat. Children will look at the pages again and again.

Duncan, Beverly. *Explore the Wild: A Nature Search-and-Find Book.* New York: HarperCollins, 1996. ISBN 0-06-023596-9. Duncan has a wonderful idea for introducing children to seven habitats across North America: deserts, grasslands, tundra, arctic, kelp forests, salt marshes, and swamps. Each painting of the habitat is preceded by text explaining the animals and plants that live there. Students can try to find as many species as they can in each painting. An excellent book for comparing and contrasting habitats.

Dunphy, Madeleine. *Here Is the Wetland.* Illustrated by Wayne McLoughlin. New York: Hyperion Books for Children, 1996. ISBN 0-7868-0164-6. This is a wonderfully illustrated book, with frogs that look like they are jumping off the page. A cumulative text shows how one thing leads to another while introducing various wetland animals.

Dunrea, Olivier. *Deep down Underground.* New York: Macmillan, 1989. ISBN 0-02-732861-9. A counting book about the creatures we might find in a soil habitat. Beginning with one wee moudiewort (mole) and ending with 10 red ants, the reader meets a host of other underground creatures. The illustrations provide much to look at and wonder about concerning the life underground. The ending is a definite surprise.

Edwards, Pamela Duncan. *Some Smug Slug.* Illustrated by Henry Cole. New York: HarperCollins, 1996. Using alliteration, the animals of Edwards's book try to warn a slug from making a big mistake as it crawls along and up a steep slope. The warnings don't work. In addition, there are animals and an "s" shape to search for among the illustrations.

Evans, Lisa G. *An Elephant Never Forgets Its Snorkel: How Animals Survive Without Tools and Gadgets.* Illustrated by Diane De Groat. New York: Crown, 1992. ISBN 0-517-58401-8. Each page begins with the statement, "The Human Way. . ." followed by an example: "Wearing a rain slicker to stay dry." This is followed by an explanation of how animals do the same thing. While some of the examples are animals from places other than North America, there are most likely animals in your area that have similar adaptations .

Fleming, Denise. *In the Small, Small Pond.* New York: Henry Holt, 1993. ISBN 0-590-48119-3. There is much to see from a frog's-eye view on this journey through the small, small pond. Fleming's clever use of words and sounds will suggest animals for children to look for as they search their pond. *In the Small, Small Field* follows the same wonderful pattern.

George, Lindsay Barrett. *In the Woods: Who's Been Here?* New York: Greenwillow Books, 1995. ISBN 0-688-12318-X. This series of books uses incredibly realistic paintings to encourage children to search for animal signs in a variety of habitats. The pages alternate between the clue and the answer. Children can guess who left each sign behind. The childlike map drawn on each book jacket can be used to inspire children to make their own maps. These books can be used before or during a nature walk or to compare habitats. Even if the animals described in the books can't be seen in your area, the book reminds us that animals do leave behind signs, and if we look carefully there is always something to find. Other books in the series are *In the Snow: Who's Been Here?* 1995, and *Around the Pond: Who's Been Here?* 1996.

Guiberson, Brenda. *Spoonbill Swamp.* Illustrated by Megan Lloyd. New York: Henry Holt, 1992. ISBN 0-8050-1583-3. *Spoonbill Swamp* is the story of two mothers, Spoonbill and Alligator, and how they care for young in a southeastern swamp. The reader learns about their habitats and the variety of animals that lives in this habitat. It makes a good companion to Guiberson's book *Cactus Hotel,* which describes life around the saguaro cactus.

Hausman, Gerald. *How Chipmunk Got Tiny Feet.* New York: HarperCollins, 1995. ISBN 0-06-022906-3. This collection of animal origin stories is a good source of stories to tell or read to the group. There is an explanation for How Lizard Got Flat, How Possum Lost His Tail, How Bat Learned to Fly, and several others.

Hines, Anna Grossnickle. *Gramma's Walk.* New York: Greenwillow Books, 1993. ISBN 0-688-11480-6. A grandmother confined to a wheelchair takes her grandson on a walk along a beach. Using wonderfully descriptive language, the author allows the readers and the grandson to go to the beach with only their imagination. This is a great book to read after a trip to prompt journal entries. Even if the children did not go to the beach, the book makes a great model for descriptive writing.

Hirschi, Ron. *Who Lives in . . . the Mountains?* Photographs by Galen Burrell. New York: G. P. Putnam's Sons, 1989. ISBN 0-399-21900-5. One in a series of books, *Who Lives in the . . . ?* Beautiful photography complement a short account of the animals that live in each the habitats. A useful series for comparing and contrasting animals and habitats. Some background information is provided at the end of each book. Hirschi is author and photographer of many wonderful books on the variety of habitats, changes in seasons, and animals.

Hiscock, Bruce. *When Will It Snow?* New York: Atheneum Books for Young Readers, 1995. ISBN 0-689-31937-1. Everybody is waiting for the first snowfall. A young boy named Robin can't wait, and he is feeling very discouraged because there is no snow. Meanwhile, the animals in the forest are getting ready themselves. Each one has a different adaptation for surviving the winter.

Lachman, Lyn Miller. *Our Family, Our Friends, Our World.* New Providence, NJ: R. R. Bowker, 1992. 0-8352-3025-2.

Laurencin, Genevieve. *I Wish I Were.* Illustrated by Ulisis Wensell. New York: G. P. Putnam's Sons, 1987. ISBN 0-399-21416-X. What if we were able to change to different animals and take advantage of their adaptations? As the little boy in this book realizes, becoming a porcupine has advantages when it comes to handling a bully. Becoming the size of a mouse makes hiding much easier. The lighthearted illustrations will give children inspiration to think about what animals they would like to be and why. Some animal adaptations would be mighty handy. This book can be used to inspire a fiction story on adaptations.

Lionni, Leo. *Pezzettino*. New York: Pantheon, 1975. ISBN 0-394-831516-X. Pezzettino (which means "little piece" in Italian) sets off to find out what he is a part of. He asks each animal, "Am I perhaps your little piece?" The answer is always the same: "How could I run fast?" or "How could I be so strong to do what I do if a piece is missing?" Finally, the Wise-one tells Pezzettino where to go to find the answer. Pezzettino learns that he is his own piece and has his own special adaptation.

Luen, Nancy. *Squish: A Wetland Walk*. Illustrated by Ronald Himler. New York: Atheneum, 1994. ISBN 0-689-31842-1. This book about wetlands begins with a walk through a marsh and all the animals one might find there. There are things to hear, smell, and see. We also learn wetlands are not just homes for a variety of animals, but that wetlands prevent flooding and provide drinking water for people. Himler's paintings make a day of stomping in the marsh look like much fun.

Machotka, Hana. *Breathtaking Noses*. New York: Morrow Junior Books, 1992. ISBN 0-688-09526-7. This nonfiction picture book starts with a photograph of a nose. Children can guess whose nose it is. The answer is on the following page, along with an explanation of how the nose helps its owner. The same pattern continues through the book, making it a good way to explain the meaning of an adaptation.

Maynard, Thayne. *Animal Olympians*. New York: Franklin Watts, 1994. ISBN 0-531-15715-6. This book is the animals' version of the *Guinness Book of World Records*. There are many great facts, photographs, and background information on animal record holders, from spitting champions to fastest flyers.

Mazer, Anne. *The Salamander Room*. Illustrated by Steve Johnson. New York: Alfred A. Knopf, 1991. ISBN 0-679-86187-4. A brilliant story about a boy who finds a salamander and brings it home. When his mother questions how he will take care of it, the boy has an answer for everything, thereby showing his knowledge of what an animal needs and how to create the perfect salamander habitat. With a little magic, his bedroom becomes the Salamander Room.

Michaels, Tilde. *At the Frog Pond*. Illustrated by Reinhard Michl. New York: J. B. Lippincott, 1987. ISBN 0-397-32315-8. A beautifully illustrated book that captures the life of a pond. The illustrations tell the story of food cycles and life cycles of pond animals. The text describes a pond from the way it looks to how it feels.

Michelson, Richard. *Animals That Ought to Be: Poems About Imaginary Pets*. Illustrated by Leonard Baskin. New York: Simon & Schuster Books for Young Readers, 1996. ISBN 0-689-80635-3. This is a great book of poetry to go along with any adaptation lesson, especially the invent-an-animal activity. Michelson has written a book of poetry about the animals that are wonderfully adapted to life in a house. There is the "Roombroom" that has special adaptations for cleaning, the "Talkback Bat" that survives a younger brother. Because these animals are pets, not wild animals, the adaptations help humans more than the animal. It is still a fun book.

Pandell, Karen. *Animal Action ABC*. Photographs by Art Wolfe. New York: Dutton's Children's Books, 1996. ISBN 0-525-45486-1. An absolutely great book for showing children a variety of adaptations as well as a model for an alphabet book. Each letter is accompanied by a photograph of an animal in action, a child imitating the animal, and a short poem. For example, "L" stands for "Leap" as penguins leap across the ice. Each action can be a way to introduce a variety of adaptations.

Perenyi, Constance. *Wild Wild West: Wildlife Habitats of Western North America*. Seattle, WA: Sasquatch Books, 1993. ISBN 0-912365-82-X. Beginning with a definition of habitat, this book introduces children to a variety of habitats. The illustrations are cut-paper collages that are fun to browse. Each illustration is accompanied by a short text. A good book for comparing habitats.

Robbins, Ken. *Air*. New York: Henry Holt, 1995. ISBN 0-8050-2292-9. Illustrated with hand-colored photographs, this unique book will change the way children think about air. Each set of pages has a photograph and text that explains one of the many things air can do. Robbins's poetic explanations of topics, such as convection, wind, and rainbows, are a pleasure to read. This book is a part of a series, including *Water*, *Earth*, and *Fire*.

Rochman, Hazel. *Against Borders: Promoting Books for a Multicultural World*. Chicago: American Library Association, 1993. ISBN 0-8389-0601-X.

Ryder, Joanne. *Under Your Feet*. Illustrated by Dennis Nolan. New York: Four Winds Press, 1990. ISBN 0-02-777955-6. A book full of questions that will get one to think about and wonder about the creatures that live under our feet in a habitat we never really see. Over the course of the year, we learn about how the lives of the animals underground are affected by the changing seasons.

Shahan, Sherry. *Barnacles Eat with Their Feet*. Brookfield CT: Millbrook Press, 1995. ISBN 1-56294-922-5. The title of the book tells the reader just one of the amazing adaptations about animals that live in rocky tide pools. A number of tide pool animals are covered in the book. Close-up photography helps identify the animals children may find on a trip to a rocky beach. The book ends with very good advice: sit still and watch.

Silver, Donald M. *One Small Square Backyard*. Illustrated by Patricia J. Wynne. New York, W. H. Freeman, 1993. ISBN 0-7167-6510-1. The books in this series are nicely illustrated but are not picture books. Each book provides a great deal of information and interesting activities. The concept behind the books is to focus on what can be discovered in a square yard of backyard, pond, seashore, and other habitats. With a few easily obtained tools, the reader can discover a variety of plants and animals in each habitat. The books cover all seasons and different times of day. Each page includes background information on plants and animals. In addition, there are many activities for children to try that help them explore and learn. This book will help them find the wonders in a place as simple as a backyard. The final pages of the book can be used as an identification guide. This is part of a series that includes *One Small Square Seashore*, 1993; *One Small Square Pond*, 1994; and *One Small Square Desert*, 1997.

Snape, Juliet, and Charles Snape. *Frog Odyssey*. New York: Simon & Schuster Books for Young Children, 1991. ISBN 0-671-74741-X. A group of frogs in a pond decide that it is time to move to cleaner waters. They pack up the tadpoles in a jar and bring their favorite diving post. Off they go, surviving a variety of hazards until they reach a nice, clean pond. The humorous illustrations lead the way as the frogs bounce along.

Sussman, Susan, and Robert James. *Big Friend, Little Friend: A Book About Symbiosis*. Boston: Houghton Mifflin, 1989. ISBN 0-395-49701-9. After a brief introduction to symbiosis, the authors combine photographs with one-page descriptions of symbiotic relationships. Only one of the relationships described is from North America, but the animals and plants covered will give readers an idea of some interrelationships involved and help them look for examples in their own area.

Wexo, John Bennett. "Animal Champions." *ZooBooks*. San Diego, CA: Wildlife Ed. Ltd., 1988. A good resource for more examples of record holders in the animal world.

Wick, Walter. *A Drop of Water*. New York: Scholastic Press, 1997. ISBN 0-590-22197-3. Incredible photographs, including many close–ups, show the reader the beauty of water as well as its important and wonderful qualities. The back of the book provides more background information and an interesting account of how the book came to be.

Zolotow, Charlotte. *The Seashore Book*. Illustrated by Wendell Minor. New York: HarperCollins, 1992. ISBN 0-06-020213-0. Reading this book is like taking a trip to the seashore. That is exactly its goal. Zolotow starts with a little boy asking his mother, "What is the seashore like?" The book is filled with incredible details of the colors, sounds, scents, and feelings of being at the seashore. Minor's paintings add to the image perfectly.

Activities

Habitat

Describe a Habitat

This activity is simple but effective, and the impact is long lasting. Simply go outdoors to a forest, pond, meadow, or any habitat. Use one or two of the suggested books as models. Give the children time to simply describe the habitat. You may want to allow them to collect a few objects for their journal that symbolize the habitat.

Habitat Box

This is a quick way to introduce the abiotic factors that affect every habitat. Put a jar of water and some soil in a box. Begin with the question, What are the parts of a habitat? Build some mystery by dramatically telling them you have two parts of the habitat in the box, but two are missing. The other two will be in the box as soon as you open it. With guessing and some clues, the students will arrive at the answer: sun, soil, air, and water.

Habitat Pictures

For a variety of activities, photographs of animals, plants, and natural scenes can be extremely helpful. Collect nature magazines and let the children cut out pictures. Put the word out for old copies of *Ranger Rick*, *My Big Backyard*, *Audubon*, and other magazines; plenty will roll in. Use pictures of different habitats to discuss how the sun, soil, air, and water vary from habitat to habitat. Having animal pictures on hand is a good back-up for those surprising rainy days.

The discussion can be extended by giving the children a chance to share their favorite habitats and why they like them it so much.

Hula Hoop Habitats

Use hula hoops, loops of ropes, or coat hangers for this activity. Randomly spread the hoops out on a schoolyard lawn. The hoops will focus the children on a small area. Each group carefully studies the area inside the hoop and records how many different plants and animals they can find. If no one in the group knows the names of the plants or animals, the children can simply make up a name that fits. After 10 or 15 minutes, move the hoops to a different place. Use an area that is more forested or one with unmowed grass. Repeat the activity. For the final habitat, use a section of blacktop or sidewalk. Gather the groups together to discuss the results. Which place had the greatest biodiversity? In other words, which place had the greatest variety of plants and animals? Which had the least? What parts of a habitat are missing from the sidewalk? How does this affect what can live there?

One extension is to give the children golf tees and have them set up a miniature nature trails inside the hoop. The golf tees can mark the interesting sites within the hoop. The children can lead trips on their nature trails.

Abiotic Factors

These activities will provide some background knowledge on each abiotic component of a habitat.

Sun: It is 92,960,000 miles away, but all life on Earth is dependent on the sun. The amount of sunlight hitting a particular habitat varies depending on where the habitat is. Sunlight hits the Earth more directly at the equator. As one moves away from the equator, temperatures fall and vary to a larger extent with the seasons and between night and day. The best way for children to see the effects of sunlight in their place is to measure the temperature and to keep track of the temperatures in the local area from the newspaper. An atlas with a map showing average high and low temperatures around the world clearly shows the effect of a change in latitude. Another way to show the power of the sun is to conduct simple experiments on heating. Which side of the school has a average higher temperature? Do darker colors heat up faster? How does surface area affect heat absorption? The answers to these experiments can lead to a discussion of their implications on the need for certain adaptations and gives good practice with the scientific method.

Soil: Life is also dependent on soil. Often unappreciated, soil is an important factor in each habitat. Soil itself can be considered a habitat. It is a clear example of the interrelationships between living and nonliving components of a habitat. These activities will help children learn just what soil is and why it is important.

Soil Dissection: Using the word *dissection* while introducing any activity definitely will get the children's attention. If you are conducting the activity outdoors, simply tell the group to find all the ingredients of soil and bring them back to a designated bucket. If you do it indoors, give the students a bucket full of soil to dissect. Lay out some paper for each group and give them a pile of soil. The students separate the parts of the soil and record what they find. It is useful to give each student a hand lens and tweezers or spoons. After discussing what they found, write a recipe for fertile soil. The recipe should include: dead organic matter, such as leaves and twigs; dead animals for nutrients; decomposers to put nutrients in the soil (decomposers are animals, bacteria, and fungus that decay dead plants and animals); rocks to provide minerals; water; and air.

Tell the students you are now going to make soil. Place a little of each ingredient in a bucket; there is still one component missing. Every good recipe tells the chef how long to cook the food. The last ingredient is the "time" it takes to make soil. To dramatize your point, drop a watch into the bucket and say "100-400 years." It takes a long time to make soil.

The Value of Soil: Is there anything children eat that does not need soil? Trace any food to its source, and you end up with soil. To show that soil is necessary to grow crops, challenge the students to use the craziest mixture of materials and try to grow bean seeds. Put the crazy mixtures in egg cartons or small cups with a couple of seeds. Compare the growth to a bean seed grown in soil. They may be able to get sprouts in the crazy mixtures, but the beans in the soil will grow better.

Erosion Demonstration: Erosion is the process of soil being worn away by wind, water, and other factors. Once eroded away, it is hard to get soil back. Use a hose or a bucket of water to demonstrate erosion on the playground or in a tray of soil in the classroom. Land is also eroded by wind and human activity. Use a fan or have the students blow on sand or soil to demonstrate wind erosion. In the area around the school, look for examples of erosion from people. Foot traffic can cause erosion. Look for a place where people have packed down the soil. Discuss why plants would have a hard time growing where a great deal of erosion is taking place. Plants prevent erosion, especially on hillsides. Compare how much soil is eroded away when water is poured over ground with plants growing and ground without plants.

Air: Air is a mixture of gases that carries what both plants and animals need—carbon dioxide and oxygen. These molecules have been exhaled and inhaled by plants and animals for millions of years. A dinosaur breathed the same oxygen you are breathing. Animals in aquatic habitats need O_2 from the water. Air affects the animals and plants through wind. One way land animals and aquatic animals differ is the way they obtain oxygen and the fact that it is easier to move through air than water. Air has weight; in fact, there are 32 pounds of pressure per square inch. This adds up to a lot of pressure. One way to demonstrate this is to take a sheet of newspaper and lay it flat on a table. Slide a ruler or meter stick half way underneath. Part of the stick should hang out over the table. With a swift chop you can break the stick. The air pressure on the newspaper acts as if your hand were holding the other end of the yardstick. Another good demonstration is to put an index card over a small glass of water. Quickly flip the glass over. Nothing should spill; the air pressure pushing up holds the card and water in place.

Look for evidence of how wind affects the habitat.

Water: Water is a unique substance with unique qualities. Without these qualities, life as we know it today would not exist. Making a glass of lemonade demonstrates to children these unique properties.

Give each child a glass of water and an ice cube.

Ask them to put the ice cube in. A floating ice cube may not seem like much, but it is a unique phenomena; the solid floats on the liquid. There is no other matter in which the solid state of the substance floats on the liquid state of the substance. Solid H_2O has less density than liquid H_2O. A copper penny sinks in a glass of melted copper. What makes this important is that if ice were heavier than water, ponds and lakes would freeze from the bottom up, killing most of the life in the water.

Leave some lemonade out to evaporate over the course of a couple days. The next amazing thing is that within the normal range of temperatures on Earth, H_2O can be in the liquid, solid, and gaseous forms all at the same time. Water is the only matter that can do this. Without this property, water could not be recycled. The water cycle allows the Earth to maintain life with a limited amount for water.

Pour in the powdered lemonade. What happens? The lemonade dissolves. Another important quality of water is its ability to dissolve other matter, including oxygen. Without dissolved oxygen in the water, animal life would not be able to obtain oxygen from the water.

Stir the lemonade. Remember it is easier for animals to move through air than water, which affects their body shapes.

Spill a little lemonade on your table. Use a paper towel to soak it up. Watch the water move through the paper towel. One molecule pulls another upward. Water is very cohesive—water molecules stick together. Without this cohesiveness, water would not be able to rise up from the roots of plants, hundreds of feet in the air. If the water cannot reach the leaves, photosynthesis cannot take place, and therefore no food is produced. These properties give us a clue as to the value of water.

How Much Water Is There? The water in the glass represents all the water in the world. Drink 97 percent of the lemonade. That represents all the water in the ocean. Drink another 2 percent to account for glaciers. The remaining 1 percent is the fresh water available to drink. The problem is that some of this fresh water is polluted. There are only a few drops left that are available for us to drink. We better take care of it. (Facts taken from *Project WET*, Watercourse and the Council for Environmental Education, 1995.)

Site Study

A site study is a more in-depth version of the hula hoop activity. Site studies get the children outdoors, directly comparing and contrasting the different habitats. Make it an up close and personal examination. A larger area is studied, and students find more information about each site. In each habitat the children visit, they will study and record information about the abiotic and biotic parts of the habitats. Provide them with a list of questions they will answer at each site. If possible, take a trip to different habitats, such as a field, a forest, a wetland, or a seashore. If that is not possible, a schoolyard usually has more then one micro-habitat.

Record the information they gather on a large chart. Depending on the site, the children answer some of the following questions about the habitat's components.

Sun: On a scale of 1 (sunny) to 10 (shady), is the place usually shady or sunny? What is the temperature in this habitat? What is the temperature in different places in the habitat? What is the average? How much does it vary within the habitat? How quickly will a wet paper towel dry out? Graph the temperature over the course of one day.

Soil: What color is the soil? Darker soil has more organic nutrients than lighter soil. How quickly does the soil absorb water? Pour water into a coffee can without a bottom, placed on the ground, and time how long it takes for the water to soak in. Pour the same amount each time and measure how quickly the water soaks in. How moist is the soil? Pick up a handful of the soil. Can you squeeze it together? Dig into the soil. What do you see? Is the soil rocky?

Sandy? Clay-like? Use a pointed stick to compare soil compactness by measuring how hard it is to push a pointed stick into the soil. Be sure to push just as hard each time. If you have a soil test kit available, there are other factors to compare, such as pH and nitrogen content.

Air: On a scale of 1 (windy) to 10 (not windy), is this usually a windy place? Are there any places in the area that show the effects of wind? Use the Beaufort Table to measure wind speed.

Beaufort Number	Name	Miles/Hour	Description
0	calm	less than 1	calm; smoke rises vertically
1	light air	1-3	direction of wind shown by smoke, but not on wind vanes
2	light breeze	4-7	wind felt on face; leaves rustle; wind vane moved
3	gentle breeze	8-12	leaves and small twigs in constant motion; light flag
4	moderate breeze	13-18	raise dust and loose paper: small branches are moved
5	fresh breeze	19-24	small trees in leaf begin to sway; cresting wavelets form on inland
6	strong breeze	25-31	large branches in motion; inconvenience in walking against wind
7	moderate gale	32-38	large branches in motion; telegraph wires whistle; umbrellas used with difficulty
8	fresh gale	39-46	breaks off twigs; generally impedes progress
9	strong gale	47-54	slight structural damage occurs; chimney pots and slates removed
10	whole gale	55-63	trees uprooted; considerable structural damage occurs
11	storm	64-72	very rare; widespread damage
12	hurricane	73-136	devastation occurs

(Source: taken from Environmental Factors Unit of Orleans Madison County BOCES.)

Water: Is the water fresh or salt water? On a scale of 1 (dry) to 10 (wet), is this usually a wet or dry place? Do you see any water from where you are? Is the water moving? If so, how fast? To find how fast a stream flows, record the time it takes for a cork to float 10 yards. Divide the total distance the cork traveled by the number of seconds. In a marine habitat, estimate wave size. What is the water temperature? Measure the amount of rainfall in different places.

Animals: What animals live here? What signs of animals can you find? See chapter 5 for more activities.

Plants: Are there many different plants in this habitat? Can you identify any? What kinds of plants are the most common? See chapter 6 for more plant activities.

After visiting each habitat, the children have a number of ways to compare the information gathered. One possibility is to photograph each habitat visited. If possible, allow the children to take their own pictures. The photographs combined with captions can create a display comparing the habitats. Two other methods are dioramas and murals. Using materials collected at the habitats combined with their own artwork, the students can create murals or dioramas portraying each habitat. If you can re-visit the habitats more than once over the course of the year, the children can track the changes as the seasons progress. The children can practice comparing and contrasting by using habitats and their descriptive writing skills.

Adaptations

Once the children have an understanding of habitats, they can make the connection to how plants and animals are adapted to each habitat.

Adaptation Walk

To introduce the concept of adaptations, explain some examples of what local animals do to survive in their habitat. Take a walk around the schoolyard or other nearby natural area and point out some of the ways plants and animals survive in the local habitat. The key is to emphasize local plants and animals. Even the common neighborhood animals and plants have amazing adaptations. If you don't know any, check out the children's section of any library for books on the specific animals you want to feature.

Missing Adaptations

Another way to introduce the concept of adaptation is to take away one of most important human adaptations. Use masking tape to tape students' thumbs to their own hand, making it impossible to use. Let the children try to tie their shoes and to do other everyday activities. The opposable thumb is just one important adaptation for humans.

Adaptation Examples

If it is possible to obtain bones, animal study skins, feathers, or any other animal parts, they can also be used to show children a variety of adaptations. Seeing and holding something will make the experience more meaningful. Use pictures cut from magazines to give the children other examples of adaptations. Ask the children to try to match the photographs of animals and plants to the pictures of various habitats.

Amazing Adaptations

Children can select a local plant and animal and find out some of the adaptations the animal has to aid in survival. This type of research does not always require children to write reports. They can simply find a few answers and share them on a class chart, in a class discussion, or on a school nature walk. Here are some suggestions of things for children to answer after they pick an animal: name of animal, adaptation for finding food, adaptation for finding protection from the local climate, adaptation for finding protection from predators, adaptation for finding shelter, and any other amazing adaptations.

Animal Olympics

Children love a challenge. Competing in the Animal Olympics will get them curious and excited about animal adaptations. These events match the students' abilities against the champions of the animal world. Each event has three parts. First, the students participate in the athletic event. Second, they learn about the animal champion and its adaptations. Third, they use math skills to compare the results to their own ability. Some of the animals in the Olympics are not native to the United States, and some may not be native to your area. If possible, use the examples from the place where the children live and find out the record setters in your area.

Speed: Time each student for the 100 yard dash. You can even time them for a mile run. Compare these times with the fastest animals. The fastest land animal is the cheetah. Cheetahs can reach speeds of 75 mph. That means they can cover 25 yards in one second. Cheetahs have long legs for running. Their spine is flexible, allowing them to extend their legs even further. A small head and a thin body help them stay streamlined. The peregrine falcon can dive through the sky at speeds up to 240 mph. They have narrow wings like a fighter jet. The pronghorn can run 50 mph, and the canvasback duck can fly 70 mph. A white-tailed deer runs 30 mph, a rabbit around 27 mph. To find out how many miles per hour a student runs, multiply their time for 100 yards by 17.6 (there are 1,760 yards in a mile). That will tell you how many seconds it takes to run one mile. Divide by 60 seconds to find out many minutes it takes to run one mile. Use ratios to find out how many miles can be covered in one hour.

Another way to compare speed is by number of body lengths covered in given amount of time. The common house spider can travel 330 times its body length in 10 seconds, or 115 mph. How many body lengths can a child run in 10 seconds?

Snails travel 0.03 mph; how long would it take them to travel a mile? (Answer: a day and a half.)

Long Jump: Make a starting line in a grassy area. Let the children get a running start and measure how far each of them can jump.

The animal world has some great jumpers. With incredibly strong legs and a tail for balance, kangaroo rats can jump 43 times their body length. Tree frogs can jump 100 times their body length. Fleas can jump 4 feet; that is 384 times its $\frac{1}{8}$ inch body length. How many more feet can a kangaroo rat jump than the students? If you could jump 43 times your body length, how far would you be jumping? What animal is the best jumper in your local habitat? If it is possible, use a live cricket or frog in the competition.

Wing Flap: Put the children in pairs. One student will flap his or her arms up and down as many times as possible in one minute. The partner counts how many flaps his or her partner makes in one minute, records the number, and then switches roles.

Hummingbirds can flap their wings 4,500 times in one minute. The hummingbird has ridged wings that flap up and down in a figure-eight pattern. Other birds simply flap their wings up and down. This adaptation allows the hummingbird to hover up and down and fly backward and forward. Bumble bees can flap their wings 15,000 times per minute. If you kept up the same pace, how many times would you flap in one hour? How many times could a hummingbird flap its wings in one hour? What is the difference? Some other flapping times: crow, 120 beats a minute; starling, 270 beats a minute.

Jumping Accuracy: Place a piece of paper on the ground. One at a time, the students jump off a chair and try to land on the paper without falling off. Make the paper smaller and smaller.

The klipspringer is an antelope that lives on the rocky slopes of mountains in Africa. They are excellent climbers because of their rubbery, rounded hooves. Klipspringers can jump from one rock and land on an area the size of a dime. Bighorn sheep and mountain goats also have to be able to jump from place to place on mountains without falling. What is the area of a dime? What is the area of the paper on which the child jumped?

Strength: It is a little difficult to directly compare strength of other animals to children because weights may not be available. However, there are several ways to measure the students' strength that will give them some appreciation for the strength of animals. Children can simply try to lift each other up. The students can lift greater and greater numbers of books. Even push-ups or chin-ups can be done.

There are some incredibly strong animals. Chimpanzees can lift six times their body weight. Elephants can pull 20,000 pounds. Perhaps the strongest animal is the ant. Ants can lift 50 times their body weight. Leave some crumbs on the ground near an ant hole and watch ants pick them up. The average car weighs one ton. How many cars can an elephant pull? If you could lift 50 times your body weight, how much could you lift? Find out how much a chimpanzee weighs. How many pounds can a chimpanzee lift?

Breath Holding: The students can time how long they can hold their breath.

A champion breath-holder is the sperm whale. The sperm whale can hold its breath for two hours. The oxygen in the sperm whale's body combines slowly with other substances in the body. Their heartbeat slows down, and the blood flow decreases. These adaptations save oxygen for the sperm whale. How many more seconds can a sperm whale hold its breath than you? Next time the children see a frog jump in the water, sit by the edge and wait to see how long the frog stays under.

High Jump: The children hold a piece of tape in their hands. Standing next to a wall or tree, they jump as high as they can and stick the tape on the wall or tree. Have them hold up their hands as high as possible and measure the height. Measure the height of the tape. The difference between the two measurements is the vertical leap. Powerful legs help mountain lions have a vertical leap of 18 feet. How much higher is a mountain lion's vertical leap than the child's?

Distance Traveled: The children find out how many miles the family car has traveled and the age of the car. Some animals travel incredible distances. Arctic terns migrate 24,000 miles each year, from the Arctic to the Antarctic and back. With long wings for their body size, Arctic terns are great flyers. Gray whales travel 26,000 miles a year. This translates into 115 miles a day. Discuss a way to estimate the distance a child travels in one day. Round your car's mileage to the nearest thousand. Find the average number of miles driven each year. What travels further, your car or an Arctic tern? Monarch butterflies travel 50-100 miles a day during their migration to Mexico. Many songbirds fly to Central and South America every year.

Sleeping: For one week, each child keeps track of how long he or she sleeps and finds the nightly average. Figure out how much time the children spend sleeping in the winter months. In order to survive the winter, some animals hibernate. Their bodies slow down to the point where their heartbeat may be only beat two or three times a minute, and the breathing drops as well. Bats, chipmunks, and other ground squirrels are examples of true hibernators. These animals cannot be easily woken up. Male lions often sleep 22 hours a day. Many other animals simply sleep many hours during the winter, but they can be woken up, and they do wake up.

Plant Match

Write one-half of each statement on a card. If there are more then 20 children, make up other matches or put some of the children in pairs.

Thick Bark	To protect from fire (redwood)
Thorns	To protect from being eaten (rose)
Sweet Smell	To attract insects (orchid)
Brightly Colored Flowers	To attract insects (jewelweed)
Hard Seed Covering	To protect from being eaten (oaks)
Fluffy Seeds	To float in the wind (milkweed)
Leathery Leaves	To hold in water in the desert (paloverde)
Deep Roots	To anchor the plant and obtain water (chicory)

Tendrils on Vines	To climb up walls and trees (poison ivy)
Flowers shaped for a	Landing pad for bees (lady slippers)

Mix the cards up and hand one card to each child. The children run around trying to find their match. Discuss the adaptations these plants have. If there are examples nearby, show them to the children.

Nature Did It First

Make a list of animal adaptations and how humans have created inventions for the same purpose. For example, the hooves on a deer are like human running shoes. This is another good use for cut-out animal pictures.

Cooperation Is Natural

Symbiosis is a relationship between two different species that is mutually beneficial for both species. The natural world is filled with fascinating examples of this type of cooperation. As you explore your area, look for other examples of symbiosis. This activity can also be combined with a lesson on developing cooperation and community in the classroom. Simply by taking a walk in the school yard, you can find many examples.

Introduce symbiosis with a common example. Flowers provide bees with nectar, and bees help the flowers reproduce by spreading their pollen. Another example is lichen. Lichen grows on bare rocks and tree trunks. It is a combination of algae and fungus. The algae provides food through photosynthesis, and the fungus provides the shelter by holding the algae to the surface of the rocks and trees. There are many other amazing examples, coming in all sizes. The gray Phalarope pecks tiny animals off the backs of sperm whales. The birds get a meal, and the whales get rid of parasites. Certain species of ants milk aphids for food as they offer them protection from predators.

Humans are also part of symbiotic relationships. Bacteria in our digestive system help us absorb food as we provide a home for them. All of us are dependent on the symbiotic relationship between legumes (clovers, beans, peas) and rhizobium bacteria. All plants and animals need nitrogen. The nitrogen in the atmosphere cannot be used in that form. The bacteria convert the nitrogen into a form usable by the legumes. The legumes provide shelter for the bacteria in their roots. All other living things are dependent on this relationship.

We are all dependent on trees. Many trees are involved in a symbiotic relationship with mycorrhiza fungus. The fungus grows on the trees' root tips. Tiny hairs on the fungus increase the ability of the roots to take in water and nutrients. Without this fungus, trees would not be able to obtain necessary but limited resources. The fungus gets food and safety from the tree roots.

To insure that your class understands the concept, play the "Symbiosis Game." Put the students in groups of three and bring them outside to a playing field. Each student has a different role. The animals in the symbiotic relationship are the digger and the tagger. The digger is adapted to dig for roots. The tagger loves to eat worms but can't dig. Instead, the tagger offers protection. The attacker loves to eat diggers.

To play the game, the digger squats down and starts digging a hole. Meanwhile, the tagger guards the digger from the attacker as he or she tries to run in and touch the digger. If the tagger touches the attacker, the digger is safe, and the digger and tagger get their food. If the attacker touches the digger, he or she gets to eat. Students can switch roles after each tag.

Give the digger a spoon and tape the tagger's fingers together to make the adaptations more realistic. Play this game in a large area so each group can run around without interfering with each other.

Invent an Animal or a Plant

This is a good culminating project and a way to evaluate the children's understanding of the connection between habitat and place. Each child will invent and create a model of an animal or plant that is adapted to live in the schoolyard. The first step is to study the habitat and to observe the conditions.

The children may want to refer to habitat site studies and the research they did on local animals and plants. Before the students work on their own, lead them through a class example by inventing an animal that could survive in the bathtub.

Discuss the bathtub habitat. An animal or plant living in a bathtub would have to contend with a varying water supply that can leave the place dry for most of the day. The color of the habitat is white. Draining water has a great deal of suction. People come in on occasion. There are very few other plants and animals. Ask the class to think of adaptations to survive in a bathtub habitat. The animal will need adaptations to protect itself from weather conditions and local predators as well as for finding food, water, and shelter. Finally, they will need an adaptation to reproduce. Some ideas may be suction cups to avoid being sucked down, white skin, and a piercing tongue to suck out toothpaste.

The main project will be to invent an animal or a plant for the schoolyard. The children can refer to their site study to consider what makes the schoolyard habitat unique. What abiotic and biotic factors will have to be considered in designing an animal in this habitat? The students can make a model of their animal or draw a detailed picture. As an extension, the children can write a short essay explaining each adaptation.

A fun way to share the projects is to go out in the schoolyard and set up the animals. A simpler approach is to use magazine pictures to cut out parts of various animals and combine them to create the new animals.

Natural Selection

An extension of learning about adaptations is an understanding of how adaptations are developed. This activity introduces children to the idea of natural selection.

Use a box of colored toothpicks to demonstrate natural selection. Split the class into two groups. Use 50 toothpicks, 10 of each color. The game can be played outdoors or indoors. One group will hide the "toothpick worms." The other group will search for them. The only rule for hiding is that at least one part of the toothpick must remain showing. After the searchers collect as many as they can in two minutes, count the results. Make a chart showing how many of each color were found. Switch roles and repeat for several rounds. Any toothpick that is not found should be returned by the child who hid it and given out to the next group to be hidden. After each round, record the results. After totaling the numbers for each color, ask the students which color has the best chance of reproducing. Whichever color is caught the least will reproduce the most. Suppose red is the least likely caught. Because the red ones are caught less, they can reproduce more and pass the color trait down. If more yellows are caught, they will have less babies. There will eventually be less yellows.

To demonstrate that in a given population there is a variability within one trait, have the children measure their foot size. List the results on the chart. Use this example: The water level is rising around the world. People with longer feet will have a great advantage. In the following generations, it will be more and more likely that long-footed individuals will reproduce. Eventually, the population will consist of people with bigger feet.

Natural selection takes time and many generations. If a habitat changes rapidly, the animals and plants cannot keep up. They will die out if there is no other place to go. Animals and plants can adapt, but only over a long period of time. As an extension, you may want to use some of the timeline activities discussed in chapter 5. Use these activities to help children see the scope of time.

Folktales

For thousands of years, people around the world have used stories to explain why things are the way they are. Some of the most common stories are those that explain why animals are the way they are. These stories not only answer those questions but teach other lessons and entertain the listeners.

Children can write stories about local animals that explain why they are the way they are. For example, how did the rabbit get big ears? How did the chipmunk learn to sleep through the winter? Why do prairie dogs dig? We have all witnessed the power of storytelling while teaching. Perhaps in the middle of a math lesson you ended up sharing a story from your own life; suddenly, fidgeting kids stop, listen, and lean forward, eyes glued to you. Storytelling has an incredible power to teach and to entertain. Having that hold on an audience makes storytelling an extremely effective teaching technique.

Begin by reading, or better yet telling, stories to your class. Give them time to read some by obtaining an assortment of Native American folktales and letting them choose which ones to read. When they are familiar with the genre, they can start writing and telling their own.

Each child should pick an animal about which they are interested in learning more. The next step is a little research, and if possible, direct observation of the animal. Learning more about the animal's adaptations makes the story interesting and realistic.

Armed with a topic and some facts, the children can plan out their stories. They should select one trait of the animal and think of a story explaining how the animal got that trait. Planning is essential for a good story, despite what children say. By spending time planning, the child is less likely to get halfway through the story and decide it is not any good, give up, and start over. The plan should include the characters, the setting, and the plot. There needs to be a beginning, a middle, and an end.

Once the child has a plan, it is time to write a rough draft. Because the stories will most likely have talking animals, the project is a good place to teach about punctuation and writing dialogue.

After revising and editing, the children are ready to share their stories. Children can read them to other classes; better yet, they can tell them.

Another option is for children to learn traditional Native American folktales that explain animal adaptations. Children can pick their favorite stories to learn for themselves. There are a number of good books to read on storytelling. Here are some basic pointers: Listening to other storytellers will help. Read the story out loud many times before telling it in public. Practice. Know the story. Don't memorize; tell the story. Use an echo chant to be sure people are listening and to make the audience participate. The audience responds with a certain word or sound every time the teller says a certain word or sound. For example, whenever I say chipmunk in a story, the audience squeaks. Another traditional method is to simply say "Ho" every once in a while, and the audience responds with "Hey." Tell stories in a circle. Consider the audience when deciding what story to tell. Don't rush, speak clearly, pause for effect, and change the pace of your voice once in a while. Make eye contact with the audience. On occasion, focus on one child and speak directly to that child. If you use hand motions, keep them simple so that they do not become a distraction. If you are going to use different voices for different characters, be absolutely sure you are able to maintain the same voice throughout the story. Give credit to the people who told the story first. Have fun. Light a candle to begin each storytelling session. It isn't as good as a campfire, but it creates a sense of ritual and ceremony in the telling.

(Most of these suggestions come from Michael Caduto and Joseph Bruchac's excellent book *Keepers of the Earth.*)

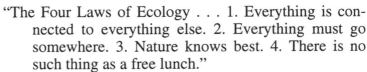# Chapter Four

How Does the Place Work?

"The Four Laws of Ecology . . . 1. Everything is connected to everything else. 2. Everything must go somewhere. 3. Nature knows best. 4. There is no such thing as a free lunch."

Barry Commoner

"All living things are interwoven, each with the other; the tie is sacred, and nothing, or next to nothing, is alien to ought else."

Marcus Aurelius Antoninus

"When we try to pick out something by itself, we find it hitched to everything else in the universe."

John Muir

Introduction

Having an understanding of how the natural world works is an important part of connecting to any place. This knowledge is soon coupled with the realization that all parts of a place are interrelated. These principles apply to any place in the world. The activities in this chapter demonstrate a variety of the most important interrelationships that make the world work. The overall goal of these lessons is to help children understand the basic facts of ecology.

Everything is connected to something else. Everything needs something else; everything affects something else and is affected by something else. Every action causes another action. What happens matters. What we do matters. Showing children the power and the effect of interrelationships helps show them that what they do matters; each of them has an effect on the world and is affected by the world. The question is, will it be a positive or a negative effect?

Ecology is the study of the interrelationships between living things and between living and non-living parts of the environment. Understanding ecological principles begins with seeing the world as a set of interrelationships. This chapter focuses on some of the major cycles that make life on Earth possible: food, water, carbon, and nitrogen cycles, and the process of succession. Each cycle is taught with physical games and outdoor activities that help children see the cycle in action.

Teaching children about these cycles helps them understand that all living things, including humans, are part of many interrelationships. Although these cycles are complex, we can teach children a basic understanding of each cycle. Knowledge and understanding as well as mystery and wonder foster strong connections. Knowing how something works helps one both appreciate and care for it. Knowing how our home, our ecosystem, works is a key part of being part of where one lives. This knowledge is also the base that is needed to begin to understand the impact human actions can have on the environment. Before anyone understands the Greenhouse Effect, they need to know what the carbon cycle is. Learning how these cycles create a balance and a system shows how incredibly and wonderfully they all fit together.

Books to Use

Asch, Frank. *Water.* San Diego, CA: Harcourt Brace Jovanovich, 1995. ISBN 0-15-200189-1. Asch tells us water is many things: "Water is dew, water is ice and snow." Each reminder of the many forms water can take is accompanied by bright, multicolored illustrations that look like they were fun to make. Children can continue adding to the list of what water is.

Bernhard, Emery. *The Way of the Willow.* Illustrated by Durga Bernhard. San Diego, CA: Harcourt Brace Jovanovich, 1996. ISBN 0-15-200844-6. A willow branch falls off a tree in a storm. A dog discovers the branch, plays with it, and drops it in a river, where it is used by a beaver and then by an osprey. The stick finally ends up in the ocean. Rediscovered washed up on a beach by a young boy, the stick is used to make a mobile. The book demonstrates both the way one thing can lead to another and the water cycle. The book includes instructions for making mobiles.

Birch, David. *The King's Chessboard.* Illustrated by Devis Grebu. New York: Penguin Books, 1988. ISBN 0-14-054880-7. A king in ancient India gives his wise man a reward. His request is to have one grain of rice for the first square on the royal chess board, then doubled for the second squared, doubled again for the third, and so on. The king soon learns that what he thought was a silly request actually meant giving the wise man a great deal of rice. This ancient folktale shows just what exponential growth can do.

Bunting, Eve. *Red Fox Running.* Illustrated by Wendell Minor. New York: Clarion Books, 1993. ISBN 0-395-58919-3. Bunting's words and Minor's paintings capture the edge of fear in a red fox as he desperately searches for food on a cold winter day. This book provides an interesting look at the food cycle.

Cunningham, David. *A Crow's Journey.* Morton Grove, IL: Whitman, 1996. ISBN 0-8075-1356-3. A crow begins his journey by asking where the melted snow on the mountain goes. He follows the snow through streams and rivers, over waterfalls, past the village, and to the ocean. Cunningham's paintings show each stage of the journey with stunning beauty and realism.

Goble, Paul. *I Sing for the Animals.* New York: Bradbury Press, 1991. ISBN 0-02-737725-3. Using pictures from some of his many books about the Plains Indians, Goble has written a poetic and beautiful book about the interconnectedness of life. His words remind us that all lives have a role to play and that humans are part of this web. This book is both a celebration of life and a reminder to value all life.

Griffin, Sandra Ure. *Earth Circles.* New York: Walker, 1989. ISBN 0-8027-6843-1. This unique book combines the story of a mother and child on a spring day with a series of poems written in the shape of circles that represent the endless cycles. Each poem is about one of the many interrelated cycles that are part of our environment: life cycles, the water cycle, the cycle of high and low tide, and others. The illustrations were drawn with pencil.

Jeffers, Susan. *Brother Eagle, Sister Sky: A Message from Chief Seattle.* New York: Dial Books, 1991. ISBN 0-8037-0969-2. Using Chief Seattle's famous speech about the interconnectedness of life, Jeffers has created a book that helps children understand that "The Earth does not belong to us. We belong to the Earth." Despite the controversy over the exact words and the author, this speech has a very powerful message.

Lauber, Patricia. *Who Eats What?* Illustrated by Holly Keller. New York: HarperCollins, 1995. ISBN 0-06-022981-0. A simple and straightforward description of food chains and how they become food webs. The colorful and cartoon illustrations diagram food webs and show simple activities children can do to learn more about food cycles.

Locker, Thomas. *Water Dance.* San Diego, CA: Harcourt Brace Jovanovich, 1997. ISBN 0-15-201284-2. Locker's books are always stunning to look at, and this book also beautifully describes the many forms water takes as it moves through the water cycle. Each page is a short poem connected together like a water cycle. The book ends with some scientific background on each step of the water cycle.

Manson, Christopher. *The Tree in the Wood.* New York: North/South Books, 1993. ISBN 1-55858-192-8. Manson has adapted an old nursery song to show how interrelated everything is. One thing leads to another as a tree in the wood helps others; so many wonderful things happen, and they all eventually make their way back to the tree. The illustrations give a sense of old-fashioned wood cuts.

Marlke, Sandra. *Creepy, Crawly Baby Bugs.* New York: Scholastic, 1996. ISBN 0-590-55829-3. Stunning close-up photography gives the reader a view of the life cycle of a variety of insects. The reader will learn of many adaptations insects have for their life cycles.

McLerran, Alice. *The Mountain That Loved a Bird.* Illustrated by Eric Carle. Saxonville, MA: Picture Book Studio, 1985. ISBN 0-88708-000-6. A barren mountain sits alone for years and years until a bird appears. Each year the bird visits but is forced to leave because the mountain is so barren. The mountain is sad to say goodbye and cries a tear that becomes a stream. The bird leaves a seed behind that slowly grows into a tree. The rock turns to soil, more plants come, and the mountain slowly changes. There is finally enough forest for the bird to stay.

Miller, Edna. *Mousekin's Woodland Birthday.* New York: Prentice Hall, 1974. ISBN 0-13-604405-0. A young mouse ventures through the woods and learns how all the other animals' babies are born and grow.

Myers, Christopher A., and Lynne Born Myers. *McCrephy's Field.* Illustrated by Normand Chartier. Boston: Houghton Mifflin, 1991. ISBN 0-395-53807-6. Joe McCrephy left his farm to help raise goats in Wyoming. After the first year, the fields on his farm were covered with flowers: the next year, blackberries and trees sprouted. Animals moved in, and more plants grew. As the forest changed, the animals changed. Fifty years later, Joe came back to a place he barely recognized. A beautiful story showing the effects of succession.

Newton, James R. *Forest Log.* Illustrated by Irene Brady. New York: Thomas Crowell, 1980. ISBN 0-690-04007-5. A Douglas fir falls to the forest floor in the Pacific Northwest. Over many years, the fallen tree becomes part of the soil. Along the way, a variety of animals find food, water, or shelter from the fallen log. The log acts as a nurse to help other plants grow. Death helps life in this endless cycle.

Ring, Elizabeth. *What Rot! Nature's Mighty Recycler.* Photographs by Dwight Kuhn. Brookfield CT: Millbrook Press, 1996. ISBN 1-56294-671-4. A rotting pumpkin is used to introduce what happens to plants and animals when they decompose. The photographs are intriguing, especially the close-ups of decomposers in action. The simple text is supported by additional information at the end of the book.

Roop, Peter, and Connie Roop. *One Earth, a Multitude of Creatures.* Illustrated by Valerie A. Kells. New York: Walker, 1992. ISBN 0-8027-8192-6. Although the book focuses on the Pacific Northwest, the message applies to life everywhere: One thing leads to another, and a variety of animals lives in each place. Each animal is introduced along with the word used to define a set group of these animals. For example, a pod of whales, an army of caterpillars, and a smack of jelly fish.

Schwartz, David. M. *How Much Is a Million?* New York: Lothrop, Lee & Shepard, 1985. ISBN 0-688-04049-7. How long do you think it would take to count to a million? It would take much longer than you think. This book helps children get a sense of just how big a million actually is, let alone a billion.

Activities

 ## Big Picture

To get the big picture, children need to see that everything in the world is connected to something else. Everything is interrelated. Put the children in groups of four or five. Give them large pieces of paper, the bigger the better. For 10 minutes, they write or draw anything in their community. The drawing should be simple. The idea is to put down as many different items as possible. Plants, animals, machines, houses, or whatever they think are just a few of the possibilities. Ask for a few examples from their papers and write them on a chalkboard. Suppose you start with a tree, an ice cream cone, a bird, and a television. Ask the group for ways in which any of the objects are connected. The bird lives in the tree. The tree provides wood for a table that holds up the television. Draw arrows connecting the items. Once everyone has the idea, let them draw the connections on their pictures. They can even draw arrows connecting something on their paper with another group.

The two important points to make at the end of this activity are that no object exists in isolation and there is more than one way in which objects are interrelated.

 ## Resources

Another effective way to demonstrate all the interrelationships that go into a single item is to trace back all the ingredients for a child's favorite food. Pick a food the children like, such as pizza. Create a large chart showing all the resources needed to make a pizza. Trace back each ingredient to see all the resources needed to make the food. For example, pizza needs cheese, the cheese comes from a cow, a cow needs grass, the grass needs a farmer, a farmer needs tractors to plow the fields, as well as sun, soil, air, and water just to name a few. All foods require many resources. As an extension, children can make their own charts.

Interrelationships Scavenger Hunt

This scavenger hunt can start off as an interpretative hike. Point out various examples of interrelationships. Look for examples the children may not otherwise notice. To see the effect of shade on a tree, compare the size of the leaves on the same species of tree in the forest and in an open place. Consider the way a vine uses a fence to help it grow, or a log in a stream that creates a pool of water in which water striders can live. Excess water from a drainpipe creates a moist habitat that allows different plants to grow. One part of a field is not mowed, so wildflowers grow. A squirrel accidentally plants an oak tree. Try showing the children how one thing leads to another. After the children have seen enough examples, they can search for their own. The hunt can be as simple as telling them to search for examples of interrelationships and see what they come up with, or they can be given more focus. For example: Find an interrelationship between a plant and something made by humans. Find an interrelationship between two animals. Find evidence of an interrelationship between a decomposer and a log. Find evidence of an interrelationship between something people did and animals in the area. Eventually, children may hit upon the realization that everything they see is part of an interrelationship.

One Thing Leads to Another

There is a cause for every action. The cause may not always be evident. Start with any simple natural event, like a log that falls, a wave that hits the shore, or a storms that washes leaves into a stream. Begin the story with the initial event. From there, ask a child to make up what happens next; then the next child takes the story one step further, and so on, each child contributing a line. Try to keep the story at least semirealistic. At the end of the story, call attention to how the story develops and how each event is interconnected even though it may not seem like an obvious connection.

Food Cycle

In any outdoor setting, give the group a few minutes to find signs of life. Using what they find, introduce the parts of the food cycle: producers, consumers, and decomposers. A leaf can represent a producer, an insect or a bird sighting is a consumer, and a worm or a mushroom is a decomposer. Plants are producers. They can take sun, soil, air, and water and produce food. All other living things must eat other living things. Only plants can create their own food. Animals can be considered consumers because they consume food. They can be divided into two groups: secondary and primary consumers. Primary consumers eat plants directly and are also known as herbivores. Secondary consumers eat other animals. They are also called carnivores. Omnivores eat both plants and animals. They can either be primary or secondary consumers, depending on what they are eating. People are omnivores. Decomposers are living organisms that feed off of dead plants and animals and recycle them back into soil.

Food Cycle Game

This game is a fun way to learn the parts of a food cycle. Divide the children into two lines standing shoulder to shoulder, facing each other about 15 feet apart. Mark home base lines about 20 yards behind each group. In the game, the students play the role of producers, consumers, or decomposers. Each part has a different symbol.

Producers: The students reach for the sun and say "ahhhhhhh" because plants take sun, soil, air, and water and produce food.

Consumers: The students stretch their arms in front, opening and closing them, like alligators, each time saying "chomp, chomp." Animals can't make their own food; they need to eat other living things.

Decomposers: The students wiggle their fingers and say "eeeeeeee." Decomposers live off dead plants and animals, thereby returning nutrients to the soil.

To play the game, each team huddles together and decides which part to play. The groups return to the starting line and face each other. On your signal, each group displays their symbols. Depending on the signal, one group will chase the other. The activity is based on the children's game "Rock, Paper, Scissors." Producers chase decomposers (plants need good soil), decomposers chase consumers (dead animals are decayed into soil), and consumers chase producers (animals eat plants).

If both teams pick the same part, the teams return to the huddle and pick again. A student is caught if they are tagged before crossing the home base line. If caught, they join the other team; if not, they stay on the same side. Don't worry if it takes a few rounds for everyone to remember where to run.

Local Food Cycles

Once the children know the parts of a food cycle, show them local examples of producers, consumers, and decomposers that make them up food cycles. Make sure they realize humans are part of food cycles as well. The children can draw pictures of the food chain they are a part of during that day. As the children learn about local plants and animals, they can see how they all fit together in food cycles.

The children search an area for examples of each part of the food cycle and record the number of possible food cycles they find. Some examples of a food chain in action are fungus on a log, a half-eaten leaf, remains of a dead animal, or scat.

Predator/Prey

The Native Americans in the northern part of this continent believed that the wolf and the caribou were really one animal. The wolf needed the caribou for food, and the caribou needed the wolf to keep their population in check. This game demonstrates how the relationship between predator and prey helps both groups of animals. Divide the group into three parts. For a class of 25, call 12 students "leaves," eight "mice," and five "owls." It is helpful to give each child a sign or color to distinguish them from other groups. The mice chase the leaves, the owls chase the mice. Play each round for about 30 seconds. When children are tagged, they will give their marker to whoever tagged them, and then stand next to the teacher until the round is over. Before starting the next round,

Any mouse tagged by an owl becomes an owl.

Any leaf tagged by a mouse becomes a mouse.

Any mouse that did not tag a leaf becomes a leaf.

Any owl that did not tag a mouse becomes a leaf.

This game demonstrates the need each part of the cycle has for each other part. Keep track of the numbers of each group. The children can graph the results. Point out what happens if there are no predators (owls); at first, the mice population does well, but eventually there will be no leaves left. The mice need the owls to control their population.

There Is a Limit

Each habitat has a limited number of species it can support. Animals need water, food, and shelter to survive. Whichever one of these needs is least available is called the limiting factor. Use blue, green, and brown paper to represent food, water, and shelter, respectively. Spread 60 sheets or more of each color of paper. The children, acting as deer, have one minute to gather as many pieces of paper as they can. At the end of the round, the children count their complete sets. Any child with five or more sets survives, and anyone with fewer decomposes. You may have to adjust the numbers, depending on the size of your group.

After each round, record the number of deer that survive. Repeat the game a number of times. Discuss what happens when too many "deer" use the habitat. By having a couple of the children act as wolves by running around and tagging deer, you can show the importance of predators in keeping the population in check.

Food Webs

Any given animal or plant is not limited to one food cycle. In fact, a better symbol of the way plants and animals are interconnected is a food web. One way to display the interrelationships of a food web is to make an actual web. Each child represents an animal or a plant in a local habitat. Each child writes the name of the plant or animal they are representing on a card and sits in a circle. Stand in the middle with a ball of string. You represent the sun, soil, air, and water. Begin by asking who needs sun, soil, air, and water. For example, the child representing the aspen tree says "me." He or she must give you a reason before connecting him or her to the string. Then ask who is connected to the aspen tree. The child representing the mouse volunteers. Maybe the mouse needs food, maybe the mouse dies and becomes part of the soil, or maybe carbon dioxide from the mouse helps the plant. The children have to hold the string hooked around one finger. Next, ask who needs the mouse. Repeat until everyone is connected. Discuss the fact that all the parts of the habitat are connected and that there are many ways the habitat can be interconnected. Lay a big poster with the name of the habitat on top of the web to symbolize how the web holds up a habitat.

Another way to set up the web is across the room. Attach the signs of each member of the community around the room. Staple or tape string to the signs. The advantage of this method is that is can be a permanent reminder of how a habitat is made up of countless interrelationships. Use animals and plants the children are familiar with or even the ones they have studied in past activities.

Energy in a Bucket

Energy moves through the food chain, beginning with the sun. Each living thing in the food chain takes in energy and gives out energy. Along the way, most of the original energy is lost. These games explain what happens.

You will need four buckets, two of which are filled with water, and four cups. Poke one hole in the bottom of two cups and poke two holes in the bottom of the other two cups. The holes represent the energy loss from the consumers. Divide the class into two relay teams. Put the buckets of water in front of each team. Put the empty bucket about 20 yards away. The buckets with water represent plants, and the water represents energy. Plants are able to convert sunlight to usable energy for animals. Give the cup with one hole to the first person in each line. That cup represents an herbivore. The student stands next to the bucket. Give the second cup to the second student in line. This cup represents a carnivore. This student stands in the middle between the full and empty buckets. When you say "go," the herbivore scoops up some water, carries it to the carnivore, and pours it in his or her cup. Then the herbivore throws his or her cup back to the next student in line and waits in the carnivore spot. Meanwhile, the carnivore carries the water to the empty bucket, pours the water in, and throws the cup back to the carnivore spot. The next student in line scoops up some water, brings it to the new carnivore, stops, and throws it back to the line, while the carnivore runs to the bucket. Continue the cycle until the plant energy bucket is empty. Whichever team has the most water left wins. The game clearly shows how much energy is lost at each stage of the food chain.

Gather the group together around the two buckets. Ask what happened to the energy. Most of the energy was wasted. In a food chain, 90 percent of the energy is wasted at each step. This fact has a significant effect on how many animals any particular habitat can support.

Candy Energy

To further demonstrate the loss of energy at each step of the food chain, put 100 small candies in a cup. Tell the class this represents 100 units of the energy that a plant made from the sun. Ask for a volunteer to be an herbivore. Give the student 10 candies and throw the rest in the garbage. This has a dramatic effect on the class. Ask, "What percent is wasted?" The answer: 90 percent. Ask for a volunteer to be a carnivore. Ask, "If 90 percent is wasted, how much does the carnivore get?" The answer: one candy.

Discuss the implications. First of all, the carnivore needs many plants and herbivores to support it. Look around the community. There are plenty of plants, and the most common animals are herbivores. In order to have carnivores, there needs to be enough producers to support enough herbivores to support a few carnivores.

The Food Pyramid

This energy loss can be visualized in the shape of a pyramid. The base is the producers, the next level primary consumers, and the top level secondary consumers. Use five children to make a pyramid representing local animals. Use two children on the side to represent decomposers and to act as spotters.

Biodiversity Blocks

To demonstrate the importance of biodiversity, make a larger pyramid with 17 blocks, cubes, or boxes. Label each block for an animal or a plant with which the children are familiar from their studies of the area. The base will be made up of seven blocks that represent plants and decomposers in the area. The next level will be six blocks labeled with the names of herbivores in the area. The third level is three boxes representing carnivores, and the last block on top is the highest carnivore in the area, past or present. You may want to make this block represent people. Make another pyramid with the same dimensions, except this time label the boxes with only two different species. Label the boxes in the consumer's row with only two species. Use species that were in the first pyramid for the second.

Suppose all the barrel cactus in an area are killed. Pull the boxes marked barrel cactus out of both the pyramids. What happens, which pyramid crashes? Biodiversity helps create a stable community.

This is a good opportunity to discuss why each individual species is important. There are a variety of reasons, from the species' own individual right to live to a human need for the plant because it may provide a life-saving medicine.

Measuring Insect Diversity

The children will collect insects from two different habitats and compare the diversity of species. In each place, the collection methods should be the same. The children can study the biodiversity of life under a rock, or you can give them a bucketful of soil. The children can compare the biodiversity in different places. Sort the insects into groups by species. You or the children do not need to know the names. Count the number of species and the number of individuals. To find insect diversity, divide the total number of species by the square root of total number of individuals.

Populations

A population is the number of individuals of a species in a certain area. Populations can change for a number of reasons. Ecologists try to estimate populations in order to better understand the community. Population studies can help an ecologist learn about the health of a community. Over- and underpopulation of a species can be a problem.

Estimating Plant Populations

Explain to the class that as ecologists, they are going to estimate the number of clover plants growing on the schoolyard lawn. If there are not any clovers, choose another plant that is found in a lawn and is growing in moderate numbers. Plantains or dandelions are usually available. Designate a large rectangular area for the study. If possible, use the same area as in other schoolyard activities to reinforce the idea of getting to know one place very well. This is just one of several activities that could be conducted as part of an in-depth study of one particular spot. Discuss methods the children could use to estimate the clover population.

Counting every clover is accurate but impractical. Guessing is easy but not accurate. A simple and effective method is to mark off several one-square-meter areas. The children count and record the number of clover in each square. Find the average of all the squares surveyed by the students and multiply the average clover population per square meter by the total area of the lawn. Discuss why surveying more squares makes the estimate more accurate and the importance of randomly picking the squares to survey. Once an estimate is determined, discuss how the information might be used. For example, knowing the population of a plant can help determine how the area will be managed.

Animal Populations

Plants do not move, which makes it easier to estimate their populations. Animals move. Discuss how scientists can estimate animal populations without counting the same one twice. One method is capture and release. The formula for estimating animal populations by marking the captured animals is easy to use. N = estimated population, m = number of animals marked the first time, M = number of animals marked the second time, T = total number of animals captured the second time: N/m = t/M; compare to actual amount.

Life Cycles

The best way to learn about life cycles of animals and plants is to see all the stages of one of the cycles. Animals have a variety of ways of reproducing. Some animals are born live and some in eggs; some undergo metamorphosis and some don't; some have many, many babies, and a few manage to survive; whereas some have one or two offspring and provide them with a great deal of care. During their explorations, have the children focus on finding examples of the life cycle of local animals. They might find eggs, nests, larva, pupas, or babies. Try raising animals, such as hamsters, gerbils, meal worms, butterflies, or other small animals. If a child finds some insect eggs, collect a few of them in a jar and wait to see what happens over the next few months. Understanding and accepting the life cycles of other animals will help children learn about and feel comfortable with their own life cycle. A careful search of even a small outdoor area should provide results.

Population Growth

What Would You Rather Have?

One way to demonstrate population growth is to tell the children the following situation. For a month, each of you does some yard work at my house. I will either pay you $1 a day for each day or a penny the first day, two the second, four pennies the third, and so on, doubling the amount of pennies each day. After everyone has made a choice, figure out who made the right decision. After 20 days, the dollar-a-day group has $20. After 20 days, the doubling pennies group has more than $5,200. Here is how: day 1, 1 penny; day 2, 2 pennies; day 3, 4 pennies; day 4, 8 pennies; day 5, 16 pennies; then 32; 64; 128; 256; 512; 1,024; 2,048; 4,096; 8,192; 16,384; 32,768; 65,536; 131,072; 262,144; and finally 524,288 pennies in 20 days, or $5,242.88.

This exercise demonstrates just how quickly a population can grow without any checks. It demonstrates how quickly something can become a pest, which is reason enough for predators.

What Is a Million?

Understanding numbers helps children make sense of population. A number of math activities can be used to show children the size of these numbers. Ask the students how long it would take to count to a million. After they make predictions, allow them to use calculators to make an accurate estimate. Assuming one could count nonstop at an average of 2 seconds per number, it would take approximately 23 days. This dramatically conveys the size of one million. These extension activities will also help children get a better sense of how large a million really is. Have the students try to collect a million of something. Pick a small object. Figure out the distance it would take if you lined up one million of the objects from end to end.

Carbon Cycle

The carbon cycle is just as important as the food cycle. All living organisms are made up of similar chemicals. These organic compounds are rich in carbon. Each ingredient is critical. To introduce the carbon cycle, have the children search dead leaves, fungus, worms, and other creatures of the soil that are involved in recycling soil. They are a good introduction to the carbon cycle.

Divide the group into three teams. One will be the producers, one the consumers, and the last team the decomposers. It is helpful to have each group wear some sort of marker in order to tell them apart. Carbon dioxide is one of the gases in our atmosphere. All living things need carbon. Plants can take carbon dioxide out of the air and make food. Animals can't use the carbon dioxide directly, so they eat plants or animals. When animals and plants die, the carbon is put back into the soil and air by decomposers. (Carbon is also returned to the atmosphere when animals breathe and when plant matter is burned.)

In the game, leaves represent carbon. On your signal, producers run out and grab as many leaves as possible. As they run around picking up leaves, the consumers chase them. If a producer is tagged by a consumer, the producer gives all the leaves to the consumer and sits down for 15 seconds before reentering the game. Meanwhile, the decomposers are chasing either consumers or producers. If tagged by a decomposer, the leaves (carbon) are thrown back on the field, and the student sits down for 15 seconds before reentering the game.

After the students are exhausted and ready to sit still and listen, you can review how carbon cycles through the environment. Remind them of the importance of the leaves and animals they found at the beginning of the activity. One hopes they have new-found respect for decomposers. Without the decomposers, carbon would be locked up in the dead producers and consumers and would be unavailable for new plants and animals.

Nitrogen Cycle

The necessity of nitrogen for making protein makes this another key cycle for the living world. A search for four leaf clovers is a good way to introduce the lesson. Even if no one finds one, they are about to learn why clover is a special plant.

The most common gas in our atmosphere is nitrogen. Seventy-eight percent of the air we breathe is nitrogen. All living things need nitrogen. The problem is that plants and animals can't use the nitrogen in the atmosphere unless it is changed into a different form. Fortunately, there are things that can do this; nitrogen fixing bacteria, certain fungi, and blue green algae! These organisms live in oceans; in the roots of legumes, such as clover, peas, and beans; and in the soil. Once converted, plants use the nitrogen to grow, consumers get their nitrogen by eating plants, and the nitrogen is returned to the soil by the decomposers when plants and animals die.

In this game, there will be four groups. Spread out popcorn, plastic links, or gram cubes to represent nitrogen. Popcorn is a good marker to use outdoors because it doesn't have to cleaned up. Markers that can be connected, such as gram cubes, symbolize the nitrogen being connected. The markers represent nitrogen. The first group will be bacteria. They run out and connect as many markers as possible. The second group will be the producers. They chase the bacteria. When tagged, the bacteria passes the nitrogen along and sits down for 15 seconds. From here on, the game is just like the carbon cycle game. Don't worry, they will not mind playing again. After running around, they will be ready to discuss the implications of the nitrogen cycle.

Another game is Water/No Water. To prepare for the game, use two sets of coffee cans or two buckets. Label one "water" and one "no water." On 3-by-5-inch cards, write a number of animals, plants, animate, and inanimate objects on cards. Dog, cat, rocks, ice cream, tulips, table, ice cream, cars, and the like are all possible items. Divide the group into two teams. This is a relay race; the first person in line will hand out the cards. The children run down and decide in which bucket to put the card. If the item on the card needs water, they put it into the "water" bucket; if not, it goes into the "no water" bucket. The winning team is the one that finishes first, plus the one with the most cards in the correct bucket. After the race, bring the buckets back and go through the cards to see if the cards are in the correct place. Any card in the "water" bucket is correct. Any card in the "no water" bucket is automatically wrong. Everything needs water at some point in its existence. For example, the table is made from wood, from a tree, and the tree needed water. The car needs water in its radiator, the person who made the car needed water to drink. This simple game can be used to teach a variety of concepts; for example, Soil/No Soil, Air/No Air, or Sun/No Sun.

Water Cycle Juggling

Another important cycle is the water cycle. Simply put, water is evaporated as a gas into the air by the sun. The molecules float around the atmosphere and condense on particles of dust and fall to Earth as rain, snow, sleet, or other precipitation. The rain may fall either directly into a body of water or fall somewhere else where eventually it ends up being evaporated again off a body of water or through plant leaves. The cycle has been going on since water was ever on the Earth, with the same molecules circulating around.

To play, the children will represent the steps of the water cycle. The number of steps you use will depend on the number of children with which you are working with. The basic steps are Sun, Evaporation, Cloud, Water, Body of Water, and Ground Water. If you have a group of 25 children, write each step five times on five different index cards. Pass all the cards out to the entire group. The children ask around and find everyone they need to create a complete set. If you have more children, make another set, or do so if you want larger groups and more steps. For example, add cards for oceans and lakes, snow, ground water, or wind.

Once the groups have been formed, the children are arranged in order, and you have explained the basics of the water cycle, give each group a tennis ball that represents a water molecule. The goal is to pass the ball around the circle as fast as possible. Because a water molecule can go from ocean to clouds, or clouds to river, or any other combination, the children can throw the ball anywhere in the circle. They should call out the role they are playing to further emphasize the steps of the water cycle. Add more tennis balls to each group to increase the challenge.

Where Does the Water Go?

Where does the rain go that falls on a street, lawn, or other places in the your area? Take a look at a puddle with the children and discuss where the water will go. Is it going to evaporate directly or flow into the ground? When it rains on the land in your area, to what body of water does it flow? If there is a stream nearby, trace the stream on foot if possible, if not by map.

Succession

Another principle of ecology is that everything is always changing. Habitats do not stay the same. The process of one habitat changing to another is called *succession*. Eventually, a pond fills in and becomes a marsh that turns to a field and then to a forest. As the habitat changes, the animals that live there also change. Some animals have to move, and new ones move in. Succession can be a slow process, as when a field becomes a forest. However, events such as hurricanes, fires, or human disturbances can reset the process.

Let It Grow

Find a patch of lawn that can be marked off from mowing or any other kind of disturbance. The children can observe changes to the lawn over the course of the year. If possible, keep the area marked off for a number of years. One group of children can compare their observations to the students from previous years. This overgrown spot can be the site of a number of other activities in this book.

Search the area around your school and community for places where fields are turning to a forest and other examples of succession. One way to observe succession in a forest is to see if the seedlings sprouting and growing on the forest floor are the same as the adult trees. Aspens and birches are trees that are quick to grow in a disturbed area. Eventually, other species crowd them out. Often there will be many dead aspens and birches surrounded by other trees. If the seedlings are different from the mature trees, there may be a change someday. If possible, look at the edge of a pond. Leaves and branches are slowly filling in the water. Search for places where succession is held in check by the actions of people. A lawn is one example.

Cartoons

Children can make cartoons showing stage by stage how a habitat can slowly change. For example, a man cuts his foot with his lawn mower and decides he is never going to cut his lawn again; what will happen? Or a beaver comes along and makes a dam on a stream. What will happen?

Flip Books

Flip books can be used to show any of these ecological principles. Children can create books that show one animal eating another in a food chain or how water moves through the land and sky. A flip book creates a simple animated cartoon Yellow stickie pads or a set of index cards work great. The child makes about 30 simple drawings of the habitat changing slightly from one habitat to another in each drawing. The more drawing and the slower the changes in each drawing will make the cartoon even better. Flip the pages of the pad, and the drawings become an animated cartoon. The cycles can be illustrated using flip books. Children will enjoy showing them to each other.

Ecological Magic

Teachers are true magicians. What could be more magical than making knowledge appear and making ignorance disappear? But having a few extra tricks doesn't hurt either. Children love magic. Whenever I perform a trick and my class stares at me in wide-eyed wonderment, I have captured their attention and can slip in some learning.

I use magic to grab my student's attention when I teach a variety of ecological concepts. All the magic tricks are explained in this chapter for convenience. The suggested tricks can be used in conjunction with lessons from a variety of chapters. Even when I teach children magic tricks, they learn how to follow directions and the concept of practice makes perfect. Below are five simple tricks to get you started. One other piece of advice: Practice really does make perfect. The patters are just suggestions. Adapt the trick and what you want to get across to the objectives of that particular activity.

These tricks are just the beginning. Once you have mastered these, learn new ones. Many tricks can be adapted to teach children ecological concepts as well as other important skills and facts. Even if you simply use the tricks to entertain, they will help you be a more effective teacher. Good teachers are good entertainers.

Name That Animal

Effect: A student picks the name of an animal out of a hat and tells the rest of the class. You walk in from another room and name the animal.

Set-up: Ask the class to name different animals. As they call out different names, write them down on a scrap of paper. The trick is to write down the same animal on every scrap of paper. After all the papers are in the bag, ask a student to pull one paper out of the bag. Leave the group while everyone hears which animal was picked. When you come back, build some drama by stalling, then call out the animal's name.

Patter: Use the animals they suggest to create a review on one of the ecological cycles (How the Place Works).

Animal Senses

Effect: Hand a stick to a student and tell him or her to pass the stick around. Leave the room, and when you come back you will be able to tell who touched the stick last.

Set-up: Pick one student to be your partner. The student will secretly tell you who touched the stick by imitating the person who touched it last. For example, if the person is sitting with his or her legs crossed, your secret partner sits with his or her legs crossed. Glance at your partner and see whom they are imitating. The trick is easier when the students are sitting or standing in a variety of positions instead of sitting at their desks.

Patter: Discuss with the students how animals use their senses to observe their surroundings (Adapting to the Place).

Costs

Effect: The students watch while you make a quarter disappear into your elbow.

Set-up: Tell the students that you can make a quarter disappear. Begin rubbing the quarter into your elbow with your right hand; put your left hand on your neck. Pretend to drop the quarter. Bend down and pick up the quarter with both hands (this is important). Begin rubbing again. Drop the quarter again and pick it up with both hands. Repeat once more. This time secretly pick the quarter up with your left hand and slip the quarter down your shirt while rubbing your right hand on your elbow. With a few magic words lift your hand off, and the quarter is gone.

Patter: Discuss the costs of environmental problems (Protecting the Place).

Endangered animals

Effect: The students will see you make a small animal disappear from under a handkerchief.

Set-up: This trick also requires advance planning with a secret partner. Hold a small plastic animal under a handkerchief. Walk around the group and ask the audience members to reach up and touch the animal to make sure it is still there. Go to your partner last. Your partner will secretly take the animal. Keep your fingers in place so that it looks like the animal is still there. With a few magic words, lift off the handkerchief, and the animal is gone. If you want to make the animal reappear, repeat the same procedure. This time your partner puts the animal back.

Patter: Discuss endangered species. Remind them that once an animal is extinct, they are gone forever, and no amount of magic will bring them back (Protecting the Place).

Deforestation

Effect: A toothpick is wrapped in a handkerchief. The students hear the toothpick break. When the handkerchief is unrolled, the toothpick is back together.

Set-up: To prepare this trick, you will need a handkerchief with a hem and two toothpicks. Slip one toothpick in the hem. Now show the audience the handkerchief and the other toothpick. Carefully fold the handkerchief with the toothpick in the middle. Hand the handkerchief to a student. Tell him or her to break the toothpick. Be sure he or she breaks the toothpick in the hem. Say a few magic words and unwrap the handkerchief. There is the toothpick, good as new.

Patter: Discuss forest resources. Forests can be renewable if the proper practices are followed (Protecting the Place).

Chapter Five

Animals of the Place

"Out of the earth/I Sing for them/a Horse Nation/ I sing for them/the animals."

I Sing for the Animals, Teton Sioux

"You only need sit still long enough in some attractive spot in the woods that all its inhabitants may exhibit themselves to you by turns."

Henry David Thoreau

"I came to learn that worthwhile observations of birds and animals and insects were great in proportion to the smallness of territory covered. . . . To be a good naturalist one must be a stroller or a creeper, or better still a squatter in every sense of the word."

William Beebe

Introduction

Local animals can be the subject of a variety of activities that will help children connect to their place and learn more about wildlife. We share our place with a variety of neighbors. We all benefit by paying more attention and taking the time to learn more about them. Animals are everywhere. My two-year-old son, Zack, finds them no matter where we are. He is keyed in. I remember listening to a fellow teacher describing a field trip she just took with her class. She was thrilled at the fact she heard a woodpecker for the first time. I was thrilled for her, but I also wondered. I had just moved to Long Island and had already heard and seen many woodpeckers. All she had to do is start paying attention; they were there all the time.

We are animals. This is a fact about which we should constantly remind ourselves. We have the same needs as any other animal; we share the world with them. There is a natural connection between children and animals that we can use to foster a deeper sense of place. E. O. Wilson, Paul Shepard, and others have explained this connection with the concept of biophilia. *Biophilia* is the innate emotional attachment humans have for animals and other living things (Wilson, 1996). It has only been recently in our evolution that we have not shared a close day-to-day existence with other animals. For the vast majority of our time as a species, we have lived as hunters and gatherers in competition and cooperation with other animals. We still crave this connection.

Take advantage of the presence of animal life in any place and children's fascination and interest. Don't forget those small creepy, crawly creatures. Children can find them, hold them, see them. This can have a much longer and more important impact then learning about animals from pictures or videos. A focus on charismatic megafauna such as pandas, whales, and tigers limits the connections to millions of other species with which we share our world.

This chapter covers a number of activities that bring the magic of animals into children's lives through observation, research, and role-playing. Many of the activities not only teach children about animals but also the skills scientists use, such as classifying, experimenting, observing, and developing a conclusion. These skills are crucial for an educated public that can understand scientific issues of the day. Role-playing the lives of animals is a spontaneous reaction for many children. Take advantage and use it to teach. These games help children feel a part of the animal's world. They can be away to learn facts and foster a emotional connection.

All children begin with this deep affinity for other animals. As educators, we can help children hold on to that sense of connection and use that connection to motivate a desire to learn and care for the place in which they live.

Books to Use

Aragon, Jane Chelsea. *Salt Hands.* Illustrated by Ted Rand. New York: Penguin Books, 1989. ISBN 0-14-050321-8. Rand's beautiful illustrations grace this short story of a young girl and a deer. In the middle of the night, she awakens to "a rustle of a breath." She walks outside with salt in her hands. A deer approaches and licks her hands clean in a moment of meeting between a child and a deer.

Bash, Barbara. *Urban Roosts.* San Francisco: Sierra Club Books, 1990. ISBN 0-316-08306-2. Bash tells the story of birds that live in our big cities. She includes numerous facts about killdeers, barn owls, starlings, and other urban birds that explain how they are adapted to city life. The illustrations themselves convey even more information and help the readers to know where to look to see birds in the city.

Baylor, Byrd. *Hawk, I'm Your Brother.* Illustrated by Peter Parnall. New York: Macmillan, 1976. Rudy Soto has always want to fly like the hawks he sees around his home. One day he brings a baby hawk home to raise. Only by letting the hawk free does Rudy learn how to fly like a hawk. A good story to help children think about their special animal.

Behnke, Frances L. *What We Find When We Look Under Rocks.* Illustrated by Jean Zallinger. New York: McGraw-Hill, 1971. This book provides fascinating information on several common creatures that children are almost certain to find when they dig through soil, look in the grass, or lift up a rock. From slugs to ants, children will be interested in how these animals live. The text is accompanied by detailed black-and-white drawings that add even more information.

Bergman, Donna. *City Fox*. Illustrated by Peter E. Hanson. New York: Atheneum, 1992. ISBN 0-689-31687-9. We all know that foxes live in the country, but in this book Ellie teaches us they also live in the city. Her neighbor Mrs. Kindley tells her all about the one she sees and cares for. Ellie wants to see City Fox for herself. When Mrs. Kindley is too old to take care of City Fox, she shows Ellie how to do it. They sit up one night and watch and wait for City Fox to appear in the moonlight. Muted pencil drawings add a unique illustration style to this book.

Bowen, Betsy. *Tracks in the Wild*. Boston: Little, Brown, 1993. ISBN 0-316-10377-2. This guide to animal tracks focuses mainly on wildlife of the North Woods, such as moose, martins, and ravens. The tracks are complemented by beautiful woodcut illustrations of each animal. The text describes facts about the animals as well as sharing some of the author's personal experiences. Quotes from a variety of Native Americans grace the book and add to its power. Even if the children are from other places, the book will serve as a wonderful model.

Brown, Ruth. *The Picnic*. New York: Dutton Books, 1992. ISBN 0-525-45012-2. The story of a picnic told from the point of view of the chipmunks, mice, moles, and rabbits that live in a meadow. A baby and a dog become fearsome creatures from the point of view of the animals. Fortunately, the rain drives the humans away. When the sun comes out, the animals can have their own picnic.

Bruchac, Joseph. *Fox Song*. Illustrated by Paul Morin. New York: Philomel Books, 1993. ISBN 0-698-11561-9. A story that shows the close relationship between Jamie and her great-grandmother. After her death, Jamie finds comfort in what she was taught and strength by her relationship with a fox she meets in the forest.

Buchanan, Ken, and Debby Buchanan. *Lizards on the Wall*. Illustrated by Betty Schweitzer-Johnson. Tucson, AZ: Harbinger House, 1992. ISBN 0-943173-77-9. While lying in bed, the narrator tells the readers all about the two lizards on the wall. The rhyming text makes for fun reading as we learn what the lizards eat and what they do. The book captures the appreciation that develops when one closely observes an animal.

Bushnell, Jack. *Sky Dancer*. Illustrated by Jan Ormerod. New York: Lothrop, Lee & Shepard, 1996. Jenny sees a red-tailed hawk in her backyard. Everyday she goes out to watch the hawk. Meanwhile, farmers discover that a hawk has been killing local chickens. Jenny knows it is not her hawk. She knows the hawk is there for her. When a local farmer tries to shoot her hawk, Jenny screams just in time to scare it away. Aside from being a beautiful story of the friendship between a girl and a hawk, the book prompts a discussion about humans and predators.

Christelow, Ellen. *What Do Authors Do?* New York: Clarion Books, 1995. ISBN 0-395-71124-X. This book is a good way to show children how authors work. They may be surprised by how much time is spent on revising and thinking about revising. The book is not specifically aimed at nature writing, but the advice and humorous drawings are universal.

Denslow, Sharon Phillips. *Woollybear Good-bye*. Illustrated by Nancy Cote. New York: Four Winds Press, 1994. ISBN 0-02-728687-8. When Joe Dean Cattleberry announces he is moving away, Miss Rosemary decides to make him captain of the Woolly Bear Week team. Each grade in the school tries to catch the most woolly bear caterpillars. Only by climbing Miss Rosemary's special tree do the third graders win. In the spring, they watch them fly off as Isabella tiger moths. An entire school collecting woolly bears is not such a good idea, but catching a few and having a special tree is magical.

Ehlert, Lois. *Feathers for Lunch*. San Diego, CA: Voyager Books/Harcourt Brace Jovanovich, 1990. ISBN 0-15-230550-5. A cat escapes to the outside and discovers plenty of possible lunch meals in the form of house sparrows, mourning doves, goldfinches, and other common birds. Children will enjoy the story and illustrations as they learn to identify common backyard birds.

Ehlert, Lois. *Nuts to You!* San Diego, CA: Harcourt Brace Jovanovich, 1993. ISBN 0-15-257647-9. A mischievous gray squirrel ends up inside rather than outside in this adventure. Tempted by nuts, he is lured back outside. This playful, brightly colored book ends with factual information on gray squirrels.

Fleischman, Paul. *Joyful Noise: Poems for Two Voices*. Illustrated by Eric Beddows. New York: HarperTrophy, 1988. ISBN 0-06-021852-5. A fascinating and wonderfully written book of poetry about insects. Each poem is meant to be read by two voices at the same time. Each poem blends information on insects with beautifully written words. A great model for children.

Gaffney, Michael. *Secret Forests*. Racine, WI: Western, 1994. ISBN 0-307-17505-7. This oversized, wonderfully illustrated book is a definite attention-getter with a great concept. A variety of insects are shown in their natural habitat. Children can try to find them camouflaged in the pages. Each habitat is complemented with an identification guide that explains something about each insect.

Gove, Doris. *One Rainy Night*. Illustrated by Walter Lyon Krudop. New York: Atheneum, 1994. ISBN 0-689-31800-6. A mother and child set off to collect animals for the nature center at which the mother works. It is a regular outing because they never keep an animal in a cage for very long. They collect on rainy nights to finding the most reptiles, amphibians, and insects. The illustrations capture a rainy night. The book is a great way to begin collecting animals for temporary study.

Horowitz, Ruth. *Bat Time*. Illustrated by Susan Avishai. New York: Four Winds Press, 1991. ISBN 0-02-7445541-0. Leila finishes dinner and waits impatiently for "Bat Time." Darkness approaches as she goes through nighttime routines. Finally, after a bath and stories, it is time. Leila and her father walk out on the porch. Canadian geese fly by, a skunk appears, and suddenly bats flutter above their heads. A good introduction to an incredible but often misunderstood animal. Bats are in more of our communities than we realize. Ask the children what unpopular animals they like and begin a discussion of animal stereotypes.

Kudlinski, Kathleen V. *Animal Tracks and Traces*. Illustrated by Mary Morgan. New York: Franklin Watts, 1991. ISBN 0-531-10742-6. A handy reference for finding signs of animals. The book covers much more then tracks. There are suggestions for finding lunch spots, sheddings, and even scents. There are activities and a tracking quiz. A great book to use in preparation for a hike and as a source of information.

Lavies, Bianca. *Compost Critters*. New York: Dutton Books, 1993. ISBN 0-525-44763-6. The setting for this book is a compost pile. The close-up photography in this book is incredible. Children will be amazed and excited when they discover compost critters for themselves by looking under rocks, logs, and leaves. The text includes interesting information and reminds us how important these critters are for making the soil productive.

Lerner, Carol. *A Backyard Full of Birds in Winter*. New York: Morrow Junior Books, 1994. ISBN 0-688-12819-X. This book and its companion *A Backyard Book Full of Birds in Summer* (1996) are perfect guides to common feeder birds. The books begin with suggestions for attracting birds. Each book covers a variety of western and eastern birds. The illustrations will help identify the birds, and the text is filled with a wealth of information. Whether you read a passage to the children or simply have the book available on the windowsill near the feeder, this book is a delight.

Lesser, Carolyn. *Dig Hole, Soft Mole*. Illustrated by Laura Regan. San Diego, CA: Harcourt Brace Jovanovich, 1996. ISBN 0-15-223491-8. This story of a star-nosed mole written with alliteration and rhymes is a wonderful example of combining animal facts into a story. We see the star-nosed mole dig through the earth and into a pond. Regan's illustrations bring to life a normally unseen world.

London, Jonathan. *Gray Fox*. Illustrated by Robert Sauber. New York: Viking, 1993. ISBN 0-670-84490-X. London describes the gray fox's life through the seasons. The male fox raises a family and runs the forest until he is killed by a passing car. The body is found by a boy who carries the fox to a secret place in the woods to bury. With lush paintings, the book captures the sadness of death and the beauty of life.

McDonald, Megan. *Insects Are My Life*. Illustrated by Paul Brett Johnson. New York: Orchard, 1995. ISBN 0-531-06874-9. A wonderful book about a girl who loves insects. She studies them, reads about them, and watches them despite the fact the her classmates are not as interested. Finally she finds Maggie, a friend to share her passion.

McNulty, Faith. *A Snake in the House*. Illustrated by Ted Rand. New York: Scholastic, 1994. ISBN 0-590-44758-0. A boy catches a small garter snake in a jar and brings it home. The snake promptly escapes. After surviving a variety of close calls in the house, the snake finds a surprising way to get back to the pond. A book for discussing what one can learn from collecting animals, as well as from letting animals go.

Melville, Herman. *Catskill Eagle*. Illustrated by Thomas Locker. New York: Philomel, 1991. ISBN 0-399-21857-2. Using a short passage from Melville's *Moby-Dick* and his own incredible paintings, Locker has created an inspiring story of an eagle and all it can see. The story is a look at the mountains from the eagle's point of view. In the introduction, Locker explains how the Catskills inspired many artists and writers in the late 1800s in a new appreciation of nature. A way to start a discussion of what places and animals inspire the children.

Nail, Jim. *Whose Tracks Are These? A Clue Book of Familiar Forest Animals*. Illustrated by Hyla Skudder. Niwot, CO: Roberts Rinehart, 1994. ISBN 1-879373-89-0. Animal sign clues are given for a variety of common forest animals. Children can hear the clues described and guess the animals. The information provided goes beyond just the animal tracks.

Oppenheim, Shulamith Levy. *Fireflies for Nathan.* Illustrated by John Ward. New York: Tambourine Books, 1994. ISBN 0-688-12147-0. Nathan is visiting his grandparents and wants to know what his father was like as a little boy. His grandparents tell him about the fireflies. That night, using the same jar his father did, Nathan and his grandparents sit outside waiting to catch fireflies. While they wait, there is much to see. Just like his father, Nathan catches a jar full, and just like his father, he tells his grandmother to let them go. This is one of the few books I have found with African Americans characters.

Pine, Jonathan. *Backyard Birds.* Illustrated by Julie Zickefoose. New York: HarperCollins, 1993. ISBN 0-06-021039-7. Similar in format to his book *Trees*, Pine writes about six backyard birds: house sparrows, starlings, robins, wrens, ruby-throated hummingbirds, and the common night hawks. Each chapter can be read alone and tells the story of the bird's life in elegant language.

Robertson, Kayo. *Signs Along the River: Learning to Read the Natural Landscape.* Boulder, CO: Roberts Rinehart, 1986. ISBN 0-911797-22-X. Focused on western habitats, this book uses elegant black-and-white drawings that remind us that signs in nature are not limited to animals tracks. Sounds, scents, and sights all tell a story, no matter where one lives. Each picture is explained in further detail in the back of the book.

Rockwell, Anne. *Our Yard Is Full of Birds.* Illustrated by Lizzy Rockwell. New York: Macmillan, 1992. ISBN 0-02-777273-X. Common birds are pictured in a story of what a young child sees in his backyard. The simple text includes some information abut each bird.

Ryder, Joanne. *Catching the Wind.* Illustrated by Michael Rothman. New York: Morrow Junior Books, 1989. ISBN 0-688-07170-8. In this story, a young girl hears the music of goose calling and is transformed into a Canadian goose. She joins the flock and spends the day as a goose until her own home calls her back.

Ryder, Joanne. *Chipmunk's Song.* Illustrated by Lynne Cherry. New York: E. P. Dutton, 1987. ISBN 0-14-054796-7. Incredible illustrations full of detail will capture a child's interest in the life of a chipmunk. A careful observer will notice hidden birds and animals throughout the book. Ryder's words tell the reader about the life of a chipmunk through the seasons. Cherry's illustrations put the reader literally in the story will the chipmunk.

Ryder, Joanne. *The Snail's Spell.* Illustrated by Lynne Cherry. New York: Warne, 1982. ISBN 0-7232-6197-0. Ryder asks the reader to imagine that they are becoming a snail. Slowly, you get smaller and smaller, fitting into the garden hidden among the leaves. Cherry's detailed paintings from the point of view of a snail make it easier to imagine the small yet interesting world of a snail.

Ryder, Joanne. *When the Woods Hum.* Illustrated by Catherine Stock. New York: Morrow Junior Books, 1991. Beginning with some background on cicadas, this book is a stunning account of the life cycle of the periodical cicadas. Ryder tells us their story through the eyes of a father and daughter who take a walk in the woods. The book captures the magic of such a rare event. Every 13 to 17 years, thousands of cicadas crawl out of the ground and make the forest hum with their music. The book also describes the changes in a family over the same period. After reading this book, you will want to find your own red-eyed cicadas and keep track of the years that pass. This book is a great reminder of the amazing life in our own backyards. One of many wonderful books by Ryder that are worth reading to children.

Sandved, Kjell B. *The Butterfly Alphabet.* New York: Scholastic, 1996. ISBN 0-590-48003-0. The photographs in this book are amazing. Close-up photography of butterflies' wings reveals letters of the alphabet. The text tells us of the beauty of butterflies, and the photographs remind us of what we can find if we look carefully. A great way to start a butterfly garden.

Savageau, Cheryl. *Muskrat Will Be Swimming.* Illustrated by Robert Hynes. Flagstaff, AZ: Northland, 1996. ISBN 0-87358-604-2. A truly special story about a Native American girl named Jeannie. She loves her home near the lake in town. The only problem is that at school Jeannie is teased by the kids who live in the other part of town. They call her "Lake Rat." Her grandfather tells her a story and shows her a way to rise above the children who tease her and know what is special about being a Lake Rat.

Selsam, Millicent. *How to Be a Nature Detective.* Illustrated by Ezra Jack Keats. New York: Harper & Row, 1963. A detective looks at clues to figure out what happened. An animal tracker has to do the same thing. An animal detective can look for clues just about anywhere. Keats's illustrations give the reader the chance to figure out a variety of scenes, including challenges in our own homes.

Selsam, Millicent, and Joyce Hunt. *Keep Looking.* New York: Macmillan, 1989. ISBN 0-02-781840-3. Beginning with a remainder to sit still and watch, the book shows the reader many backyard and forest creatures. There are mammals, birds, and insects to see. The last page of the book gives readers a chance to test their skills by searching the illustrations for various animals.

Sheldon, Dyan. *The Whales' Song.* Illustrated by Gary Blythe. New York: Dial Books for Young Readers, 1990. ISBN 0-8037-0972-2. Blythe's paintings are stunning, and Sheldon's words make this a wonderful book about the magic that can happen between children and animals. A young girl listens to her grandmother's stories of giving gifts to the whales. One night, she brings a flower to the water. That night she hears the song and sees the whales.

Sill, Cathryn. *About Birds.* Illustrated by John C. Sill. Atlanta, GA: Peachtree, 1991. ISBN 1-56145-147-9. Incredible paintings of birds set the tone for a wonderful introduction to the world of birds. A simple text tells the reader what birds do. "Baby birds hatch from eggs. Most birds fly, but some swim and others run." Children can think of examples from their place that match the examples in the book.

Slepian, Jan. *Lost Moose.* Illustrated by Ted Lewin. New York: Philomel, 1993. ISBN 0-399-22749-0. A young moose is separated from its mother and ends up lost. A young boy meets the moose on his morning walk. The boy, thinking he has discovered one of Santa's lost reindeer, follows the moose through the forest. They end up back at his vacation cabin. Suddenly, the moose's mother returns and is confronted by the boy's mother. Both are ready to protect their offspring. Silently, the moose returns to the forest. As usual, Lewin's illustrations are captivating. The book shows the magic of an encounter with wild animals and a realization that many basic needs are the same.

Smucker, Anna Egan. *Outside the Window.* Illustrated by Stacey Schuett. New York: Alfred A. Knopf, 1994. ISBN 0-679-84023-0. A very interesting book from a different point of view. Birds in a nest look at a young boy and ask all sorts of questions about his life. What does he eat? Where does he sleep? What is he doing? The full-page illustrations show the reader just how the young birds imagine the answers their mother gives.

Sturges, Philemon. *Ten Flashing Fireflies.* Illustrated by Anna Vojtech. New York: North-South Books, 1995. ISBN 1-55858-420-X. A counting book that adds and subtracts ten fireflies. The book can serve as a model for the children's own counting books based on plants and animals in their community. The fireflies painted by Vojtech seem to actually glow. The children in the book capture fireflies, count them, and then release them. Letting your lawn grow a little longer between mowings means more fireflies.

Thornhill, Jan. *Wild in the City.* San Francisco: Sierra Club Books, 1995. ISBN 0-87156-910-8. Realistic paintings and a puzzle to solve will help children pay attention to common wildlife in an urban area. Another interesting aspect of the book is the demonstration of how one small event leads to another and how lives become interrelated.

Torres, Leyla. *Subway Sparrow.* New York: Farrar, Straus & Giroux, 1993. On a New York City subway, a sparrow is trapped inside the closing doors. Three very different people come together to help the sparrow escape to freedom. A beautiful story of how even a sparrow can connect people together and to an animal.

Wilson, E. O. *In Search of Nature.* Washington, DC: Island Books, 1996. ISBN 1-55963-215-1. A good introduction to the writing of one of our most important scientists.

Yolen, Jane. *Bird Watch.* Illustrated by Ted Lewin. New York: Philomel, 1990. ISBN 0-399-21612-X. Another wonderful book by Yolen. This collection of poetry about birds not only captures the wonder of birds but also our connection and attraction to birds. Children will recognize many familiar birds in Lewin's watercolors and will enjoy Yolen's use of language to describe birds and their lives.

Yolen, Jane. *Owl Moon.* Illustrated by John Schoenherr. New York: Philomel, 1987. ISBN 0-399-21457-7. A young girl is finally old enough to go owling with her father. They head off in the cold of winter. Occasionally hooting like great horned owls, they walk further into the forest. Suddenly and silently, an owl flies in and they share a stare. Beautiful paintings capture the wonder when humans and animals share a moment with each other.

Activities

Finding a Totem Animal

In many Native American cultures, each person has a totem animal. This animal was linked with the child by common traits, dreams, family tradition, or personal events. Many tribes believe that animals and people shared a common ancestry and could talk to each other at one time. Having this personal connection with an animal was a way of showing how people shared a kinship with other animals, that people and animals shared the same world. Native Americans believed that animals have a spirit like humans and that they share human qualities. This was not anthropomorphism; it did not trivialize animals but made them equal and subject to respect. When looking for strength, one could turn to a wolf or find patience in the turtle. By watching animals, people learned lessons in survival. The separateness that exists between humans and animals did not exist. Friendship with animals is an important way to break the barriers between humans and nature.

One could learn from animals just as one learned from people. It was understood that when taking the life of an animal for food, the dead animal deserved respect and ceremony. Many native peoples around the world share these ideas. One look at the many sports teams named after animals or the number of last names such as Wolf or Crane reminds us that the idea of gaining strength and knowledge from animals is nearly universal and not far removed from our own lives.

Through their research and outdoor experiences, children can discover their own totem animal. As they learn more about animals, let them select a local animal that reflects their personality and whose traits will inspire them.

Once they have selected an animal, each can create a symbol or draw a picture of the animal. The totem animal can be the subject of research or kept as a private decision. It may take time for a child to decide on his or her own totem animal, and it may change over time. It will mean different things for different children.

Totem animals are a serious aspect of Native American culture. It would be insulting and disrespectful to think this activity can replicate their beliefs. The goal of this activity is to simply give children a glimpse of another culture's view of animals, to see animals from a different point of view, and perhaps to gain closer connection to their place by connecting to one particular animal.

During an outing to a nearby natural area, the children can assume the role of their animal. In a given area, they can try to find a place they would use for shelter, a source of water, and food. For animals that are carnivores, they may be able just to find a sign of their food. Give them time to be the animal and to see how the woods look a little different from that point of view. The children can take each other on a tour of the area and let the children explain what they found.

Animal Watch

This is a simple but powerful activity. How often do we stop and simply sit and watch an animal, any animal? Give the children a chance to simply stop and watch. This works particularly well with silent sits. On the other hand, animals appear at any given time. If possible, take the time to watch a spider spin its web, or an ant to carry a bread crumb to its home. Watch what the birds are doing in the field. Pause during your lesson if a hawk flies over head. Watch what they do. Set an example when something happens by.

Charades and Twenty Questions

Charades, like Twenty Questions, is one of those games that are truly oldies but goodies. Children love to act like animals, and charades is a perfect game for this desire. Give volunteers slips of paper with the animal they should imitate. Two or more children can come up with a skit showing interaction between animals. Twenty Questions is a good way to practice questioning and classifying skills. Give children a card with a local animal written on the front. The children hold the card so that other people can see it but they cannot. The children mill around asking questions until they figure out what card they have.

Animal Needs

Animals need food, water, and shelter in the place in which they live. In the outdoors, ask the children to pretend they are an animal that would be native to the area. Give them time to search for a shelter, something they would eat (or in the case of a carnivore, a sign of an animal they would eat), and a place to find water. Be sure to give clear boundaries before they search.

An extension for the activity is to make bird nests. All you need are tweezers. The tweezers represent the bird's bill. Using the tweezers, the students try to make a bird's nest. No hands are allowed, only the tweezers. If possible, return to the nest later to see how it survives in inclement weather. For younger children, you can make the tweezers optional.

Classifying

Using animal pictures from magazines, the students can classify the animals in a number of different ways. Using a variety of characteristics, the children can classify the animals into various groups. Simply by studying each animal's basic characteristics, the children will learn more about local wildlife. They will also be practicing a very important scientific skill. Another source of animals to classify is the running lists the children have kept of all the animals they have seen.

Another aspect of classifying is identification. It is fun to know an animal's name. When getting to know your neighbors, it is good to be able to call them by name. Younger children can make up their own names for the insects, birds, and mammals they find. Older children can use field guides to find out the common names. See the bibliography for suggested field guides. Depending on the age and your objectives, spend some time going over how to use the books and vocabulary. Pictures alone will not always be enough. The text may have some information about the animal that helps identify it or eliminates it from consideration. Some of the plant identifying activities could be used to help identify animals.

Finding Animals and Identifying Animals

Identifying animals in the outdoors is a little harder; they move, and they can't always be counted on to be where you want them to be when you want them to be there. That is why it is a good idea not to overlook insects. They are easy to find, there are many of them, and if a child can catch them in a bug box, there is time to watch them.

Catching Insects

Insects and other invertebrates are everywhere if we look. Insects, salamanders, frogs, and toads have a distinct advantage for children. They are common, and they are small enough to hold. Take advantage of these qualities so that children can have some direct experience with animals. Pick up rocks, look under logs, and examine the grass. Another way to gather insects for observations is to hold a white sheet of paper under the branches of a bush and shake. Insects will fall on the paper and can be collected in a plastic tray for observation. Try collecting insects by setting a trap. Dig a small hole in the ground and sink in a cup. Put a small piece of fruit on the bottom and use a piece of wood for a roof. Put two or three small rocks on the top of the cup to hold up the wood, creating a small space between the wood and the cup for the animal to crawl in. This will allow the animals in, but they will not be able to get out. Try setting out various baits to see what they like and do not like. And remember: never underestimate how many or what kinds of things children can catch with their bare hands.

Pond Animals

Aquatic insects are fascinating as well. They are not very hard to catch, and they are worth the effort. There is nothing better than visiting a pond. Do not worry if you are not a pond animal expert. The pond itself will do the teaching. This kind of direct contact will help children connect to the place where they live. All you will need is a pond, some buckets, a net, and old sneakers. Use the net to scoop up leaves and muck. The creatures are in there. Fill one bucket with clean pond water. This will be the place to put all the animals that the children find. Your job is to scoop up pond water and muck. Let the water drain off and dump the wet leaves in a tray. Show the children how to search carefully through the leaves for anything that moves. Anything that is moving can go into the clean water. If a child is uncomfortable using his or her hands to pick up an animal, there is always at least one person who will volunteer; otherwise, spoons, sticks, or leaves all work well. Each tray of leaves should be put back into the water after the search is completed. There are still animals in the leaves, and they will die if left on the shore.

Some children will dive right in, and some won't, but once they realize how many creatures there are to find, the hesitancy vanishes. A variety of insects, nymphs, snails, tadpoles, frogs, and newts can be found. The children will be surprised at the amount of life in a pond.

Even if a trip cannot be arranged, try to bring in a bucketful of pond water and leaves. It is sure to be one of the highlights for the year.

Once the class has a tray full of animals, there are plenty of possibilities. Activities can be as simple as counting the different species and trying to identify some of them. Sometimes identifying insects is difficult because there are so many different species. Don't worry; try making up names. A population survey, sketching, observing, and field research are all possible activities. The important thing is that the children have direct contact with the animals that live in a pond.

Bird Identification

Birds and mammals are also interesting; they are just harder to find sometimes. One way to introduce field identification is to use a picture of a local bird and a copy of a page from a field guide with that bird and a few others. Hold the picture up to the class and give them time to look at the field guide page and figure out what bird it is. Use other pictures to help point out some of the key characteristics for identifying birds, such as body shape, color, size, beak shape, and habitat.

Another way to get a good look at animals in order to identify them is to set up a bird feeder. Simple feeders can be built out of plastic milk jugs or milk cartoons. Simply cut out the sides and hang the feeder in a tree. If a tree is not available, bird feeders can be attached to a pole in the ground; you can even put bird food on the ground. Bird feeders can be made by spreading peanut butter on a pine cone and sprinkling bird seed all over it. Then simply hang the pine cone in a tree.

Children can try to identify the birds and take field notes on bird behavior. Some of the behaviors the students can watch for are: Do the birds feed alone or in groups? Do the birds feed on the ground or in the trees? Is there a pecking order among the birds? How do the birds act at the feeder? How many birds come to the feeder? If it is not possible to make bird feeders, simply ask your students to make observations of the birds they see in their neighborhood.

Animal Signs

In the case of mammals, finding animal signs is a good way for learning who else lives in the place. It may be the only way. Among the signs children may find on their outings are tracks, droppings, left over food, bones, homes, and pieces of fur or feathers. Go on a hike and find as many animal signs as possible.

Animal Sign Box

For classroom practice, make an animal sign box. Gather as many animal signs as possible, such as droppings, nests, feathers, bones, pellets, chewed-on nuts and pine cones, tufts of hair, and any other signs. Line a large box with plastic and cover with leaves, sticks, and soil. Put the animal signs in the box hidden among the forest materials. Put the box on display and give the children an opportunity to look inside and find all the animal signs.

Track Trap

There are ways to find more tracks. Make a wood frame of about 4-by-4 feet. Put lime inside the frame. Animals follow paths just like people. There are places they are more likely to walk in than others. With the children, try to think like a fox or any other local animal. Where would you walk? Set up the frame on an animal path or at least where you think an animal lives. Put some peanut butter or other bait in the middle. Overnight, animals will walk in to investigate and leave their tracks.

Snowfall means tracks. Take a walk after a snowfall, and you will amazed at all the traffic that usually remains hidden. Muddy places on the trail or near water are also good places to look.

Mystery Tracks

Even if the children can't find any animal tracks, they can still learn about tracking.

Following animal tracks can tell us much information about an animal without ever seeing the animal. Children can learn what the animal eats, does, and where it goes. Children can practice this skill by leaving tracks for each other to follow. While one person keeps his or her eyes covered, the other leaves a set of tracks. After the tracks are laid, the other child follows the tracks and tries to figure out how they were created and what the track layer did along the way. If tracks can't be laid, children can draw track scenes. Another way to make tracks is to walk with wet shoes over pavement.

Observing Animals

With close observation, we can see that animals still surround us and share our world. To learn about animals, wildlife biologists study animals in their natural habitats and make observations of their behavior. A readily available subject for learning to observe wildlife is other children. I prepare the children by telling them they are going to watch some truly wild animals. We discuss that being an observer means paying attention and trying to make sure our actions do not affect the behavior of the animals we are watching. This is a good chance to practice note-taking skills as well. As observers, the children need to spend the available time observing and just taking enough notes to remember the key points. Once everyone is ready, take them to recess, the lunchroom, or some other place where children are in action and let them observe. The children should not interact with the children they are observing; they should pay attention and take notes. It is best for each child to select one person to focus on during the observation time.

After making their observations, the children can compile the notes in a report or simply use them for a class discussion. Begin with the question, What did you learn about children from your observations? This will be an opportunity to make a distinction between facts and theories. The children will often start off with a statement as if it is fact, when in reality it is a theory. A good theory explains an observation and is based on facts. They should be able to back up any theory with facts they observe. "The boy in the red shirt was mad" is a theory because he stormed away from the swing, shouted at the other kids, and told the teacher something—the facts that back up the theory.

Children can also observe other animals. This can be done outdoors on a trip by simply lifting rocks, logs, and leaf litter to observe various soil animals. Once aquatic insects settle down in a tank, they also can be observed. With notebook in hand, children can watch and record the actions of a single animal as long as possible.

Pets at home also can be the subject of observations on a regular basis. A bird feeder at home can provide opportunity for a chance to observe animals. Keep a bird feeder journal next to the window. As the children observe birds, they can record what they see in a class bird journal. Even if the animal is only seen for a short time during an outing, children can become better observers and more aware of what an animal is doing.

Pictures of animals from magazines can also be used to make observations. The students can study a set of photographs and make a list of facts. From these facts, they can develop a theory about the animal.

As the children discuss their theories, they will learn there can be more than one. Only more observations will help determine which theory is more accurate.

Animal Experiments

Biologists also learn about animals by conducting experiments. A variety of invertebrates can be used to learn about animals and learn how biologists do their work. The first step is to find animals to study. Under almost any rock or log are plenty of animals: beetles, snails, crickets, pill bugs, sow bugs, and millipedes. Aquatic animals, such as crabs, snails, and crayfish, can also be used. Different children can study different animals depending on what they catch. Another possibility is to order class sets of animals from a biological supply house. A great animal for study is a mealworm. They take virtually no care and are very inexpensive. Just put them in a container of oatmeal. They can live their whole life cycle in the same container. They are usually available in a pet store where they are sold to feed pet lizards.

To begin the study, children can simply make some observations about the animals' behaviors. More information can be gathered simply by capturing and keeping some of these animals for a short period of time and conducting simple and safe experiments. Discuss what is and is not ethical about experimenting with live animals. A good experiment follows certain guidelines. This activity will help teach this all-important concept about science.

Asking the Question. The first step is to pose a question. For example: Do snails prefer a certain color paper?

Hypotheses. After considering the options, children predict an answer to the question. This should be recorded on a lab sheet.

Conducting the Experiment. The children need to take the time to plan an experiment that will answer the question as accurately as possible and does not harm the animal. To conduct a good experiment, everything has to be fair. This means that all the variables have to be kept the same except the one that answers the experiment's question. Put four pieces of colored construction paper in each corner of a tray. Place the snail in the middle and wait to see which paper it hides under. The colored paper should all be the same size and the same distance from the animal at the start of the experiment. A comparison that is easy for the children to understand is a race. If Sue and Judy are racing to see who is the fastest, each one should race the same distance, start at the same time, and one of them should not wear boots and the other sneakers. The reason for keeping all the variables the same is that the results of the experiment can be interpreted accurately. If the colored paper in the snail experiment is different colors and different distances, can we be sure that the snail chose the paper because of the color or because to the distance? Once the experiment is planned and all the necessary materials are gathered, the children conduct the experiments. They may need to make adjustments after the first try. It is a good idea to repeat the experiment more than once to see if the results are consistent each time and not just random choices by the animal. A good experiment has a control to be sure the results are not simply random. For example, if I were experimenting to see if music makes the snails go into their shells, I should leave some snails alone to see if they go into their shell no matter what.

Observations. The children report their results and develop theories based on the facts they observed. Depending on the experiment, graphs and tables can be used to organize and present the information gathered.

Suggested experiments are: What food does the animal prefer? Provide the animal with a choice of food. Does the animal prefer to be in the open or under a shelter? With a cardboard shelter, create a dark place and a bright place in the container. What surface material does the animal prefer? Provide the animal with a choice of surface materials. Does the animal prefer wet places or dry places? Use a moist paper towel and a dry one. What color does the animal prefer? Provide the animal with several choices of colors. There are experiments that can be conducted with animals that are not captured. What food do birds at the feeder prefer? What foods will ants carry back to their nests?

Other information that can be gathered about the animal include size, weight, and speed—how fast does the animal move 10 body lengths? Is this faster than a human for its size? Obtain a map of the community and mark the locations where the animal is found. Write a description. Observe and record the animal's behavior. Can the animal be taught to go to a certain place for food? How would you train the animal to do this? What is the animal's life cycle?

Animal Research

Local animals make a natural topic for a research project. If possible, the students can write a report on a local animal they have some personal connection to; let it be their choice. Their direct observations and feelings can be helpful for the report. Some of the information can be gathered by personal experience. The information they gather can be published for a wide audience. A major factor in motivating students to write and then revise is knowing the audience for their work is more than just a teacher. The children can write books that are bound and can put in school and local libraries. Try making a temporary nature trail with laminated index cards attached to coat hangers. Children in younger grades will enjoy reading the work. The research can be put together as a nature guide for a local nature preserve or museum. Contact a local preserve and find out if they are interested. They may even be able to help with printing costs. There are also many places to publish the writing the children produce. Knowing that there is an audience beyond the classroom not only is a great motivator but a model for others on where the emphasis of environmental education should be: the place in which we live. Here are some places to publish the finished projects: Simply make copies of the children's writing and distribute to other children. Create class books. Send student writings to a local newspaper; perhaps they will be interested in a regular column on local animals. Make an intercom announcement of fun facts on local wildlife. Writing contests are another way to publish their books. There are many local writing contests; keep your eyes open. Nationally, the Global Rivers Environmental Education Network, (GREEN) sponsors the River of Words Poetry Contest each year. Another good source of information on writing contests and other markets for young writers is *The Market Guide for Young Writers* by Kathy Henderson (Cincinnati, OH: Writer's Digest Books, 1997). Set up bulletin boards in public places outside of the school. Grocery stores and local libraries are just a couple of places that might be interested. Do not forget the World Wide Web—there are lots of possibilities for publishing there.

As with any other writing project, it is better to break the writing into steps. Writing is a process; each step is just as important as any other. Evaluate the children's efforts based on how they do along the way, not just on the end product.

Pick an animal. Before the children choose an animal, brainstorm a very long list, so there are plenty of choices. Focus on animals the children have had direct experience with in their lives. From the beginning, let them know there will be an audience. If you don't know exactly what that will be, tell them that this will be one of the projects the class will work on.

Brainstorm a list of places to gather information. Encourage them to think beyond books and encyclopedias—interviews, videos, television, letter writing, the Internet, atlases, other reference books, nonfiction books, and their own observations are all place to get information. Another factor to discuss is that when one looks for a book, there may not be an entire book on that particular animal, but there may be another book that has a chapter on the animal or at least a few pages. The children need to think of related topics that may lead them to more information on their animal. They will have to be information explorers. It takes creative thinking to find books that may have one more piece of information. Learning to use an index is very helpful.

Taking Notes. Children need to be taught how to take notes. They need to be shown how to abbreviate the information in order to have more time and avoid mistakes. It is important to model taking notes before the children do it themselves. One way to is to write your own report modeling each step of the process. Write out each step on large chart paper. Each note fact should be numbered on sheets of paper. By writing down note facts and using them to write the rough draft, the report will be in the child's voice. Use a different sheet for each source of information, and they need to record the title and author on the top of the sheet. This is most useful when it comes to doing some fact-checking. The children will need constant reminders to record the source of information. You will need to guard against the children writing misinformation because they misunderstand what they are reading. It helps to be able to check a source when a child writes that bullfrogs eat lily pads.

Once the children have gathered enough note facts, it is time to organize. Gather a large collection of nonfiction picture books. Use nonfiction picture books as models of the variety of ways information can be presented. They do not have to be about animals. After reading one of the books to the group, we discuss how the author presented the information. For example, the author may have used a map. Another used a question/answer format, and another wrote in the animal's point of view. The children read the books on their own and look for ideas. We gathered together again to share the discoveries on a chart. For each book, record the author, title, and technique. After a couple sessions, you will have a long list of ideas for your books.

Outlines. The children next make an outline for their book. The outline can be very simple, basic phrases. For example:

The Common Crow

    a. Describe a Crow _____

        _____

    b. What It Eats _____

        _____

    c. Crows and People _____

        _____

    d. Amazing Facts _____

        _____

      The children also write down any of the techniques that they plan to use. Next, they color-code their note facts. Each outline section is given a different color. For example, any fact that describes a crow's appearance is marked green, any fact about breeding is marked purple. Then the green note facts are numbered in order. The students continue this until the facts are organized. There will be information that doesn't fit. The children can have an amazing fact paragraph, or they may simply decide not to use the information.

Now the children follow the plan and write a rough draft. Writing on every other line will help them have room for revising later. It is a hard habit to remember, but they can put a check on every other line before starting. The rough draft is the place to get the information down on paper; there will plenty of time for revision later.

Revising and editing. These suggestions for revising are helpful for any type of writing. Again, remind the children that because these reports will be read by the public, it is important to make them the best that they can. I constantly remind them that there will be people reading their writing who will not be able to turn around and ask you what something means. The writing has to make sense. Revising is their opportunity to make changes, reorganize, and improve their report. Good revising requires trust between the writer and the editor. Writers of works for children need to learn that the goal of the editor is to make the writing better. Whenever possible, I have the children revise my own writing. I want them to know I practice what I preach. I want them to know I trust their suggestions; it is simply a wonderful way to model what I expect of them. After the children write what they consider a finished report, I ask for volunteers to share their reports. We make suggestions as a group. Then the children go back for self-editing, followed by peer editing. They are always amazed at how many ways they can change their writing for the better.

Here are some suggested revising techniques and some questions to ask yourself. Can I build on the most important part to the writing? Have I described the details well enough? Do I have too much information in some places? Is there a way to explain the same idea in fewer words? Does the lead grab the reader's attention? Does the sequence make sense? Are there any extra words?

Some things to do to help with revising are to share the writing with another child and listen to the suggestions and to read the report out loud and listen for parts that do not fit. Give the piece to someone else and listen as they read it back to you. Use a tape recorder to record the research and play it back to listen for places to make changes. Reading our own writing out loud forces one to read each word. Start at the end of the report and read the last sentence first and so on, reading each in order to pay better attention to each line. Work on another project for a couple days, then come back and do more revising. This helps writers look at the report with fresh eyes. If you are working on a computer, print out a hard copy and do some more revising and editing on the hard copy. Carefully read your report line by line to make sure the punctuation is correct. Suggest editing conferences with the teacher. I save this conference for last. I want the children to do the best they can on their own. I want them to become independent writers who can make their own decisions and catch their own editing mistakes. Then I will step in like a magazine editor and work with the students to make the final corrections. There should also be some other adult editors involved to clean up any other spelling and grammar errors, especially if the work will be read by an audience outside of the school. Volunteer editors may need to be reminded to let children find and correct as many mistakes as possible to keep the children's voice.

Depending on how the final drafts are being used, publish the children's work. The effort it takes to find an audience outside of the classroom is rewarded by the effort that will motivate children to write.

Evaluating a report like this should not be focused solely on the final product. We need to evaluate the process. I break it up into four sections: gathering information, organizing information, rough draft, and final copy. Each one is worth 25 percent.

Gathering Information: evaluated on effort, amount of information, and creative information search techniques.

Organizing: use of other writers, does the plan make sense?

Rough Draft: use of information, organization, creativity, and revising.

Final Draft: mechanics, style of writing, and content.

Animal Art

In conjunction with the animal research, the children can create an artistic representation of the animal. There is no reason to limit the illustrations to one medium. There are many possibilities. Many children are overly concerned with realism when drawing animals. If it is not realistic, it is bad, is the common view. Leslie Marmon Silko writes about the traditional Pueblo artists. They never attempted to create any realistic image of any animal or plant. They focused on the essential features of the deer, squash, or whatever they were drawing. The Pueblo believed that each living being was a unique individual. A realistic drawing would represent just one particular deer. Instead, they created symbolic images that represented all deer. This tradition has an important message for children artists.

The children can make masks of their animals using paper bags and a variety of scrap materials. They can cut out magazines pictures of the animals to create a collage. Shoe box dioramas are a way of conveying information about the animals and their habitats. Clay, papier mâché, or plasticine are other ways to create images of each animal. If the children are going to draw, give them the chance to experiment with a variety of paints, pastels, crayons, or markers. Interesting images can be created by cutting out geometric shapes in construction paper and piecing it together. Whatever the medium, the object is to create an image that will capture someone's attention.

Puppet Shows

Another way to share the knowledge they learn is through skits, puppet shows, and charades. Small groups of children can write, plan, and design skits or puppet shows that tell a story and share facts about the lives of the animals.

Puppets can be made from paper bags, old socks, boxes, paper plates, or simply by drawing the animal on cardboard, cutting it out, and gluing it to a stick. Taking on the role of an animal is a natural and effective way to gain closeness to an animal.

Chapter Six

Plants of the Place

"To learn about a tree go to a tree."

Matsuo Basho

"To plant a pine one need be neither god nor poet; one need only a shovel."

Aldo Leopold

Introduction

Consider the miracle of plants, life created out of sunlight and water. A tiny seed grows into a tree. In the tiniest crack in the sidewalk, a plant grows. It is easy to take plants for granted. They grow almost everywhere; on the other hand, they are a constant reminder of the power of life, of a world beyond humans. All life is dependent on plants. They give us food and oxygen. Plants created a world where life could exist on land. As they produced more and more oxygen, the atmosphere went from 1 percent to 21 percent oxygen. This meant dangerous ultraviolet rays were filtered out, and there was enough oxygen for animals on land to breathe. Plants give us a food, a variety of medicines, and beauty. We surround ourselves with the plants we love and bring plants into our homes. We are just as dependent on their beauty as we are on the oxygen and food they produce.

Plants define each habitat, each place. The dominant plants of our childhood homes will always be the benchmark for comparing other places. To me, the only place that is normal is the second growth deciduous forests of my childhood. There is a comfort in being in a place where the plants are familiar. Plants can teach us ecology through their interrelationships with the land. The stories about plants can teach us history from the native peoples to the first settlers. Their lives were connected to the plants with which they lived.

The first few activities will foster a connection between a child and a single tree. Fortunately, there are at least a few trees in almost every schoolyard. Even a single tree can be the subject of a number of activities that will help children connect to their community. They can be done in a series throughout the year, or just a few can be chosen.

Depending on the number of trees available and the amount of time you have, you may want to have each child adopt a tree, and that will be their tree for the entire year. By concentrating on and studying a single tree, a child can become an expert. There is a great deal of satisfaction in being an expert.

Some activities are more general and simply geared to helping children focus attention and learn something about the plants in their area. The following activities help children understand the basics of how plants grow. By understanding plant life cycles and the miracle of photosynthesis, children will appreciate and better care for the plants in their community.

Books to Use

Arnosky, Jim. *Crinkleroot's Guide to Knowing the Trees*. New York: Bradbury Press, 1992. ISBN 0-02-705855-7. One of many of Aronsky's Crinkleroot books that can be used to teach children about the outdoors. In this book, Crinkleroot shows the readers many things about trees. There are basics about tree identification, forest ecology, and an introduction to reading the forest landscape.

Bash, Barbara. *Desert Giant*. San Francisco: Sierra Club Books, 1989. ISBN 0-316-08301-1. Bash's books are beautiful, down to the calligraphy she uses for the text. This book describes the life of the saguaro cactus and all the animals, including humans, that depend on this amazing plant. The illustrations are full of detail and information. The facts are intriguing. Aquatic insects live in the water inside the dead saguaros. Harris hawks perch on saguaros, sometimes on each others' backs.

Behn, Harry. *Trees*. Illustrated by James Endicott. New York: Henry Holt, 1977. ISBN 0-8050-1926-X. Beginning and ending with the line, "Trees are the kindest things I know," Behn's poem describes some of the wonderful ways trees help us all. Endicott's close-up illustrations of trees give his work a unique point of view.

Branley, Franklyn M. *Roots Are Food Finders*. New York: Thomas Y. Crowell, 1975. ISBN 0-690-00702-7. The illustrations are not exactly stunning, but this book does explain the function of roots and suggests several simple hands-on activities children can use to learn more about roots and how they find food for the plants.

Bunting, Eve. *Someday a Tree*. Illustrated by Ronald Himler. New York: Clarion Books, 1993. Bunting has written a number of wonderful stories that personalize the connection between children and nature. This book tells the story of a child, her family, and a special tree. The oak tree is a place for picnics, stories, fun, and daydreaming. Sadly, they discover the tree has been poisoned. The town bands together to try to save the tree, but eventually it dies. The young girl plants a handful of acorns in its place. At the same time the story tells the reader of a tragedy it also tells the story of a special relationship and a way to renew life in a personal way. This book easily prompts a discussion of the children's favorite trees.

Bunting, Eve. *Sunflower House.* Illustrated by Kathryn Hewitt. San Diego: Harcourt Brace Jovanovich, 1996. A beautiful book and a great idea. With the help of his father, a boy plants a circle of sunflower seeds. They grow into a sunflower house. For a whole summer, the boy and his friends play, camp, talk, and relax surrounded by sunflowers. In the fall, the sunflowers die despite everyone's best efforts, but soon they realize by planting seeds they can spread the beauty of sunflowers. Even planting one sunflower can capture some of the spirit of the book and provide plenty of seeds for birds.

Busch, S. Phyllis. *Wildflowers, and the Stories Behind Their Names.* Illustrated by Anne Ophelia Dowden. New York: Charles Scribner's Sons, 1977. In this book, we learn the story of more than 40 common flowers. Each one is accompanied by a full-color painting. The text not only explains how the flower got its name but also how the flower was used in the past. The stories we learn about the flowers help us remember who they are. This is a great book to bring on a hike.

Chaffin, Lillie D. *I Have a Tree.* Illustrated by Martha Alexander. New York: David White, 1969. In strictly personal terms, a little boy explains that he has a tree and that the tree has much to offer. All seasons, alone or with friends, the tree offers plenty to do. All children should have at least one tree they consider their own.

Dorros, Arthur. *A Tree Is Growing.* Illustrated by S. D. Schindler. New York: Scholastic, 1997. ISBN 0-590-45300-9. A stunning book about trees, filled with information and realistic illustrations. The main text explains how trees grow, produce food, protect themselves, and reproduce. Sidebars provide interesting facts, and the illustrations show a variety of living things dependent on the trees.

Eastman, John. *The Book of Forest and Thicket: Trees, Shrubs, and Wildflowers of Eastern North America.* Illustrated by Amelia Hansen. Harrisburg, PA: Stackpole Books, 1992. ISBN 0-8117-3046-8. Eastman covers approximately 100 common plants seen in eastern forests. For each plant, there is information on the plant's lifestyle, associates, and some folklore. Best used as a reference book, the illustrations are lovely, but you will need a field guide for identification.

Ehlert, Lois. *Red Leaf, Yellow Leaf.* San Diego, CA: Harcourt Brace Jovanovich, 1991. Written from a child's point of view, this book tells the story of a sugar maple tree growing from a seedling in the forest to a sapling in a nursery and finally planted in the child's backyard. Ehlert shows us how a child can have a relationship with a tree. The illustrations are vivid and bold, with detailed labels. Basic information on trees and how to plant trees is provided in the back of the book. This is the perfect book to read before planting a tree.

Frost, Robert. *Birches.* Illustrated by Ed Young. New York: Henry Holt, 1984. ISBN 0-8050-0570-6. Frost's classic poem is combined with the unique style of Young in sharing the beauty and fun of birch trees.

Hall, Zoe. *The Apple Pie Tree.* Illustrated by Shari Halpern. New York: Scholastic, 1996. ISBN 0-590-62382-6. Two children tell the reader about their apple tree through spring, summer, fall, and winter. We learn how the bare branches bud into leaves and how flowers turn into apples for apple pie. The book even includes a recipe for apple pie. The robin's nest in the illustrations reminds us that we aren't the only creatures dependent on apple trees.

Heller, Ruth. *The Reason for a Flower.* New York: Grosset & Dunlap, 1983. ISBN 0-448-14495-6. This is a wonderful book with bright illustrations that give us the reasons for a flower. We also learn a great deal about how the flower makes seeds. The rhyming words can be a little awkward. The reader will also learn about other plant functions.

Hiscock, Bruce. *The Big Tree.* New York: Atheneum, 1991. ISBN 0-689-31598-8. Hiscock combines the story of a 300-year-old tree and all the tree has seen of American history, with information on how trees grow, photosynthesis, and other facts.

Krudop, Walter Lyon. *Something Is Growing.* New York: Atheneum Books for Young Readers, 1995. ISBN 0-689-31940-1. Peter plants a seed in a patch of dirt in the middle of New York City. No one noticed. The plant grew and grew and grew. With Peter's tender care, the plant is taking over the city. Professor Thornbine is called in to get to the bottom of everything. There he finds Peter taking care of the plant. A beautiful fantasy to consider next time you see a plant growing through a crack in the sidewalk.

Lewin, Betsy. *Walk a Green Path.* New York: Lothrop, Lee & Shepard, 1995. ISBN 0-688-13425-4. Lewin's book is a series of paintings of plants, from house plants to rain forests to people who care for plants. Each painting is accompanied by a short poem and an explanation about the painting and the plant. The combination is a beautiful reminder of the beauty of a single plant.

Locker, Thomas, with Candace Christiansen. *Sky Tree.* New York: HarperCollins, 1995. ISBN 0-06-024883-1. This is an absolutely beautiful book. Thomas Locker painted the same tree through the seasons. The text not only describes the tree but poses questions for each painting that help the reader focus on art and the feelings it creates. The end of the book explains how each tree painting was made.

Lucht, Irmgard. *The Red Poppy.* New York: Hyperion Books for Children, 1995. ISBN 0-7868-0055-0. Stunning, larger-than-life paintings show a red poppy grow, flower, and turn into fruit. Each detail of the process is shown. Insects crawl inside the flower to help it pollinate, and tiny seeds fall to the ground. The book ends with notes that explain each page and add even more information. The author's note also explains how the idea of the book came to be.

Oppenheim, Joanne. *Have You Seen Trees?* Illustrated by Jean Tseng and Mou-Sien Tseng. New York: Scholastic, 1967. ISBN 0-590-46691-7. Beginning and ending with the same questions "Have You Seen Trees?" this book will invite your students to pay attention to all kinds of trees, in all seasons. The questioning pattern of the book acts as a personal conversation about trees. By focusing on the details about trees, the book is a great beginning to a walk among trees. Use the book's questions to start a discussion with your class about what they have seen in the trees. Use the patterns to write a class version of the book by trying to answer the book's questions.

Peattie, Donald Culross. *A Natural History of Trees of Eastern and Central North America.* Boston: Houghton Mifflin, 1977. ISBN 0-395-58174-5. Along with the companion volume, *A Natural History of Western Trees,* this book provides the reader with a wealth of information on trees. This reference book includes plenty of wonder stories for our nation's history as Peattie weaves them together with the natural history of various trees, showing how the two are connected. Beautiful writing combined with fascinating facts.

Pine, Jonathan. *Trees.* Illustrated by Ken Joudrey. New York: HarperCollins, 1995. ISBN 0-06-021468-6. This isn't exactly a picture book; each short chapter tells a story of a different tree species. It is still an elegant read-aloud. There are also chapters on leaves and roots. The trees covered in the book are common species, such as maples, oaks, willows, and trees of heaven. Pine's passages combine facts with reminders to get up close and personal with each tree.

Robbins, Ken. *A Flower Grows.* New York: Dial Books, 1990. ISBN 0-8037-0764-9. This book tells the story of an amaryllis flower from bulb to sprout to flower to seeds and back again. There is also a section at the end explaining how to care for amaryllis bulbs. The illustrations are a stunning combination of color-tinted photographs. Much more than the words, the pictures tell the story of a flower growing.

Sanders, Jack. *Hedgemaids and Fairy Candles: The Lives and Lore of North American Wildflowers.* Illustrated by Dawn Peterson. Camden, ME: Ragged Mountain Press, 1993. ISBN 0-07-057233-X. A great reference book filled with stories and facts about wildflowers. Children can use it for research, or you can simply carry it along on a hike. The book is organized by season, and Peterson's illustrations will help with identification.

Sanders, Scott Russell. *Meeting Trees.* Illustrated by Robert Hynes. Washington, DC: National Geographic, 1997. ISBN 0-7922-4140-1. A story based on one of the many walks the author took with his father as a child. He writes hoping to inspire more parents and children to go out and meet trees. Through the story, Sanders shows a number of ways one can interact with a tree, from wood working and field study to playing. The book also acts as a field guide to a few common eastern tree species, including devices for remembering their names. The detailed illustrations tell the story as well as provide information about trees and the animals with which they interact.

Tamar, Ericka. *The Garden of Happiness.* Illustrated by Barbara Lambase. San Diego, CA: Harcourt Brace Jovanovich, 1996. ISBN 0-15-230582-3. In New York City, Marisol's neighbors are starting a garden. Marisol wants to help, but she has no seeds. Finally, she finds some bird seed and plants it in a crack in the sidewalk. It grows into a huge sunflower that brightens the whole street. When winter comes, Marisol is sad that the sunflower has to die. But in the spring, even more seeds grow into sunflowers. No matter where, flowers help.

Thornhill, Jan. *A Tree in a Forest.* New York: Simon & Schuster Books for Young Readers, 1992. ISBN 0-671-75901-9. This is the story of one maple tree as it grows over 200 years. Each illustration shows the variety of life in a maple forest. Over time, the tree grows, and the world around it changes. Thornhill mixes story with a wealth of information about trees and forests.

Velghe, Anne. *Wildflowers: A Garden Primer.* New York: Farrar, Straus & Giroux, 1994. Full-color pages of wildflowers alternate with text describing the flowers and including loads of interesting information. Each flower is numbered and can be matched with its name at the back of the book, along with more fascinating facts. A wonderful and easy-to-use reference and identification guide for wildflowers.

Wexler, Jerome. *Flowers, Fruits, and Seeds.* New York: Prentice-Hall Books, 1987. ISBN 0-13-322397-3. Bright photographs show the reader the variety of plants, fruits, flowers, and seeds. A simple text explains how the flowers turn into fruits that produce seeds.

Activities

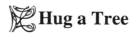Hug a Tree

This activity is a great way to introduce each student to a tree. This is a great activity to increase sensory awareness, teamwork, trust, or as a way for each student to pick a tree for his or her in-depth study. It is simply a great activity.

The only materials needed are blindfolds; use strips of cloth or even T-shirts. Put the students in pairs. Explain that one student will be the guide and the other will be introduced to a tree. The guide will put the blindfold on his or her partner. Carefully, they will lead their partner to a tree. At the tree, the students will use their other senses to get an image of the tree in their mind. When the child is ready, his or her partner will lead him or her back to the beginning. The guide should zigzag around a bit to make it a little more difficult for the child to find the tree. Once the blindfold is off, the child tries to find the tree.

There are some important safety considerations. Be sure to stress that this is no time for joking. The guide should always have his or her hand on his or her partner. When approaching the tree, the guide should put his or her partner's hands on the tree first, so no one walks face first into a tree.

The children switch roles so that everyone meets their own tree.

Personal Tree

Over a length of time, a child can adopt a tree. The tree should be growing in a place the child can visit regularly. At each visit, the child can do any number of activities or simply record journal entries. To begin, encourage the students to use all their senses, to be patient, and to really observe the tree. Have a contest on the first day to see who can write down the most observations. Other possible journal entries: How does the tree change over the year? How does the tree feel? How does the tree sound? What shapes do you see in the tree? What animals are on the tree? What questions would you ask the tree? What do you think the tree would say? How old do you think the tree is? Can you find other trees in the area that are the same as yours? How are the seeds from your tree dispersed? What has the tree seen standing there all these years? How does human activity affect your tree? How does your tree affect humans? Describe the leaves, bark, or buds. Use a hand lens and record what you see. Record the date of the first buds, first leaves, first flowers, first fruits, and when the leaves fall. Draw the tree. Draw one part of the tree. Press a leaf from your tree at different seasons of the year. Estimate how many leaves your tree has.

Tree Size

There are a number of ways to estimate the size of a tree.

Student Size

Stand a student of known height next to the tree. Using the student as a benchmark for the rest of the class, estimate the size of the tree. For example, if Jill is five feet tall, stand her next to the tree; how many Jills tall is the tree?

Ruler Method

Each student holds a ruler in hand and walks away from the tree. At about 50 yards, the students stretch out their arms and line the tree up, with the top of their fist at the bottom of the tree and the top of the ruler in line with the top of the tree. Next, turn the ruler sideways, keeping the fist in line with the bottom of the tree. Another student walks out from the base of the tree and stands in line with the end of the ruler. A third student measures the distance from the base of the tree to the spot where the second student is standing. That distance is the height of the tree.

Ratio Method

Put a meter stick in the ground next to the tree. Measure the length of the meter stick's shadow. Then measure the shadow of the tree. Comparing the ratios can give you the height to the tree. For example: the shadow of the meter stick is two meters. The shadow of the tree is 60 meters. $\frac{1}{2} = ?/60$.

Leg Method

Ask a child to walk away from the tree and periodically stop, bend over, and look through his or her legs. When he or she sees the top of the tree, stop. Measure the distance back to the tree. That length will be the height of the tree. Use more than one method and compare the results.

 ## Other Measurements

Circumference

To measure the circumference of a tree, wrap a string around the tree at a height of four-and-a-half feet. Measure the length of the string to find the circumference. Asking the children how to measure the circumference of a tree is a good problem-solving question.

Crown Width

To measure the crown spread, put stakes in the ground, marking the distance from one end of the crown to the other at the widest point and narrowest point. Measure the distance between the stakes and find the average.

Leaf Size

The children can put leaves on graph paper, trace the outline, and then estimate the area of the leaf. Use this to estimate the surface area that can absorb sunlight. The children can also compare the variations between trees of the same species in different places.

Tree Age

The children find the circumference of their tree. Then have them find the diameter by dividing by 3.14 (*pi*). To get the approximate age, multiply the diameter by the coefficient form in the table below:

White elm, tulip, chestnut	2.5
Black walnut	3
Black oak, plum	3.5
Birch, sweet gum, sycamore, oak, red oak, scarlet oak, apple	4
Ash, white ash, pine, pear	5
Beech, sorghum, sugar maple	6
Fir, hemlock	7
Shagbark, hickory, larch	8

(Adapted from *Arithmetic Teacher*, January 1994.)

Bark Rubbings

With paper and crayons, students can make rubbings of the tree's bark and leaves. Colored chalk, charcoal, or pencils will also work. Put the paper on the bark and rub the side of the crayon over the paper. An outline of the bark will appear. To do a leaf rubbing, put several leaves on layers of newspaper. Cover the leaves with paper and begin rubbing.

Dissect a Bud

In the spring, each student picks a bud off of his or her tree. With tweezers and a magnifying glass, the students carefully pick apart the bud and use the magnifying glass to look at the new leaves. Next, the children can select and mark one bud to check on every day. They can measure a leaf for a week to see how fast it grows. They can chart its growth rate over time.

Tree Seeds

Students should collect seeds from their trees and figure out how the seeds are dispersed. They can try to estimate the number of seeds produced. Some seeds, such as acorns and black walnuts, are spread out by squirrels and other animals that hide the seeds. Most of the time, these animals never find them. The seeds of maple trees, tulip trees, and many others are spread by wind. Some even float on water, like the coconut.

Leaf Classification

Ask the children to collect five different leaves. After collecting all the leaves, the children spread them out in front of them. The children can classify the leaves into two groups. Next, they can classify the leaves into three groups. They can record how many different ways they classified their leaves into two or three groups. Use this activity to introduce identification methods.

Find My Plant

Children can describe a plant to a partner and see if he or she can find it.

Tree Identification

Many field guides use keys to help identify various plants and animals. A key asks the reader a series of questions about the characteristics of the subject. At each question, the choices narrow toward one particular species. In order to use the keys in any field guide, there will be important vocabulary to learn. Use the information in the guide to help you and the children learn the important characteristics. Often the children will rely solely on the pictures to identify animals and plants. Encourage them to take the time to read the descriptions to avoid simply guessing. Many times, a single characteristic makes a plant unique, whereas in other cases, other species can be quite similar.

Another way to practice with keys is to make one with the children in your group. Start with a key for identifying the children in your group. Depending on the size of your group, you may want to just use part of the group for a key.

If the child is a girl, go to 2

If the child is a boy, go to 11

If the girl has blond hair, go to 3

If the child has dark hair, go to 4

If the child has glasses, Lynn

If the child has no glasses, go to 5

If the child has straight hair, go to 5

If the child has curly hair, Susie

This continues until every child has been identified. Give the children fake names and see if someone else can use the key to figure out who is who. The children can make keys using leaves, shells, rocks, or other natural objects.

Tree Book

The children pick four different leaves off of the ground. They invent a name for each one and write a description of each leaf. This is their leaf identification book. Each description should include four characteristics. Everyone switches his or her field guide and leaves with someone else. To identify the leaves, each child should make a chart to record information about the leaves. They can record characteristics, such as size, color, shape, and so forth. After making the chart, they look at the leaf identification guide to try to figure out which leaf is which.

Tree Tag

If you have an open space with a variety of tree species, you can play tree tag as soon as the children learn to identify some trees. A different tree is base during each round. For example: the caller may pick an eastern hemlock. Any student touching an eastern hemlock is safe. As the game goes on, the caller yells out a different tree every minute or so. It is a good idea to play this as a version of freeze tag. That way if someone is tagged, they have a chance to get back in the game.

Tic Tac Tree

Another way to practice tree identification is to play tree tic tac toe, or Tic Tac Tree. On cards, make a 3-by-3 array with the names of different tree species found in the area. Make several different sets of cards. The children find leaves to match the trees listed. The first to find three in a row wins.

Tree Research

Children can use the library and other resources to find out as much information as possible about their tree. Some of the questions students can try to answer are: geographic range of the tree. Identifying features of the tree. Come up with mnemonic device for remembering your tree.

• What are some of the uses of the tree?

• How did Native Americans use the tree?

• What are some fun and interesting facts about your tree?

• What special adaptations does your tree have?

Follow the same guidelines suggested in the animal chapter of this book. Once the students have gathered the information, there are a number of ways they can share the information. Children can write speeches to be given in class or when standing next to their trees. The tree can be the subject of a report or a story by weaving the facts into the plot. The students can take the rest of the class or other children on a guided tour of the tree. Other possibilities are a schoolyard tree nature trail, illustrated picture books of schoolyard trees, or even a cassette recording of each presentation to create an audio tour for other people to use.

Tree Population

Take a survey of tree species in the schoolyard or backyards or take a walk in the neighborhood. Graph the number and species of trees and use the results to discuss the status of trees in the community.

- How can the survey of trees be used to estimate the number of each species in a larger area?

- What places in the community need more trees?

- What trees used to live in your community?

- Why do some places in the community have more trees than others?

- What are the regulations for cutting down trees in your community?

Tree Map

Make a map of the trees in the schoolyard or neighborhood. Depending on the age of your students, the map can even be drawn to scale. Label the map with the names of the trees and other features in the area.

You can make a treasure hunt as an evaluation tool. Children can also create a treasure hunt by writing a set of clues that leads from one tree to another. Each clue will lead the children to a tree where there will be another clue leading to another tree. The clues can be based on tree facts. For example, "go to the tree that is used for syrup." "This tree has three needles." As the children work their way through the treasure hunt, they mark the trees on the map. One treasure hunt can be set for the entire class, or the children can work in groups. If the children are going to be spilt up into smaller groups, give each group a number. Put the clues in the envelopes and mark the envelopes with the clues with the group numbers to avoid confusion.

Plant Art

The students go out and collect a variety of plant parts, seeds, bark, twigs, leaves, and flowers. Provide them with glue, clay, paint, string, and other materials you have on hand. Give the students freedom to create a sculpture, mobile, picture, or design. Discuss how the characteristics of the plant material affected what they were trying to do and what they could do.

Twig or Leaf Match

Collect pairs of twigs or leaves from the schoolyard. Hand out one twig to each student. The students have to search for their match. Then the pairs can search the area from which the tree or shrub came. This is a good way to put children randomly in pairs for other activities.

Round Robin

This game demonstrates how many ways we use trees in our everyday life. Divide your group into groups of four or five. Give each group a sheet of paper and a pencil. There can be no talking during the game. On "go," the children take turns writing down all the ways in which trees are part of their lives. After a student writes down one answer, he or she passes the paper to the next student. The children keep passing the paper around, adding to the list until time is up. The team with the longest list wins.

Plant Basics

Plants need sun, minerals from the soil, water, and carbon dioxide. The basic parts of a plant are designed to bring these ingredients together. Choose a plant growing abundantly so that children can pick enough for a close look. Carefully dig up some of the plants, roots and all. If possible, compare more than one species. Examine the roots, stem, and leaves closely. A magnifying glass can be very helpful. The children can record their observations in their journals. Use this opportunity to discuss the function of each part.

Roots anchor the plant in the ground and absorb water and minerals. Fine root hairs give the plant an increased surface area and the thin cell wall that allows water and minerals to pass through into the plant. Some roots spread out thinly over a wide area, and others grow deep into the ground.

Stems transport water and minerals up to the leaves and sugars back to the roots. The stems support the leaves in order to reach more sunlight. Some stems are green and help with photosynthesis, and some stems help to protect the plant and have thick bark or thorns.

Leaves gather sunlight, produce food, and collect water and carbon dioxide. The leaves also release oxygen and extra water into the air. The veins distribute water, minerals, and sugars. Leaves come in a variety of shapes and sizes, each with their own adaptations.

 Plant Life Cycle

Seeds

Have the students collect as many seeds as possible from home and school. Ask the children to put a pair of old socks over their shoes and take a walk through a field to see what seeds they collect. One method of seed dispersal is for the seeds to cling to animal hair. After the walk, the children can sort and try to identify the seeds they find. Discuss why seeds need to disperse and the various methods used by the seeds they collect. Students can invent their own seeds with unique ways to disperse them.

Sprouts

After collecting some seeds, students can plant them and see if they sprout.

This can be done with other wild plants as well. Spread the seeds on wet paper towels and count the number that sprout versus the ones that do not sprout. Put some of the sprouts in potting soil. Discuss why some seeds sprout and others do not. Try putting some seeds directly in soil and compare their growth to the soaking method. Conditions have to be just right for seeds to sprout. The seed doesn't want to waste its only chance.

Super Sprouts

Have a contest to see who can find a plant growing in the strangest place. I am continually amazed by the fact that plants will grow anywhere they have a chance. They need to have one witness to confirm the sighting. My current favorite is a Queen Anne's lace growing in the back of a tractor at my parent's housing development.

Where Do All the Seeds Go?

Go out to a tree when the seeds from the tree are still on the ground. Line the children up arms' length apart facing the tree about 25 yards away. The children will walk in a straight line past the tree and stop another 25 yards away on the other side. As the children walk in a straight line, they should count how many seeds are on the ground in the line they walk. Record the average. Return a few weeks later and repeat the same activity. This time, the children are counting the number of seedlings. At the same time, look around the general area and count the number of mature trees. Compare all three numbers. A plant must produce many extra seeds because the vast majority of the seeds never make it. Discuss what factors in the area prevent more seedlings for growing.

Pollination Watch

Bees pollinate flowers when they land on the petals in search of nectar. Children can sit in an area with wildflowers and watch bees land on flowers. How many times does the same flower get visited? Do the bees land on flowers that have already been visited? Do they know which ones have already been used? If a bee lands on a flower and takes off right away, it means there is no nectar left.

Flower Dissection

Use a magnifying glass and tweezers to dissect a flower. The children can divide the flower into each of its major parts. Petals and sepals surround the reproductive organs. They aid in reproduction by protecting the flower-attracting pollinators. The male reproductive organ is the stamen; it generally grows in a circle around the stigma. Pollen from the stamen lands on the pistil through self- or cross-pollination. In the center of stamens is the pistil, which leads the pollen grain to the ovule.

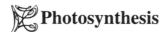 **Photosynthesis**

Can You Make Food?

A quick introduction to the magic of photosynthesis is to give students a jar of water. Ask them to make something to eat using only the water and sunlight. The only ingredients they can use are water, air, and sunlight. All life is dependent on the miracle of photosynthesis. Plants transform water and carbon dioxide into simple sugars in the presence of sunlight and chlorophyll. Water and oxygen are produced and given off by the plant.

Set up an experiment to show how sunlight, soil, air, and water work together. Sprout five bean seeds in five different cups. Eliminate one of the ingredients from each sprout. Keep the rest of the factors the same. Try growing one plant without water, try growing another in a closet without light, and try growing one without soil. It is hard to set up a situation without carbon dioxide, but try covering a leaf with a plastic bag. The fifth sprout is the control in the experiment. Every experiment should have a control. The control provides a point of comparison to test the effect of the variable you are testing. In this case, the control simply sits out, and nothing is done to it.

Photosynthesis Game

This is another game to reinforce an important concept; all you need are bits of colored construction paper for sun, soil, air, and water (sun = yellow, soil = black, carbon dioxide = red, and water = blue). Mix them up and spread them around. The children run around trying to collect as many as they can in a given time. (Plants do not usually run, but for the purpose to this game they do.) Photosynthesis only takes place when all four parts are together. After all the bits are collected, the children count their complete sets to see how much food they produced. Depending on the number of bits you make and the number of children you have, decide how many complete sets is enough for each "plant" to survive. There is competition between plants for the ingredients needed for photosynthesis. Just like food, water, or shelter limit the population of animals, sun, soil, air, and water are limiting factors for plant growth.

Plant Stories

Many of the common plants (otherwise known as weeds) have a rich and colorful history: the dandelion, for example. Use these stories to remember and identify some of the local plants. Once the children learn some of the plant lore, they can plan a way to share that information with others. The simplest way is to have the group lead other children on plant walks around the schoolyard.

Once the children have identified some of the plants in the area, they can learn some of the uses Native Americans and other people have for the plants. Find the stories told about the plants. Are there folk tales about any of the plants about which you and the children are learning? Aside from books, try talking to naturalists at local nature centers. These stories not only help one remember the names of the plant but teach us a few of the stories of the land.

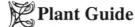Plant Guide

Drugstore contact paper is a great invention for preserving pressed flowers. The preserved flowers can become a field guide to the place where the children live. When picking wildflowers, be sure only to pick the most common species. Be aware of local regulations.

Invent a Plant

Children can invent a plant that is adapted to a certain habitat. See the invent-an-animal activity in chapter 3 for a more detailed explanation. In the case of the plant, there needs to be adaptations for finding sun, soil, carbon dioxide, and water. Like animals, the plants will need adaptations for reproducing and protection.

Chapter Seven

A Place in History

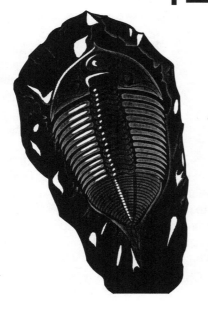

"A people without history is like the wind on the buffalo grass."

Sioux saying

Introduction

The place where each of us lives is a combination of the past and the present. It is a combination of geologic history, natural history, and human history. All those stories combine to make the place. Knowing the human past helps us learn how to live today and is necessary for learning all one can about the place and as a way to prepare for the future. When children know the past of the place in which they live, they have a connection to the chain of history flowing toward them, through them, and past them.

Teaching history can be as hands-on as teaching science. If we want children to know what life was like years ago, simply reading about it is not enough. They have to see it, live it, and act it out. They have to do what people did long ago. It is amazing how many ways there are to do this once one begins to think along these lines. There are activities in this chapter that can be done in any part of the country, and others that can be adapted to the way in which the people lived in your area. Each educator in each place will have to learn about life in his or her place and may need to do some research on the aspects of the place that make it unique.

A great deal can be learned about living with the land from the Native Americans that lived in and still live throughout North America. The first inhabitants needed to know a great deal about the land in order to survive. There was an intimacy with the place that most of us no longer have. They needed to know what plants were good to eat, what plants made the best baskets, where the fresh water spring was located, and so much more. They had to have a knowledge of the land that allowed them to survive. This knowledge is still useful today. They also had to take care of the land because their lives were so closely tied to the land. These close connections meant a different way of looking at the natural world. Although we can't recreate their world, we can learn many helpful lessons.

The activities in this chapter will help children learn something about Native American life by participating in activities that demonstrate how they lived. Each tribe had its own culture and way of doing things. Learn about the tribes in your area. These activities are very general but will show children why Native Americans needed to know so much about the place where they lived. The activities will introduce children to some of the aspects of Native American culture, but you will need to fill in the specific facts about the Native Americans in your area. Find out how the native people lived with the land, and in the process the children will learn a great deal about the place in which they live.

The native people in each region were a unique group; although they shared many of the same aspects of their culture, there were also important differences. It would be disrespectful to teach children about Europe as if each country were the same. It is the same with the native people of North America. There are some other considerations to make when teaching children about Native Americans. Avoid stereotypes and generalizations, even positive ones. Before dressing children up like Native Americans, think about whether you would have children dress up as Orthodox Jews. Use individual tribal names instead of lumping Native Americans into one big group. Although this chapter is about the history of your place, it is important to teach children that Native Americans are not just part of history; they are part of the present as well. Native Americans live on and off reservations around the country. They combine modern-day life with their traditional values just like everybody else.

It is easy to romanticize and stereotype native people's views of the natural world. We can teach about and learn from it, but that doesn't mean it can become our view. Each of us has to look at our own culture, religion, and traditions for stories, knowledge, and values about the natural world. Once I began to look, I discovered a long tradition in Judaism of ecological consciousness. I realized that my feelings about the natural world brought me closer to Judaism, not farther away. I don't have to become something I am not. Children can look at their own religions and ethnic backgrounds for folk tales, beliefs, and knowledge about the natural world.

Other activities in this chapter focus on the life of the early settlers. Their arrival changed things drastically for the native people and for the land. It is easy to forget how much the first settlers learned from the native people and how, in many ways, the settlers lived similar lives. These settlers lived lives that were also closely tied to the land. While they shaped the land, the land shaped the people. The activities presented can serve as a general introduction to a study of more specific aspects of your place.

Other activities are more general and will help the children get a sense of the scope of time and history in the place where they live. As the children participate in these activities, pay attention to what they discuss while they are engaged in the work. The issues they bring up about building shelter, finding food, and making tools while at work will be the basis for wonderful discussions.

For more information, go to the local historical museum and local library. People there will be glad to speak with you and the children. Additional places to find information are local environmental groups, government offices, libraries, and community newspapers. A couple telephone calls, and you have several lessons planned.

Books to Use

Appelbaum, Diana. *Giants in the Land*. Illustrated by Michael McCurdy. Boston: Houghton Mifflin, 1993. ISBN 0-395-64720-7. This is one of the books that inspired me to see the connection between place-based environmental education and picture books. This is the story of white pines. In colonial times, the white pine was reserved for the king and only for his quest for lumber to build ships. After the revolution, the white pine continued to have a significant meaning and use to the people in the Northeast. The pen-and-ink drawings have an old fashioned style that fits perfectly with the text, especially if you read this story under the needles of a white pine.

Baylor, Byrd. *And It Is Still That Way*. New York: Charles Scribner's Sons, 1976. ISBN 0-684-14676-2. There are many beautiful collections of Native American folktales. I included this one specifically because of the source of the stories. Baylor collected these stories from Native American school children in the Southwest. They are short, beautiful stories that children will enjoy.

Baylor Byrd. *Before You Came This Way*. Illustrated by Tom Bahti. New York: E. P. Dutton, 1969. In her usual wonderful style, Baylor asks the reader to think about who came before. Bahti's illustrations of rock art images help take the reader back in time and ask more questions than there are answers.

Baylor, Byrd. *When the Clay Sings*. Illustrated by Tom Bahti. New York: Aladdin, 1972. ISBN 0-689-71106-9. Baylor's poetic text raises countless questions about the pottery fragments left behind by the Anasazi in the Four Corners area. What did the designs mean? Why did they make them? The book also describes the magic of holding something or seeing something left behind by people from long ago. Bahti's Caldecott award-winning illustrations capture the uniqueness of the Anasazi designs.

Begay, Shonto. *Ma'ii and Cousin Horned Toad*. New York: Scholastic, 1992. ISBN 0-590-45390-4. Ma'ii is a coyote that doesn't like having an empty stomach. He goes off to see Cousin Horned Toad, who is a hard worker and has plenty of corn. Ma'ii tricks Cousin Horned Toad, only to find himself the one with all the trouble. This is a good example of a coyote trickster folk tale as well as a reminder not to be greedy.

Bruchac, Joseph. *A Boy Called Slow*. Illustrated by Rocco Baviera. New York: Philomel, 1994. ISBN 0-399-22692-3. This picture book biography of Sitting Bull beautifully describes a child's life among the Lakota people. The paintings have a darkness that creates a captivating power. This is also an example of a biography that focuses on one part of the person's life.

Bruchac, Joseph. *The First Strawberries*. Illustrated by Anna Vojtech. New York: Dial Books, 1993. ISBN 0-8037-1331-2. Bruchac has retold many wonderful Native American folktales in picture books and in several collections. Any of his books are worth reading to children and will serve you well. The ones listed here are some of my favorites. When the world was new, a man and a woman lived happily together. Unfortunately, they had a fight, and the woman walked off. The man could not catch her so he could apologize. With the sun's help, he finally has his chance. This is a good example of a story where humans speak to and receive help from nonhumans.

Bruchac, Joseph. *The Great Ball Game*. Illustrated by Susan L. Roth. New York: Dial Books, 1994. ISBN 0-8037-1539-0. The birds and the animals are having a great argument about who is better. They decide to have a ball game to decide. The birds do not want the bat, but the animals decide to accept him. Just as the animals are about to lose, Bat saves the day and wins the game for the animals. This folktale fits the pattern of stories in which animals talk as well as one that explains why a particular natural phenomenon occurs. The cutout collage illustrations are plenty of fun.

Bruchac, Joseph. *Many Nations: An Alphabet of Native Americans*. Illustrated by Robert F. Goetzl. Mahwah, NJ: BridgeWater Books, 1997. ISBN 0-8167-4389-4. Each letter of the alphabet is represented by a different tribe. This book is a simple and powerful way of showing the diversity of Native American life in North America.

Bruchac, Joseph. *The Story of the Milky Way: A Cherokee Tale.* Illustrated by Virginia Stroud. New York: Dial Books, 1995. ISBN 0-8037-1737-7. A young boy stays up to watch who is stealing the people's corn. He sees a mysterious dog with strange light eat the corn. The people decide they must scare the dog away so that the corn will be safe. The villagers wait up one night until the dog comes. When he does, they make such a racket that the dog runs into the sky, spilling cornmeal all the way. His trail becomes a band of stars we call the Milky Way. This is a good example of a folktale that explains something about the world and how it came to be. It is also a subtle way to learn something about the importance of corn in many tribes.

Carrier, Lark. *A Tree's Tale.* New York: Dial Books for Young Readers, 1996. ISBN 0-8037-1202-2. This is the story of Mai-Methung, a path tree. Hundreds of years ago, Native Americans bent trees in order to make trail markers. Through the year, Mai-Methung sees people come and go and the forest go, come back, and now fall again in the face of development.

Cherry, Lynne. *A River Ran Wild: An Environmental History.* San Diego, CA: Harcourt Brace Jovanovich, 1992. ISBN 0-15-200542-0. Cherry's story of the Nashua River in Massachusetts shows the changes that one single river went through. Each page shows someone using the river, from Native Americans through colonial days to the industries that polluted the river. She concludes with the story of how local people saved the river and cleaned it up so that once again the water is clear enough to see the pebbled bottom. Even the border illustrations convey information about the life and times of this river.

Collier, John. *The Backyard.* New York: Viking, 1993. ISBN 0-670-83609-5. A beautifully illustrated book about a boy and his backyard. He knows that before his house was there, there was a farm, and before that there were cowboys, and before that were Native Americans, and so on all the way back to the beginning.

de Paola, Tomie. *The Legend of the Bluebonnet.* New York: G. P. Putnam, 1983. ISBN 0-399-20937-9. The Comanche people were suffering from a long drought. The tribe's shaman went out to the hill to pray to the Great Spirit for help. He told the people they had to sacrifice their most valued possessions. No one would, except a young girl named She-Who-Is-Alone. One night, she throws her doll into a fire. In the morning, the rains come, and flowers cover the hills. This is one of many folktales that shows how even the poorest person can make a difference and help others.

Dragonwagon, Crescent. *Homeplace.* Illustrated by Jerry Pinkney. New York: Scholastic,1990. A family takes a walk to a place in a forest, where they find bits and pieces of the home that was once there. Listening carefully, they can hear the sounds of the people: a girl brushing her hair, a squeaking chair, dinner conversation. The family left the forest and came back.

Duke, Kate. *Archaeologists Dig for Clues.* New York: HarperCollins, 1997. ISBN 0-06-027056-X. This book is part of the Let's Read and Find Out series. The style is somewhat reminiscent of the *Magic School Bus.* Text combined with carton balloons tell the story of what archaeologists do on a dig. There is a great deal of information, and the illustrations are lively. Children will have a good idea of what an archaeologist does after reading this book.

Edwards, Richard. *Ten Tall Oak Trees.* Illustrated by Caroline Crossland. New York: Tambourine Books, 1988. ISBN 0-688-04620-7. This counting book is the story of what happens to 10 oak trees from colonial days until today. Between human and natural impacts, one by one there are no trees left until a young boy plants one.

George, Jean Craighead. *Acorn Pancake, Dandelion Salad and 38 Other Wild Recipes.* Illustrated by Paul Mirocha. New York: HarperCollins, 1995. ISBN 0-06-021549-6. George has written a unique cookbook. There are several recipes for using common, easy-to-identify plants. You will be surprised how much you can make with dandelions, acorns, and plantains. The recipes also include information about each plant. You may also want to try *The Wild, Wild Cookbook: A Guide for Young Wild-Food Foragers*, also by George (Thomas Y. Crowell, 1982).

Goble, Paul. *Adopted by the Eagles.* New York: Bradbury Press, 1994. ISBN 0-02-736575-1. Goble has retold many of the folktales of the Lakota people; they are all worth using. His words and illustrations do these stories justice, and he takes great care in making his work accurate and respectful. Any of his books would be good to use. This story is about two close friends. One friend betrays another while hunting horses. He survives and returns home. The reader will learn about Lakota life as well as see the possibility for friendship with animals.

Goodchild, Peter. *A Spark in the Stone.* Chicago: Chicago Review Press, 1991. ISBN 1-55652-102-2. A reference book for learning about Native American technology and life styles. Chapters include food, shelter, baskets, and more. Some of the projects are a bit complex for groups of children, but others lend themselves to teaching a class. In either case, the background information is welcome.

Houston, Gloria. *My Great-Aunt Arizona.* Illustrated by Susan Condie Lamb. New York: HarperCollins, 1992. ISBN 0-06-022606-4. Houston has written a biography of her Great-Aunt Arizona, a true unsung hero. Arizona grew up in the mountains, became a teacher, and taught countless children to reach for their dreams. This book will serve as an excellent model for children's own unsung hero biographies as well as telling the story of a woman connected to the place where she lives. It is a book full of love.

Lasky, Kathryn. *My Island Grandma.* Illustrated by Amy Schwartz. New York: Morrow Junior Books, 1973. ISBN 0-688-07946-6. A young girl describes her summer with her grandmother on their special island. Her grandmother teaches her to swim, what plants to eat, where the blueberries grow, and much more. From morning to night, Grandma shares her sense of wonder and all the remarkable things on this special island. The book is a beautiful reminder of what a child can learn from an elder.

Leeuwen, Jean Van. *Going West.* Illustrated by Thomas B. Allen. New York: Dial Books for Young Readers, 1992. ISBN 0-8037-1027-5. A young girl and her family head west. There are things to bring and things that must be left behind. The trip is hard, but the family arrives and begins to settle into the place. The passage about Native Americans is a bit condescending, but overall the book does capture life on the prairies and the idea of moving and settling into a new place.

Lyon, George Ella. *Dreamplace.* Illustrated by Peter Catalanotto. New York: Orchard, 1993. ISBN 0-531-05466-7. A family vacation to the Southwest takes a girl back in time to the Anasazi. In her dream, she sees the way they lived in a place with so little water, how they made what they needed, and lived off the land. When the water was gone and sickness came, the Anasazi vanished and left behind the houses in the stone.

Lyon, George Ella. *Who Came down That Road?* Illustrated by Peter Catalanotto. New York: Orchard, 1992. While walking down a road with his mother, a boy asks, "Who came down that road?" With each answer, he asks, "Who came before that?" The answers go back through the Civil War, back to the settlers, and back past the Native Americans to when the land was an ancient sea. The books ends with a perfect statement for our understanding of history. "Questions! Questions crowded like a bed of stars, thick as that field of goldenrod."

Macaulay, David. *Motel of the Mysteries.* New York: Scholastic, 1979. ISBN 0-590-47236-4. It is the year 4022, and archaeologists discover a ruin in the ancient country of Usa. Strange artifacts and treasures are discovered. Macaulay reminds us that the present day will one day be the past. By showing readers our own culture from a different point of view, we are reminded that what is normal is in the eye of the beholder. The book demonstrates how difficult it is to understand the past when seen through the eyes of the present.

MacGill-Callahan, Sheila. *And Still the Turtle Watched.* Illustrated by Barry Moser. New York: Dial Books for Young Readers, 1991. ISBN 0-8037-0931-5. This book is based on a true story that began hundreds of years ago. A Delaware Indian carves a turtle in a rock overlooking a river. As the years go by, the turtle watches over a changing land. Eventually, the turtle almost vanishes under graffiti and neglect until it is brought to the New York Botanical Garden where children can touch its history.

Martin, Rafe. *The Rough-Faced Girl.* Illustrated by David Shannon. New York: Scholastic, 1992. ISBN 0-590-46932-0. Cinderella-type stories are found in folktales around the world. This is the Algonquin version, set on the shores of Lake Ontario. Like all Cinderella stories, good triumphs over evil. The rough-faced girl uses her faith and good thoughts, not a fairy godmother, to overcome evil. It delivers the message that even the most unfortunate have a chance.

McDermott, Gerald. *Arrow to the Sun.* New York: Penguin Books, 1974. ISBN 0-14-050-2114. A boy goes in search of his father. His journey takes him to the sun, where he passes a series of tests proving his power and that the sun is his father. This Pueblo story is one many folktales involving someone taking a journey in search of something as well as an opportunity to prove themselves. McDermott's stylized illustrations helped this to become a Caldecott award-winning book.

McDermott, Gerald. *Raven: A Trickster Tale from the Northwest.* San Diego, CA: Harcourt Brace Jovanovich, 1993. ISBN 0-15-265661-8. The people live without light. Raven decides to help. He flies off in search of light. When he discovers the place where light lives, he changes himself into a baby and steals the light so the world can be seen. It is another trickster tale as well as a story that shows an animal helping people.

McLuhan, T. C. *Touch the Earth.* New York: Promontory Press, 1971. ISBN 0-88394-000-0. A collection of quotes from Native Americans.

Miner, Horace. "Body Ritual Among the Nacirema." *American Anthropologist* 58 (1956). Further information on the lives of the Naciremas.

Oughton, Jerrie. *The Magic Weaver of Rugs.* Illustrated by Lisa Desimini. Boston: Houghton Mifflin, 1994. ISBN 0-395-66140-4. Dramatic illustrations capture the beauty and starkness of the Navajo lands in this story of how the Navajo people learned to weave. Two women set off to find a way to help their people. High on a mesa, Spider Woman uses her magic to teach them how to weave beautiful rugs. Despite losing faith in what Spider Women shows them, the women return to their people and teach them how to weave. Prosperity comes to the people.

Perl, Lila. *Hunter's Stew and Hangtown Fry: What Pioneer America Ate and Why.* Illustrated by Richard Cuffari. New York: Clarion Books, 1977. ISBN 0-8164-3200-7. This book, along with *Slumps, Grunts, and Snickerdoodles: What Colonial America Ate and Why*, provides much background information on food through American history as well as suggested recipes to try with children.

Primary Voices. National Council of Teachers of English 4:3 (1996). This entire issue of *Primary Voices* is devoted to bringing Native American literature into the classroom. Articles discuss how to respect native cultures and suggest a variety of literature to use. The bibliography of books organized by region is invaluable.

Ross, Gayle. *How Turtle's Back Was Cracked.* Illustrated by Murv Jacob. New York: Dial Books for Young Readers, 1995. ISBN 0-8037-1278-8. This book provides one of several explanations of how turtle's back was cracked. This version begins with Possum and Turtle eating persimmons. Turtle is tricked by Wolf. Then Turtle's friend Possum accidentally kills Wolf. Turtle brags of his bravery. The other wolves try to get their revenge on Turtle. Using tricks similar to Br'er Rabbit, Turtle escapes with just a cracked back. This folktale is an example of how people and animals talk to each other.

Ross, Gayle. *The Legend of the Windigo.* Illustrated by Murv Jacobs. New York: Dial Books for Young Readers, 1996. ISBN 0-8037-1897-7. This Algonquin legend explains where mosquitoes came from. A terrible monster made from stone terrorizes a village. While heating rocks for a sweat lodge ceremony, a young boy realizes they can destroy the Windigo with heat. The people trap the Windigo in a pit and set him on fire. His body and evil heart explode into tiny bits that still plague people today as mosquitoes. The book explains the importance of sweat lodges in the lives in many native peoples.

Rounds, Glen. *Sod Houses of the Great Plains.* New York: Holiday House, 1995. ISBN 0-8234-1162-1. In the past, the shelters in which people lived were directly influenced by where they lived. In a place with few trees, such as the Great Plains, sod houses were the only choice. This book provides step-by-step instructions for building the sod houses as well as the advantages and disadvantages of living in a sod house. Snakes sometimes fell through the roof. Rounds's illustrations capture the vastness of the great plains in a simple style.

San Souci, Robert. *The Legend of Scarface: A Blackfeet Indian Tale.* Illustrated by Daniel San Souci. New York: Doubleday, 1978. ISBN 0-385-13247-6. Scarface loves a young woman named Singing Rains, but she promised herself to the Sun. Scarface vows to go to the Sun to release Singing Rains from her promise. His journey takes him far away. Scarface shows his honesty and bravery throughout. When Scarface saves the life of the Sun's son, he is rewarded. Even though this folktale is an example of a journey, it also shows the rewards of acting justly toward both people and animals.

Sanders, Scott Russell. *Aurora Means Dawn.* illustrated by Jill Kastner. New York: Bradbury Press, 1989. ISBN 0-02-778270-0. In 1880 Ohio, a family heading west is caught in a terrible storm. They want to return to the east. When the storm clears, they must work their way through downed trees to reach Aurora. This is a good book to use if you are studying the arrival of the first settlers of European descent. Sanders's focus on just one of the many difficulties actually makes the book a more powerful statement about the effort people exerted to start a new life.

Sanders, Scott Russell. *Warm As Wool.* Illustrated by Helen Cogancherry. New York: Bradbury Press, 1992. ISBN 0-02-778139-9. This book is a follow-up on *Aurora Means Dawn*. Newly arrived and suffering from the cold, a mother knows she needs sheep and their wool to keep her family warm. With money she saved, she manages to buy a small flock. The flock gets smaller because of disease and accidents. The illustrations show how she manages to shear, wash, card, spin, and finally weave warm clothes for everyone. The author's note at the end helps put the book in perspective.

Scieszka, Jon. *The True Story of the Three Little Pigs.* Illustrated by Lane Smith. New York: Scholastic, 1989. ISBN 0-590-44357-7. This is great picture book based on the story of the "Three Little Pigs" but from the wolf's point of view. The story is told well, and the illustrations are wonderfully funny. A great way to begin a discussion on the fact that many times, it all depends on who is telling the story.

Sewall, Marcia. *People of the Breaking Day*. New York: Atheneum, 1990. ISBN 0-689-31407-8. A first-person narrator tells the story of the Wampanoags, People of the Breaking Day. The Wampanoags lived in southeastern Massachusetts. The reader learns what life was like for the Wampanoags throughout the year: the foods they ate, the games they played, their family life, and much more. Watercolor illustrations help to convey more information.

Sheldon, Dyan. *Under the Moon*. Illustrated by Gary Blythe. New York: Dial Books for Young Readers, 1994. ISBN 0-8037-1670-2. Jenny finds an arrow-head in her backyard. She tries to imagine what it was like when the arrowhead was made but can't. Jenny decides to camp out in her tent and wait. In a dream, Jenny sees the people who left the arrow-head. Blythe's paintings based on photographs of the Sioux have their own dreamlike quality.

Sloane, Eric. *ABC Book of Early America*. New York: Doubleday, 1963. Sloane is a wonderful artist whose illustrations of early American life are full of detail. This book will show children many of the tools and other aspects of life in the early history of the United States.

Sorensen, Henri. *New Hope*. New York: Lothrop, Lee & Shepard, 1995. ISBN 0-688-13925-6. The book begins with a young boy asking his father about the statue in the park. The boy's father tells a story that begins with a broken wagon axle in 1885. With the wagon broken, Lars Jensen decides this will be a good spot to build his new home. Soon, the black-smith joins him, then farmers, and more and more people until the town of New Hope is built. The illustrations provide added detail about the period in history. The young boy learns that Lars Jensen is his great-great-great-grandfather.

Steptoe, John. *The Story of Jumping Mouse*. New York: Mulberry Books, 1984. ISBN 0-688-08740-X. This Caldecott Honor Book is illustrated with unique black-and-white drawings. They tell the story of a mouse who follows his vision to the far-off land. Along the way, he sacrifices to help others and is rewarded with magic powers. His long journey is a success, and he is transformed into an eagle.

Stilz, Carol Curtis. *Grandma Buffalo, May, and Me*. Illustrated by Constance R. Bergum. Seattle, WA: Sasquatch Books, 1995. ISBN 1-57061-015-0. A young girl named Poppy takes a camping trip with her mother to touch her family tree. They visit a variety of places in Montana as Poppy learns about the lives of her "Grands." She learns to fish, plant a garden, and feed a buffalo just like her great-grandma. A good inspiration for a search of one's own family ties to the land.

Stroud, Virginia A. *A Walk to the Great Mystery*. New York: Dial Books, 1995. ISBN 0-8037-1636-2. Dustin and Rosie are off to spend the day with Grandma Ann. Grandma Ann is not like any other grown-up. She is a medicine women, a healer. The three of them set off to find the Great Mystery. Along the way, Grandma Ann shows them many special plants, rocks, and other unique things. She explains to them about her medicine tools. She leads them to special places, and they learn what the Great Mystery is, the spirit in all living things. A wonder-filled story that shows how traditional knowledge was once passed along. The book has the potential to generate an interesting discussion because Grandma Ann's view of life differs from a Judeo-Christian outlook.

Turner, Anne. *Heron Street*. Illustrated by Lisa De-simini. New York: Harper & Row, 1989. ISBN 06-026184-6. A marsh in the Northeast undergoes many changes over the years. The sounds of the marsh grass in the wind, of the pilgrims, of school children, and of the Revolutionary War are all sounds of change. The marsh gets smaller and smaller as time goes on. The heron flies away, but the remaining marsh grass still calls, "Shhh-hello, hsss-hello."

Webb, Denise. *The Same Sun Was in the Sky*. Illustrated by Walter Porter. Flagstaff, AZ: Northland, 1994. ISBN 0-87358-602-6. A grandfather takes his grandson on a hike into the Arizona desert. Together they find rock carvings left behind by the Hohokam. Standing in the desert, feeling the power of these carvings, the boy realizes that there is a connection between himself and the past. They share the same sun and more.

Weller, Frances Ward. *Matthew Wheelock's Wall*. Illustrated by Ted Lewin. New York: Macmillan, 1992. ISBN 0-02-792612-5. More than 100 years ago, Matthew Wheelock built his stone wall. With care and patience, he built a wall that would last. Generation after generation of Wheelocks lived on the land. The wall never faltered because "The small ones need the big, the big ones the small."

Wessels, Tom. *Reading the Forested Landscape: A Natural History of New England*. Illustrated by Brian D. Cohen. Woodstock, VT: Countryman Press, 1997. ISBN 0-88150-378-9. A wonderful book that will change the way you look at forests, especially if you live in the Northeast. Wessels explains a variety of forest patterns that helps one learn what has happened to the forest and why. The clues, he explains, tell the story of the history of the forest.

Wright, Courtni C. *Wagon Train: A Family Goes West in 1865.* Illustrated by Gershom Griffith. New York: Holiday House, 1995. ISBN 0-8234-1152-4. An African American family heads west in this story of one family's efforts to start a new life. The book captures much of the effort and hardship everyone endured. The encounter with Native Americans will be a good place to stop and discuss a variety of issues.

Activities

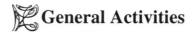

General Activities

Our Elders

To find out more about their place, children can interview people who have lived in the community for a long time. These first-hand conversations will tell the children a great deal about what the place was like years ago. For interviewing tips and ideas for lessons, see the Hero Biography Lessons in chapter 8. In fact, these interviews can easily become biographies in their own right.

It is a good idea to brainstorm some questions that will help the children find out as much as they can about what life was like in their community in the past. Some possible questions are: What did this place look like? What did you do for fun? What has been the biggest change? What about life today? Do you think it should be changed to the way it was back when you were a child? What was the state of the environment when you were a child? Are there any local legends, folktales, or stories you remember?

The interviews can be shared orally, by video, or in written form. The interviews can be compiled into a living history document. If it is not possible for each child to interview one person, invite someone to come to the class. The children can do a group interview. These interviews can turn into continuing relationships for some of the children. Children can learn to value the stories, knowledge, and experience of the community's elders.

Timelines

Timelines are way for children to gain a sense of the passage of time through a visual aid. A good place to start is a timeline of the children's lives. Mark off a 15-yard line. The scale for this timeline is one yard = one year. Ask the children to share a major event in their lives and the year that it happened. For example, at age six Billy rode his bike. Ask Billy to stand at the year six mark. Ask for a few other volunteers, each one standing on the timeline at the year that marks their event. Children can also write their own personal timelines on paper.

You can extend the timeline further into the past. Depending on the lesson, you may choose to go back in time to pre-Columbian times, or even further back to the geologic formation of your area. Discuss with the children how the scale will have to change depending on how far back the timeline will go. Two aspects of timelines I always find startling is how little time humans have been on Earth compared to history of the planet and how little time people of European descent have spent in North America compared to native people. We often don't realize that dinosaurs lived on the planet far, far longer than humans have. Discuss how much further the timeline will go into the future. As a class project, make a community timeline for the past 500 or more years.

Some important timeline events:

4.6 billion years ago, Earth is created

3.5 billion years ago, life begins

405 million years ago, life lives on land

360 million years ago, first insects

200 million years ago, dinosaurs appear

136 million years ago, flowering plants appear

65 million years ago, dinosaurs disappear

300,000 years ago, oldest known human remains

20,000 years ago, native people migrate into North America

500 years ago, Christopher Columbus arrives in the Americas

150 years ago, Civil War in the United States
(Adapted from Caduto and Bruchac, *Keepers of the Earth*, 1989.)

Point of View

As the children travel back in time, there will be a need to understand and to appreciate different cultures. It is important for children to realize that there is more than one point of view about most things in the world. There is usually a variety of ways to solve a problem. Being able to put oneself in somebody else's shoes will allow students to appreciate diversity rather than to fear differences. It will have the added benefit of helping to ease conflicts. This is an important part of understanding and learning about other cultures. When discussing historical events, discuss the fact that there can be more than one point of view about an event. What did the British think about the Revolutionary War? Even the word *his*tory tells us something about point of view. These activities also help as part of any lesson on the many sides of environmental issues.

Squares

Hold a chess board up for a short time. Ask the students how many squares they see. Record the answers. Do not allow them to discuss the answers. Hold the board up again. Give them more time and allow them to discuss the answers. Record the different answers. Let them discuss their ideas again. There will be more of a consensus, even if they all do not agree. The whole activity symbolizes that problems don't start with answers; we work toward an answer and reach more of a consensus by sharing different points of view.

Nacirema

Tell the students the following story. "I was watching public television last night. There was a show about a country that did some pretty strange things. For fun, they play a game where two groups of men fight over a dead animal skin. When the people are sick, they go to a person who gives them bad tasting food, sticks them with sharp needles, and gets paid for it. These people poke holes in their bodies and put metal through the openings. In each home there is a shrine with a special chair that holds water. The men wear tight ropes around their necks. They keep animals that bite in their houses."

By this time, the kids will be giggling a little bit. Ask them what they think of these people. Some will say they are weird, strange, or crazy. A couple of kids might figure out who the Naciremans are. Maybe you have. "Nacirema" is American spelled backward. Ask the students what you were describing about American life. In case you haven't figured it out, the story describes: football, doctors, earrings, toilets, ties, and dogs. This is an eye-opening activity for children and adults (Miner 1956).

Martian Landing

Every culture is made up of several aspects. Before studying another culture, it is good to have a working definition and a point of comparison. They can begin by looking at their own school culture. I use 10 aspects of culture: shelter, food, transportation, religion, clothes, technology, economy, government, entertainment, a child's day, and language.

A good place to start is with your own culture. Give them the following assignment or journal entry: A Martian lands in your backyard and wants to understand what life is like in this place. He has questions about what people do for fun, food, government, religion, education, and transportation. The children can write a short essay explaining their culture to a visiting Martian. They can find magazine pictures that capture various aspects of the elementary school culture.

Schoolyard Archaeology

When we teach our students history, we ask them to trust us. We tell them about places and things from long ago. The only proof they see are books. Unfortunately, children do not always believe us or books.

Studying archaeology will help students see that information in history books is not made up. The information did not come out of thin air. It is important for children to see how we study history. By participating in an archaeological dig, students will see first-hand how artifacts are discovered, how facts are gathered, and how a theory is developed. All you need is a place to dig; even a sandbox will work.

Fact/Theory

The next step in the training is to learn the difference between a fact and a theory. For this activity, I lay several items out in front of the class. Try to pick objects with which the students are unfamiliar. I tell them that they are archaeologists who have just discovered artifacts from an ancient culture. We generate a list of facts about the items by simply describing the objects' basic characteristics: height, weight, composition, and color.

Next, we develop possible theories for the object's use. First, we simply brainstorm, then we evaluate which theories make the most sense. I emphasize to them that a good theory should be based on as many facts as possible. Through the discussion, we come up with an understanding of the difference between a fact and a theory. I also point out that a good theory can become a bad theory as more facts are discovered. The Flat Earth theory made sense for a while, until more facts proved it incorrect.

The Dig

Now that the students are trained, they are ready to dig. Prior to the dig, you will need to prepare the site. First of all, you will need a dig site. Basically any area that the children can dig up will work. Ideally, you will find a place where the students will actually find artifacts. For this activity, artifacts need not be ancient. They can be anything created by humans. If needed, such artifacts as rusty pieces of metal, old nails, and bits of glass can be buried in the site. For safety reasons, when an item is found, the adult leader should pick it up. I ask each class whether they want me to plant objects or not. They always vote against planting artifacts. They want the true challenge of finding an artifact. They always manage to find some type of artifact; one is enough.

Next, use rope to mark off a square over the dig site. Wrap a piece of tape around the rope every twelve inches. This will be used as a grid for marking the location of each artifact. You also will need trowels, buckets, plastic bags, rulers, clip boards, paper, pencil, and, if possible, a sieve to sift the dirt.

There are three jobs during the dig:

The Diggers. They simply fill the buckets with dirt.

The Sifters. They take the buckets and sift through the dirt, looking for any artifacts.

The Measurers and Recorders. When an artifact is found, they have two tasks. First, they measure the depth of the hole where the artifact was found. This is important for dating the relative age of the artifact; the deeper, the older. The second measurement is to record the location using the grid. The recorders take down the following information on each artifact: location, length, depth, and other details. After recording the information, the object is numbered and put in a plastic bag. Being accurate recorders is the key to learning more facts.

I explain each job to the students and emphasize that all the jobs are necessary for a successful dig. When the students start finding artifacts and things get going, you will have to remind them to stick to their jobs. Rotate the children through each job. Chances are the measurer/recorders will need the most help once things get going.

After the dig, there are several possible follow-up activities. Based on the facts, develop theories about what happened at the site. The students can make graphs that display the information. The students record the location of the artifacts they found on a grid and make a map of the dig site.

The children love the dig, and it demonstrates how we find answers, develop theories, and work together. These are useful skills for studying history and learning about anything else.

Cemetery Search

A cemetery is a good place to find out about the place in which you live. There are a number of simple activities that can be done on a walk through the cemetery in your community. Start by talking to the manager. Then search the cemetery to answer the questions.

- What are the different nationalities represented in the cemetery?
- Who is the oldest person buried here?
- Why is the cemetery located where it is?
- Who are some of the notable people buried there?
- What was the average lifespan during different periods of time?
- How are the older tombstones different from the newer ones?
- What types of designs were used to decorate the tombstones?
- What do some of the epitaphs say?
- Is there a certain period when many people died around the same time?
- Why?

The natural area in a cemetery can be a place for many of the other activities described in this book.

History Top Eleven

Here are 11 basic questions everyone should know the answers to about the place where he or she lives.

- Who are the Native Americans that lived and perhaps still live in your place?
- What happened to the Native Americans?
- Do Native Americans still live in the area or were they forced to resettle elsewhere?
- Where are they now?
- When did the settlers come to your area?
- What crops were grown?
- How did they produce food?
- What was it about this place that attracted them?
- How has the land changed?
- What animals and plants are now extinct, and what animals and plants have been introduced?
- How does the geography of your place affect the history and development?

Feel free to turn this into a homework scavenger hunt. It can also become a survey for adults or children on what they know.

What Happened Here?

Pick one spot or one tree and ask the children to close their eyes Ask them to imagine what the spot looked like 1,000 years ago, 500 years ago, 200 years ago, 100 years ago, 50 years ago, and what it will look like 100 years in the future. What has this spot seen? How has the land changed? How have the people and the animals changed?

If possible, label trees in the area with a sign that identifies the tree, gives an approximate age, and states an event that was going on at the time. For example: "This tulip tree is 200 years old. The Constitutional Convention began 200 years ago." Tie a rope connecting several trees. On laminated cards, the children can write brief accounts of life in the past. The trees are eyes to the past, and the rope serves as a timeline to the past.

Ask the children to find out who owned the house they live in before they lived there. Challenge them to go back as far as they can in their own backyard's history. Involve parents and check the town records.

Murals

Painting a big picture is fun. There is something exciting about standing on the paper you are painting. Use large sheets of paper, big paint brushes, and bright colors. Start with a small sketch, then move on to the bigger paper. The mural can start with the Native Americans before contact with the Europeans and then move on through time. Before starting, discuss what the key elements of each section will be. Have the children think about what symbolizes each period in the place they live.

Put emphasis on the everyday lives rather than the wars. As an extension, the scenes can be compared to national, statewide, and international events.

Place-Names

The place-names in your area tell a story. Many are taken from Native American words; others come from early settlers. Some are geographically based, and some are simply one person's personal whim. The children can try to find out why the places are named as they are, for whom or what they are named, and what did that person do? Challenge the class to see who can find the most. Some sources of information are: town recorders, historical societies, and the local library.

Activities Related to Native Americans

Folktales

Folktales are a wonderful way to learn about the culture of native peoples. Stories were more than entertainment for Native Americans; the stories were told to teach, to preserve history, to keep heroes alive, and to have fun. Stories were used to educate and to teach right from wrong. Without a written language, oral tradition was the key to the survival of the culture. Reading and hearing folktales can teach us some of the same lessons.

Gather together as many folktales from Native American tribes in your area as you can. Try to find a Native American from the local area who is interested in sharing some stories.

Depending on how many you have found, the children can read them on their own, or you can read a number of the stories to them. If you are going supplement with folktales from other tribes, be sure the children understand that the folktales are not all from the same Native American nation. It is important to remember that folktales had a sacred meaning in traditional Native American culture. These stories and the traditions they represent deserve our respect. One way of doing this is to be aware of where the story came from.

The project consists of finding patterns in the various folktales. After hearing or reading a folktale, the children will do two things. First, they will write a short summary of the folktale. The next step is to make observations about the folktale. There is not an exact definition of observations. Observations are the ideas the children learn from the story, lessons from the story, what they notice, and patterns that develop between stories. It means reading between the lines. It is what the children learn beyond a basic summary of the story.

Some common observation are animals talk, people learn lessons from animals, heroes go on adventures, spirits exist, animals help people, certain traits are rewarded and others are punished, visions and journeys can transform someone, there is magic, and hunting is important. The search for patterns can demonstrate aspects of Native American life. I have suggested just a few of the many good picture book folktales. Try Hazel Rochman's *Against Borders: Promoting Books for a Multicultural World* and *Our Family, Our Friends, Our World* by Lyn Miller-Lachmann for more book suggestions. As usual, your local library will have plenty of good ones right on the shelf. The Greenfield Review Press, North American Native Author's Catalog, 2 Middle Grove Road, P.O. Box 308, Greenfield Center, NY 12833, is a great place for folktales and information on folktales as well as books on other Native American topics. Joseph Bruchac has written a wonderful book called *Tell Me a Tale: A Book About Storytelling*. Aside from including some folktales, the book suggests ways to find stories, to learn stories, and to tell stories. There is an emphasis on finding stories that have meaning within your own cultural history.

After they have read a number of stories, the children gather together to discuss and find patterns based on their observations. The children find a pattern by having at least three folktales with the same observation. See book summaries for examples.

As an extension, the children can do some of their own storytelling and share their stories with other children.

A Place to Live

In each region of North America, the native people lived in shelters based on the local environment. In the Northeast, where trees were plentiful, homes were made from trees and bark. In the Southwest, adobe bricks were used, and on the Plains, tepees from buffalo skins. Learn the type of shelter used by the Native Americans in your area. Children can try to make their own model shelter and test how the shelter protects from the elements.

For example, the Native Americans on Long Island lived in wigwams made of bark. On the playground, the children make miniature wigwams out of sticks and bark. We put little people on cardboard drawn with watercolor markers. After the first rain, they check to see whose person has faded.

For other places, you may need to provide materials. Even if the models are not perfect replicas, the children can learn about using local materials. If possible, make a life-sized shelter. This activity allows you the chance to discuss why the location of a settlement is important. Some of the considerations Native Americans had to make were a water source, food sources, protection from the elements, and other tribes. Children can draw pictures of a possible settlement, including the important natural features.

Look on maps of your local area and predict in what places Native American settlements were. If possible, check with a local historical society to see if your predictions are true.

Tools

Native Americans did not have metal or plastic. Ask the children to look around the room and see if there are any tools made without metals or plastic. Tools were made from stones, wood, and bones. Native Americans had great respect for the stones and were able to make amazing tools with these materials. Give the children a chance to make tools. They can attempt to make stone tools even if the perfect rocks are not readily available. Give children a chance to chip rocks; it is fun for them and will teach them a great deal as well as give them a better appreciation for the patience and skill it took to create an arrowhead. It doesn't matter if the children do not make a perfect arrowhead.

Either bring the children to a place with many rocks or provide them with plenty of choices. Quartz, flint, obsidian, and slate are good rocks with which to work. Let them choose rocks and use pressure points to break off flakes or chip them with another rock to try to make some sort of crude tool. Safety is a concern. Children should wear goggles and be reminded not to throw, slam, or bang on rocks. Once some sort of crude stone tool is made, the children can attempt to tie it to a stick. The children will soon learn that Native Americans had to know which rocks were the best to use, how to hit them, and where to find the right rocks (sometimes this meant trading with other tribes). Most of all, this activity teaches patience and care. Imagine how careful one would be with a tool that took hours to make.

When the children work closely with these materials, they begin to that see each has unique properties. It is easy to see why people believed each rock, wood, and other inanimate object in nature had its own spirit.

Having Fun

Ask the children to think about all the activities they do for fun. To begin to imagine how the native people entertained themselves, remind the children that any object made from plastic or metal would not have been available. What did native people do for fun? They told stories, played games, competed in a variety of competitions, and created art, much the same as we do today. Children will enjoy many of these same games played both inside and outside.

Unless noted, these games were played by the Algonquins. Similar games were played by other tribes across the country. Games are also important training for skills needed by the native people, and many were part of religious ceremonies.

Guess Sticks

Make a small mark on the end of one stick. Sit on the floor opposite your opponent with your hands behind your back. Shift the stick with your hand covering the marked end. Bring your hand to the front so your opponent can guess which hand has the stick with the mark.

Toss Up

Have a partner lay four sticks on the back of your hands. Your hands should be together with your palms facing down. Toss the sticks into the air and try to catch them in the palms of your hands, keeping your hands open the whole time.

Stick Game

Place a symbol or a design on one side of a stick. Toss the stick into the air. Predict whether the design side will land up or down. One point is scored for each correct prediction.

Dice Game

There were many variations to the "roll a dice" game. In this Cherokee version, six dice are put in a basket. The dice were made from beans or small pieces of wood. One side was marked, and the other was not. All the dice were placed in the basket and flipped into the air. If all the marked sides were up, the player got four points; if all unmarked sides came up, it was two points. If five out of six dice were the same, one point was scored. If not, no one scored.

Pick Up Sticks

Collect a bunch of dried reeds. Throw them into a pile. The children in the group take turns removing one stick at a time without moving another. This game was good practice for steady hands.

Hoop Throw

Although they are not traditional, hula hoops work great. To begin, hang a hula hoop in a tree, and the children can take turns throwing pine cones through the hoop. For an added challenge, roll the hoop in front of the class. The children can throw the pine cones through a moving target.

Chunkey

The game, originally played by prehistoric Native Americans, is played in groups of three. One person rolls a ball, and the other two throw spears in order to see who can come closer to hitting it. Instead of a spear, children can use a wooden dowel, a stick they find, or even another ball. The winner is the one who comes the closest to hitting the rolling ball.

Frog Race

This game was played on the Northwest coast. The children line up for a race. To run in this race, each child has to squat down and wrap his or her arms around his or her legs and grab the bone just above the ankle. The challenge is never to let go, never to fall over, and hop to the finish line. Check out Stewart Culin's book *Games of the North American Indians* (New York: Dover, 1975).

Make a Doll

Just like children today, Native American children played with toys. Dolls were made from natural objects. Give children today the same chance. See what they can make with shells, sticks, corn husks, gourds, stones, or whatever they can find.

Food

As Aldo Leopold said, "There are two spiritual dangers in not owning a farm. One is the danger that breakfast comes from the grocery, and the other that heat comes from the furnace."

What people ate depended on where they lived. Native people and early European settlers were hunters, gathers, and farmers. Native people had a much more extensive form of agriculture than most people think. Corns, beans, and squash were staples in many areas, along with many plants indigenous to specific areas of North America.

Plant a Garden

One way for children to get a sample of what life was like in the past is to grow a garden. Growing some vegetables and caring for a garden is a window into the lives of native people as well as the first European settlers. Across the country, people planted and grew crops. How many children today do not realize or understand the connection between soil and the food they eat? Lettuce and apples do not magically appear in the grocery store.

There are some requirements for having a school garden. One is a place to plant it. This area can range from some trays in the classroom to a patch of ground on the schoolyard. Access to sunlight and water are required as well.

If you are studying Native Americans, a good place to start is with corn, beans, and squash. To the Iroquois, these three vegetables were such a staple in their diet they called them the Three Sisters.

As part of the study of early settlers, find out what the major crops in your area were. Grow some of those vegetables. The children themselves can provide much of the equipment for the garden. Try to be open to ways children can use traditional methods for growing; for example, making holes for seeds with a stick. A good catalog for school gardening projects is from Let's Get Growing, 1900 Commercial Way, Santa Cruz, CA 95065 (1-800-408-1868). A great book is *Native American Gardening* by Joseph Bruchac and Michael Caduto.

One of the inherent problems with school gardens is the fact that most vegetables ripen in the summer. Three crops that are worth considering are radishes, sunflowers, and pumpkins. Radishes grow and ripen quickly and may be ready before school is out. Pumpkins and sunflowers planted in the spring will be ready the following fall. A local nursery will probably be glad to help you out with information and perhaps some equipment.

Wild Edibles

Learn some of the common wild edibles in your area. Be sure to explain the common sense rules regarding collecting wild edibles, the most obvious one being *do not eat anything unless you are sure it is edible and that you have identified it correctly.*

Two simple ways to introduce wild edibles is with teas and salad greens. A number of teas can be made by boiling twigs or leaves in water. Spice bush, white pine, eastern hemlock, strawberry, clover, and mints are just a few of the plants that can be used for tea.

Salads are another simple way to try wild edibles. The fresh leaves of dandelions, plantain, clovers, chicory, and wild onions are a good place to start.

Two books that can help are *Edible Wild Plants* by Lee Allen Peterson (Boston: Houghton Mifflin, 1997) and *The Wild, Wild Cookbook: A Guide for Young Wild-Food Foragers* by Jean Craighead George (New York: Thomas Y. Crowell, 1982).

Hunting

Some of the animal sign activities can be used to discuss the knowledge and skills needed for hunting. Use some of the tracking activities to get children to play the stalking game and to get some sense of hunting.

How Would You Use It?

Native Americans used the resources they had to make what they needed. When an animal was killed, meat was only one of the many ways the animal was used. Give the children time to make a list of all the possible ways a deer could be used. If possible, give the children the bones and skin of a deer for added inspiration. If not, give each group a picture of a deer to help inspire them to have more ideas.

Quotations

Children can discuss some quotations from Native Americans.

"Holy Mother Earth, the trees and all nature, are witnesses of your thoughts and deeds."

A Winnebago wise saying

"The White people never care for the land or deer or bear. When we Indians kill meat, we eat it all up. When we dig roots we make little holes. When we build houses, we make little holes. When we burn grass for grasshoppers, we don't ruin things. We shake down acorns and peanuts. We don't chop down trees, kill everything. The tree says, 'Don't. I am sore. Don't hurt me.' But they chop it down and cut it up. The spirit of the land hates them. They blast out trees and stir it up to its depths. They saw up the trees. That hurts them. The Indians never hurt anything, but the White people destroy it all."

Wintu Holy Women

"The Tipi is much better to live in; Always clean, warm in winter, cool in summer; easy to move. The White builds big house, cost much money, like big cage, shut out sun, can never move; always. Indians and animals know better how to live than white man; nobody can be in good health if he does not have all the time fresh air, sunshine and good water."

Chief Flying Hawk, Sioux

"Our land is more valuable than your money. It will last forever. It will not even perish by the flames of fire. As long as the sun shines and the waters flow, the land will be here to give life to men and animals. We cannot sell the lives of men and animals; therefore we cannot sell this land."

Blackfeet

"The old people sat on the ground. They liked to remove their moccasins and walk with bare feet on the sacred earth. Their tipis were built upon the earth, and their altars were made of earth . . . From Wakan Tanka, the Maker of All things there came a great unifying life force that flowed in and through all things."

Oglala Sioux

Getting Around

Today we travel from place to place at a much greater speed than in the past. Before the arrival of horses, people either ran, walked, or canoed. Even the arrival of horses did not speed things up much compared to today.

In an open area, children can find out their own pace and the speed at which they walk. One method is to time children for a 100-yard walk. If it takes Joe 45 seconds to walk 100 yards, multiply 45 (seconds to walk 100 yards) by 17.6 (number of 100 yard segments in a mile) and divide that number into 3,600 (number of seconds in an hour). Joe would walk 4.5 miles per hour if he maintained that pace. Even better, walk one mile with the children. It may be surprising how few of them have actually walked one mile. Using their time for the one-mile walk, the children can use scale on a local map to estimate how long it took native people to travel from place to place in you area. Discuss the implications this had on society.

Native American Scavenger Hunt

Here is a list of possible items that could be used for a scavenger hunt. Find something to be used to make rope. Find something that could be made into an arrowhead. Find something to use as camouflage for hunting. Find something to use for natural dying. Find something that could be used to hunt small animals. Find basket-making material. Find kindling for a fire. Find a wild edible. Find something to use as a fish hook. Find two possible sources of water. What are two natural things you could use for clothes? Find at least two animal signs. Find a place to make a good shelter. Discuss the results and what the children discovered.

Activities Related to Colonial Times

What to Bring?

When the settlers came to North America or moved west, they could only bring some of what they owned. These are some of the items an early settler may have brought along. Give the list of items to each group. The children can look over the list and pick out what they think is a necessity. The total weight of all the equipment cannot exceed 400 pounds. Each group can explain what they brought and why. Here are some possible items and what they weigh:

• dishes, 20 lbs.	• mirror, 5 lbs.	• cook pot, 10 lbs.	• hay, 50 lbs.
• corn seeds, 10 lbs.	• mattress, 10 lbs.	• sugar, 50 lbs.	• anvil, 100 lbs.
• wheat seeds, 10 lbs.	• candles, 10 lbs.	• flour, 50 lbs.	• plow, 150 lbs.
• cotton blankets, 5 lbs.	• clock, 10 lbs.	• beans, 50 lbs.	• nails, 50 lbs.
• Bible, 5 lbs.	• tool box with tools, 20 lbs.	• salt, 20 lbs.	• axe, 10 lbs.
• warm clothes, 10 lbs.		• water, 50 lbs.	• rifle, 10 lbs.
• coins, 50 lbs.	• rope, 10 lbs.	• tea, 20 lbs.	• saw, 2-person, 10 lbs.
• banjo, 5 lbs.	• butter churn, 15 lbs.	• spinning wheel, 20 lbs.	
• furniture, 50 lbs.	• rum, 5 gallons, 40 lbs.	• traps, 20 lbs.	• seeds, 10 lbs. each bag

(Greenkill Outdoor Environmental Education Center, Staff Resource Book.)

Making Butter

This is a simple activity that can be used to discuss food for the early settlers. For each group of five or six children, put some cream and a little salt in a jar. The children sit in a circle and pass the jar around after shaking it 20 times each. After several minutes, skim off the top and spread some butter on a cracker for a little snack. Begin a discussion of the differences between food production then and now. There are advantages and disadvantages for both periods.

Stone Walls

In the Northeast, tremendous numbers of rock walls were created during the 1800s. In central New England between 1810 and 1830, more stone was moved to make walls than was used to make the Giant Pyramid of Egypt (Wessels, 1997). These walls still line forests today. They are both a statement of how much has changed and how much work went into settling the land. If the children have the opportunity to see a stone wall, ask them to lift one stone to get a feel of the weight and experience one of the chores a young person would have had. The stone walls were made to keep sheep and other livestock from getting loose.

Another way for children to gain an appreciation of the effort that went into building a stone wall is to make their own small model. Using whatever rocks are available, children can stack them into a wall.

Candles

Making candles is a good activity that symbolizes much of what life was like years ago on a homestead. The setting sun effectively ended much of the goings-on in the house; the only additional source of light was candles. Candles were made primarily from animal fat. They didn't exactly smell good when they were burned, so various plant leaves were added to improve the scent.

Candles were made by simply dipping a wick into hot, liquid animal fat. After letting the wick cool, it was dipped again and again until the candle was large enough. Later, people would use metal molds or would tie several wicks to a single stick in order to increase candle production by dipping several candles at once. Traditionally, candles were made in large amounts in the fall.

Making candles shows children one way natural materials were used in the everyday life of early settlers. Children helped with essential household chores. It took time and patience to make even the simplest tools. As the children are making candles, listen to what they discuss among themselves. Many important issues will be talked about, giving you a perfect lead into further discussion of early American life.

Use a double boiler made out of coffee cans to make candles. You will also need blocks of wax, string, and assorted crayons for coloring. You can experiment with natural coloring as well.

Put the wax in the coffee can and place one can inside the other. Fill the bigger can about halfway with water. Heat up the water and melt the wax. Try adding some crayons for color. While the wax is melting, set up the wicks with the children. To make a wick, the children take a string of about 12 inches long. Fold the string in half, hold one end, and twist the other end. The twisting in the wick creates more surface area so more wax can adhere.

This activity is a little messy. If you can, do it outside; otherwise, put lots of newspapers on the floor. It is best to have about one can of wax for every 4 or 5 children. This lesson contains the possibility of hot wax dripping on someone. The children dip the wick in the wax. The key to making a candle is to dip quickly. Otherwise, the wax just keeps melting off each time. The wick is dipped in and out quickly, then it must be cooled either by being dipped again in a can of cold water or counting to 30 before dipping again. Each candle will be different. They will not look like store-bought candles. You can discuss the difference between homemade and factory-made items.

Natural Dying

The settlers used a variety of plant life to give their clothes some color. Using white T-shirts or strips of sheets, children can experiment with a variety of leaves, berries, flowers, and bark. Here are the steps to follow:

> Collect the plant material. Feel free to experiment.

> Shred the plant material and boil in water for 5 to 20 minutes.

> Strain the dye through cheesecloth or nylon stockings.

> Add a tablespoon of vinegar for mordant. The mordant sets the color and makes it last longer.

> Reheat the dye bath.

> You can test the color on some paper. Otherwise, drop in the cloth for as long as it takes to get the desired color.

> Take the cloth out and rinse it until the water runs clear. Let it dry, and you are done.

Some possible dyes: onion skins, light brown goldenrod flowers, yellow spinach leaves, and green berries, for a variety of colors.

Journals

One of the primary ways we have learned about the way people lived in the past is through their journals and letters. These documents tell the story of the daily life of men, women, and children. Children can write journal entries taking on the role of an early settler. The entries can reflect what the children have learned about life 50, 100, 200, or 300 years ago.

Fire Making

For the settlers and the Native Americans, starting and having a fire were crucial aspects of survival for warmth and cooking. A fire needs three things to burn: fuel, oxygen, and heat. Children can learn what it takes to have a fire by setting one up. Start with tinder. Tinder is some material that is easily flammable. Birch bark, hemlock twigs, and very dry leaves all work well. Put a handful of tinder in the fire area and add just a few twigs. The children can search the area for these materials. The next step is to find branches and logs to burn. Ask the children to gather more wood. Gathering firewood was an important chore for young people. A supply of fire wood was a constant need. Depending on the setting, you may want to simply stop the activity here.

If possible, show the children how to safely start a fire. Starting a fire was not as simple as rubbing two sticks together. To make this point, give the children the chance to try to start a fire by rubbing two sticks together. They may generate some heat but not enough to start a fire. Starting a fire without a match takes a great deal of skill.

Once the fire has caught, slowly add bigger and bigger sticks. If you rush and pile too much on, the fire will suffocate. Save the big sticks until the fire is burning well.

Under very careful supervision, children can have races to see how fast they can boil a pot of water or burn a string strung two feet above the fire. Try to see who can do it with the least amount of matches. Campfire food is great. Hot dogs still taste great cooked on a stick. Just wrap up a hamburger in foil and throw it in. Only an adult should remove cooked food from a fire.

Skits

Children love skits. Sometimes we forget how powerful a simple activity can be. Skits can range from a 10-minute activity that produces a quick skit to an elaborate production with scripts, props, and plenty of rehearsal. Children can act a variety of situations encountered by the settlers. Participating in the skits also teaches important communication skills.

An interesting variation of a skit is to take on a role yourself and lead the class through the events of a particular event in loyal history. The more deeply you become the character, the more the story will become part of their lives. Just as I am amazed at the power of storytelling, I am equally amazed at the power of role-playing on my part. A lesson on local history comes alive when you show the children instead of just tell them.

The skits are a good way for the children to present information they have learned through research. The children can write historical fiction using the facts they have learned. Read some examples of historical fiction to the class and make a chart showing what the facts are and how they were integrated into the story.

Make a Settlement

Look at a map of your area and pick out possible first settlement sites. What elements were needed for a good place to start?

Next, create a model settlement outside. After studying the lives of the settlers or the Native Americans, the children can make a model of villages in the schoolyard or nearby woods. Children love to create their own worlds. Creating model villages is a way to tap into that desire and apply it to the school curriculum. The children can make fire rings, stone walls, log cabins, wigwams, sod houses, or just about any item that represents the way people lived in the past. The effort the children put into making the village will teach them more than a textbook. It is an opportunity to apply what they have learned. The problems they encounter will be similar to the problems the first settlers had and will give them a base to discuss many of the issues.

Chapter Eight

Protecting the Place

"We must become believers in the world."

Robert Michael Pyle

"I would rather strike a single match than curse the darkness."

Eleanor Roosevelt

"The frog does not drink up the pond in which he lives."

Native American proverb

"In wildness is the preservation of the world."

Henry David Thoreau

"In our every deliberation, we must consider the impact of our decisions on the next seven generations."

Iroquois Confederation (attributed eighteenth century)

"One generation plants trees . . . another gets the shade."

Chinese proverb

Introduction

Twelve-year-old Andrew Holleman had a special place. When it was threatened by a developer who planned a 180-unit condominium for the woods behind his house, Andrew decided to do something. Andrew organized an opposition group. He researched the laws protecting wetlands, gathered signatures, spoke at hearings, and eventually forced the developers to end their plans (Hoose, 1993).

Children want to make a difference, and they can make a difference. The activities in this chapter are designed as the culmination of a long-term study of place that may last over the course of a school year or are reserved for children in upper elementary grades after they have participated in place-based environmental education over their earlier elementary school years. There can also be occasions when children will be inspired to take action because of an important issue that arises in their lives. As children connect with and bond with the natural world, it is natural for them to want to protect it. The motivation to help comes from love, not fear, and has a local focus.

Teaching students to be involved in the democratic process is important no matter what the issue. Environmental action is a good way for children to participate in the democratic process. We can take advantage of this opportunity to teach them how government and business works and show children that they can be part of the process. This is an important step in connecting with and being a part of a community.

Students can explore their neighborhood to observe environmental problems. Habitat destruction, litter, traffic congestion, new development, and graffiti are all possible issues to address. The students can document and create solutions to these problems. If we believe that children need wild places, the destruction of these places endangers not only wildlife but each child's opportunity for experience. When habitat is lost, animals can't just go somewhere else, and the children can't just have the experience somewhere else. We can help them have the power to protect their future.

It is also important to show children that there are not always simple answers. There can be a variety of points of view on a single issue. Being part of a community means honoring other points of view and honestly looking for a solution of which everyone feels a part.

The activities in this chapter begin with lessons that demonstrate some of the causes of environmental problems. These introductory activities demonstrate the fact that there are limited resources on Earth and the complicated nature of sharing them. They are followed by role-playing activities that lead to real-life projects children can become involved on that will make a difference on a local level.

Books to Use

Accorsi, William. *Rachel Carson*. New York: Holiday House, 1993. ISBN 0-8234-0994-5. Folk art-like illustrations grace this short biography of one of the most influential environmentalists of our time. Accorsi tells Rachel Carson's story from childhood on, as she blends her writing with her love for the outdoors and science into a lifelong career. The controversy that followed the publication of her book *Silent Spring* is discussed. Carson is a great example of a female scientist and also of the power words can make. It is a wonderful model for the children's own biographies.

Albert, Richard E. *Alejandro's Gift*. Illustrated by Sylvia Long. San Francisco: Chronicle Books, 1994. ISBN 0-8118-0436-4. Alejandro lives by himself out in the Sonoran Desert. His life is very lonely until he realizes how much life surrounds him. He sees a ground squirrel drink from his garden. Alejandro decides to build a water hole to share his water with the desert animals. His first try is not successful, but his second one works wonderfully. The desert animals come and Alejandro learns an important lesson about giving gifts. Long's detailed illustrations give the reader much for which to search. The last two pages provide interesting facts on the desert animals in the book.

Anholt, Laurence. *The Forgotten Forest*. San Francisco: Sierra Club Books, 1992. ISBN 0-87156-569-2. This story begins a long time ago when there were so many trees a squirrel could cross the country without touching the ground. Slowly but surely, the trees were cut down. Cities grew until there was just one small island of trees. Only the children knew about it, and they played there. One day bulldozers came to build a building. Even the builders were amazed at what was there and what they heard. The children took a stand to protect the trees and the builders took down the walls and planted trees instead of cutting them down.

Atkins, Jeannine. *Aani and the Tree Huggers*. Illustrated by Venantius J. Pinto. New York: Lee & Low Books, 1995. ISBN 1-880000-24-5. Atkins's story is based on the efforts of the Chipko Andolan (Hug the Tree Movement) in India. When men come to chop down the trees in Aani's village, she stops them the only way she can, by throwing her body around the trunk of one tree. Soon other women in the village do the same thing and save the trees. Today, councils in each village carefully plan how many trees will be cut down so as not to endanger the land. Each spring, new trees are planted. The illustrations are inspired by traditional Indian styles from the seventeenth century.

Ayres, Pam. *When Dad Cuts Down the Chestnut Tree*. Illustrated by Graham Percy. New York: Alfred A. Knopf, 1988. ISBN 0-394-80435-X. After learning that his father will be cutting down their chestnut tree, a child thinks of all the benefits: all the toys his father will make with the wood plus there will be no leaves to rake. But later he realizes there are many more benefits if the tree stays. The book ends with a plea to his father that saves the tree. Students can discuss the lobbying tactics used to convince the father.

Baker, Jeannie. *Window*. New York: Greenwillow Books, 1991. ISBN 0-688-08917-8. Baker's stunning collages tell the story in this wordless picture book. As a young boy grows up, the view from his window changes from countryside to suburbia to a city. As an adult, he moves away to look out another window, where the changes begin again.

Bang, Molly. *Common Ground: The Water, Earth, and Air We Share*. New York: Blue Sky Press, 1997. ISBN 0-590-10056-4. Inspired by Garrett Hardin's classic article, "Tragedy of the Commons," Bang has written a picture book that explains what happens if we use up the common land, water, and air that we share. The illustration have the potential for much discussion on environmental issues. It is a reminder of the problem of short-term benefits with negative long-term consequences.

Burleigh, Robert. *A Man Named Thoreau*. Illustrated by Lloyd Bloom. New York: Atheneum, 1985. ISBN 0-689-31122-2. A wonderfully written story about the life of Henry David Thoreau. Burleigh has managed to write a book for children that gives anyone a sense of Thoreau's life and work. Thoreau's sense of wonder and value are expressed in the quotations that have been selected. His own writing is quoted, and graceful drawings complement the book perfectly. The timeline, quotations, and organization of the book will provide children with ideas for their own biographies.

Burningham, John. *Hey! Get off Our Train*. New York: Crown, 1989. ISBN 0-517-57638-4. It is past his bed time, but a boy and his pajama-case dog take a train ride. Along the way they have a lot of fun, pick up a variety endangered animals, and bring them home. Unique illustrations and a funny text make this a good book to begin talking about endangered species.

Cone, Molly. *Come Back, Salmon*. Photographs by Sidnee Wheelwright. San Francisco: Sierra Club Books, 1992. ISBN 0-87156-572-2. The true story of school children and the river they brought back to life. Pigeon Creek flows into Puget Sound. It was polluted, and the salmon no longer laid their eggs. The children cleaned up the waters, raised salmon, and learned many important lessons. They learned that by working together they had an impact and made a difference. The story is a wonderful model for a local project.

de Paola, Tomie. *Michael Bird-Boy*. Englewood Cliffs, NJ: Prentice-Hall, 1975. ISBN 0-13-580803-0. A simple, to-the-point story of Michael Bird-Boy. He goes to the city to see who is covering the sky with a dark, black cloud. There he finds a syrup factory. With his help, the Boss-Lady converts the syrup factory to a honey factory. The bees do not cause any pollution. The book may be simple, but the message is clear and important: We have to stand up and be heard.

Elkington, John, Julia Hailes, Douglas Hill, and Joel Makower. *Going Green: A Kid's Handbook to Saving the Planet*. Illustrated by Tony Ross. New York: Viking Penguin, 1990. ISBN 0-670-83611-7. This isn't a picture book, but it does give the children a great deal of information on a variety of environmental problems, ranging from global to local. There is background information and plenty of suggestions for action children can take.

Erdrich, Louise. *Grandmother's Pigeon*. Illustrated by Jim La Marche. New York: Hyperion Books for Children, 1996. ISBN 0-7868-0165-4. Two children have a very strange grandmother. She has skied the Continental Divide, can touch away a charley horse, and brews strange teas. One day she disappears on a porpoise headed for Greenland. After a year, the children decide to go into her room after hearing strange sounds. Among all the interesting items of her life, they find three eggs. Remarkably, the eggs hatch and turn out to be passenger pigeons. Beautiful illustrations add to the story that helps one believe there is magic but is also a reminder that extinct is forever.

Ernst, Lisa Campbell. *Squirrel Park*. New York: Bradbury Press, 1993. ISBN 0-02-733562-3. Chuck and Stuart are friends. The only thing that is strange is that Chuck is a squirrel. Most of the other trees in town have been cut down for buildings, but there is still one great oak in the city park. Stuart's father is the man responsible for all the other buildings. He wants Stuart to design a park. The problem is he doesn't like Stuart's idea: too many trees and curvy paths. Instead, Mr. Ivey designs a park without the great oak and with a straight path and no forest. Fortunately, Chuck saves the day. A good book to use with the town meeting and other land use activities.

Fife, Dale. H. *The Empty Lot*. Illustrated by Jim Arnosky. San Francisco: Sierra Club Books, 1991. ISBN 0-316-28167-0. Harry owns an empty lot and is all set to sell it until he visits and sees all the wonderful animals and plants that live there.

Fleming, Denise. *Where Once There Was a Wood*. New York: Henry Holt, 1996. ISBN 0-8050-3761-6. Fleming won a Caldecott award for her artwork in *A Small Small Pond*. Her eye-catching style makes this book special as well. Once in a wood there was a meadow, a creek, foxes, woodchucks, and more. Now, "houses sit side by side twenty houses deep." The last four pages are dedicated to ways people can improve backyard habitats for animals. These suggestions are the source for many activities.

Galan, Mark. *There's Still Time*. Washington, DC: National Geographic, 1997. ISBN 0-7922-7092-4. An emphasis on environmental success stories is just as important as learning about the problems. Children need to know that there can be success. Otherwise, why try? The book describes 19 examples of animals and plants that have been saved with the help of the Endangered Species Act. The short account is accompanied by brilliant photographs. The introduction explains how the Endangered Species Act works to protect animals and plants.

Garland Sherry. *The Summer Sands*. Illustrated by Robert J. Lee. San Diego, CA: Harcourt Brace Jovanovich, 1995. ISBN 0-15-282492-8. While visiting their grandparents, two children play on the beach and in the sand dunes and learn about their importance and the life they protect. All summer they watch the animal life. At the end of the summer, a storm hits and destroys the sand dunes. Winter comes, and after Christmas, the children return for a visit. This time they bring a Christmas tree. With many other people joining in, they lay Christmas trees out to prevent further erosion and stabilize the dunes until plants take hold. The story is based on a program in Galveston, Texas. Many other coastal areas on the shore have similar programs.

Goffstein, M. B. *Natural History*. New York: Farrar, Straus & Giroux, 1979. An absolutely brilliant book. Lovely watercolors match words that simply describe both the beauty and the sadness of our world. Comparing the tiny grains of sands that hold back oceans to the possibility of what people can do, Goffstein manages to capture in a few words the need to and possibility for preserving the beauty and wonder of the world. An out-of-print book, but try to find it. Your effort will be rewarded.

Gordon, Esther S., and Bernard L. Gordon. *Once There Was a Passenger Pigeon*. Illustrated by Lawrence Di Fiori. New York: Henry Z. Walck, 1976. ISBN 0-8098-5003-6. This nonfiction account of the passenger pigeon dramatically describes the tragedy of the passenger pigeons. In the 1800s, billions of these birds were hunted to extinction. With sharp text and elegant line drawings, this book captures a bird that filled the sky in flocks that blocked the sun. By describing all the methods used to hunt the birds, the reader can imagine how so many birds could be killed. The book ends with a reminder to help birds that are endangered but still have a chance.

Greene, Carol. *John Muir: Man of the Wild Places*. Chicago: Childrens Press, 1991. ISBN 0-516-04220-3. John Muir was one of our most important environmental heroes. His actions inspired the protection of wilderness in the Sierras and other places. This short biography is a good introduction to his life and all that he overcame. The book is filled with photographs of Muir and the places he explored.

Hoose, Philip. *It's Our World, Too!* Boston: Little, Brown, 1993. ISBN 0-316-37421-2. Hoose has collected stories of children around the world who have taken a stand and made the world a better place. The stories cover a range of topics that include the environment. The stories make for motivating read aloud. The second section of the book has suggestions for successful projects.

Iverson, Diane. *I Celebrate Nature*. Nevada City, CA: Dawn, 1993. ISBN 1-883220-00-9. Iverson's book begins with a note to teachers and parents reminding them to let children explore, stomp in mud puddles, and climb trees. She explains that she deliberately left adults out of the illustrations to show that children need time on their own to explore. The three children explore a variety of places and see many wonders. The book ends with the children building a bird feeder and bird house, demonstrating one way children can help protect the environment.

Johnson, Kipchak. *Worms's Eye View: Make Your Own Wildlife Refuge.* Illustrated by Thompson Yardley. Brookfield, CT: Millbrook Press, 1991. ISBN 1-878841-30-0. A rather interesting book about creating wildlife habitats in a backyard setting. Johnson begins with the soil and shows how everything from bacteria to worms on up to flowers and insects can make a wildlife refuge. The emphasis on small creatures is welcome. There are all sorts of fun facts and good ideas for creating habitats. There is even a section on keeping a field journal.

Kroll, Virginia. *Butterfly Boy.* Illustrated by Gerardo Suzan. Honesdale, PA: Boyds Mills Press, 1997. ISBN 1-56397-371-5. Set in Mexico, this book tells the story of Emilio and his grandfather, Abuelo. They discover why butterflies come to their garage. The butterflies bring a great joy to Abuelo. The only problem is Emilio's father has painted the garage blue. The butterflies stop coming. Emilio is persistent and when the garage is painted back to white, the butterflies also come back. The story is about the power of a single child to make a difference.

Lasky, Kathryn. *She's Wearing a Dead Bird on Her Head.* Illustrated by David Catrow. New York: Hyperion Books for Children, 1995. ISBN 0-7868-0065-8. In 1896, hat styles depended on bird feathers; one thing led to another, and soon women were wearing actual stuffed birds on their heads. This fashion craze not only endangered the survival of many bird species but also made women look ridiculous. Women had enough trouble being taken seriously in that day and age, and a bird on a hat did not help. Harriet Hemenway and her cousin Minna Hall decided to do something. They formed a bird club to help save the birds. Because of their organizing and pressure, they persuaded the government to pass laws that protected birds. With a little undercover work, they even found where bird feathers were being stored. An author's note explains some of the background of this true story.

Levine, Ellen. *The Tree Would Not Die.* Illustrated by Ted Rand. New York: Scholastic, 1995. ISBN 0-590-43724-0. This is the story of the "Treaty Oak" in Austin, Texas, from the tree's point of view. The story begins with an acorn that buffaloes and Native Americans watched grow. The tree's story takes the reader through Texas history, from the Spaniards and the settlers through history to today. The tree then tells us how someone poisoned the tree and tried to kill it, but with the help of hundreds of people, the tree was saved. As usual, Rand's illustrations add even more to the story.

Lewis, Barbara. *The Kids Guide to Social Action.* Minneapolis, MN: Free Spirit, 1991. ISBN 0-915793-29-6. This is not a picture book, but it is a great reference for planning a project on a local environmental issue. There are inspiring success stories and practical advice on a range of actions. For each action, there are case studies and tips for success.

Luenn, Nancy. *Song for the Ancient Forest.* Illustrated by Jill Kastner. New York: Atheneum, 1993. ISBN 0-689-31719-0. Written in the form of a Native American folktale, this book is more of an updated version of the Lorax. A raven uses his song to teach people to stop cutting down the old forest. Like the Lorax, the raven speaks for the trees. There is some discussion at the end about the people employed by the lumber company. After listening to both books, the children can discuss how to make the forest last.

Martin, Jacqueline Briggs. *Washing the Willow Tree Loon.* Illustrated by Nancy Carpenter. New York: Simon & Schuster, 1995. ISBN 0-689-80415-6. An absolutely beautiful story about a loon and the people who work hard to save it from an oil spill. Each of the rescuers has other things to do, but they give that up to save the loon and other birds. "I have work to do," they all say. The book concludes with a note about wildlife rehabilitation that explains the cleaning procedures in detail and reminds us we all have work to do.

McVey, Vicki. *The Sierra Club Kid's Guide to Planet Care and Repair.* Illustrated by Martha Weston. San Francisco: Sierra Club Books, 1993. ISBN 0-87156-567-6. This book from the Sierra Club includes background information on a variety of environmental problems. In each chapter, there are suggestions for action to help solve the problem. There are short stories within the book describing the adventures of children solving environmental problems.

Neitzel, Shirley. *The House I'll Build for the Wrens.* Illustrated by Nancy Winslow Parker. New York: Greenwillow Books, 1997. ISBN 0-688-14973-1. Beginning with the plans to build a wren house, we learn just how a young girl puts one together. Using a cumulative text and pictures substituting for some words make this a fun book for young children to read themselves or chanting together. Parker's lighthearted pictures and the fact that the child used her mother's tools add a nice touch.

Parnall, Peter. *The Mountain*. Garden City, NY: Doubleday, 1971. Parnall's' distinctive style tells the story of a mountain that is loved to death by all the visitors who come to appreciate its beauty. The short story will provide a basis for discussion on the possible consequences of humans when they protect the places we love to visit.

Peet, Bill. *Farewell to Shady Glade.* Boston: Houghton Mifflin, 1966. One spring day, the inhabitants of Shady Glade hear a distant rumble. The birds leave, but the other animals aren't sure what to do. Lead by the raccoon, they discover terrible machines are destroying the trees. They decide to hop on a train and find a new home. For miles, the train takes them through fields, farms, and cities until they find a new place to live. The fact that Shady Glade is destroyed and the animals must move on is a powerful statement. Will animals always be able to find new places to go?

Peet, Bill. *The Wump World.* Boston: Houghton Mifflin, 1970. The Wumps live a perfectly peaceful and gentle life on Wump World. Everything is great until the Pollutians arrive. The Pollutians have already made their own planet uninhabitable, so they had to find a new place to live. The Wumps are forced underground. Eventually, the Pollutians make such a mess that they are forced to leave. Wumps come out and find the last remaining green space. A plant growing through a crack in the pavement hints at a better future. The book's message is a little obvious, but Peet's humorous drawings make the book.

Rand, Gloria. *Prince William.* Illustrated by Ted Rand. New York: Henry Holt, 1992. ISBN 0-8050-1841-7. The Alaskan oil spill was an immense ecological disaster, and it is hard to comprehend, but Rand's focus on a single girl and her effort to save a baby seal make it come close to home. Denny finds the seal and brings it home where her mother takes it to the animal rescue center. There they are able to clean it off and take care of it until the baby is old enough to go out on its own. An afterword explains how hundreds of school children raised money and volunteered to save animals caught in the spill. There is something children can do even during the worst ecological problems.

Rohnke, Karl. *Silver Bullets: A Guide to Initiative Problems, Adventure Games, Stunts and Trust Activities.* Dubuque, IA: Kendall/Hunt, 1984. ISBN 0-8403-5682-X. A good introduction to Project Adventure. There are activities for all sorts of groups, ages, and interest levels, making this book a good place to start.

Ross, Michael Elsohn. *Wildlife Watching with Charles Eastmen.* Illustrated by Laurie A. Caple. Minneapolis, MN: Carolrhoda Books, 1997. ISBN 1-57505-004-8. An interesting example from a unique series of biographies. This one combines the story of Charles Eastmen, a Sioux who grew up to be an important naturalist. He graduated from Dartmouth and became a doctor. He wrote several books on Native American life and worked with the Boy Scouts and the Camp Fire Girls. The book combines aspects of his life with information and suggestions for watching wildlife. Other books in the series include *Bird Watching with Margaret Morse Nice* (1997), *Bug Watching with Charles Henry Turner* (1997), and *Flower Watching with Alice Eastwood* (1997).

Dr. Seuss. *The Lorax.* New York: Random House, 1971. ISBN 0-394-92337-5. The classic story of the Truffula trees. When it all begins, the Lorax tries to protect the trees from "axes that hack," but the Onceler takes a long time to learn his lesson. In true Dr. Seuss style, the book tells an entertaining and thought-provoking story. At the end, discussion could revolve around how the Onceler could have used the Truffula trees but not used them up.

Swamp, Jake. *Giving Thanks: A Native American Good Morning Message.* Illustrated by Erwin Printup, Jr. New York: Lee & Low Books, 1995. ISBN 1-880000-15-6. This book is based on the Thanksgiving Address from the Haudenosaunee (Iroquois) of Upstate New York. The book reminds us that being human is an honor and we should be thankful for the water, sun, trees, animals, and everything else that is wonderful in the world.

Swinburne, Stephen R. *Swallows in the Birdhouse.* Illustrated by Robin Brickman. Brookfield, CT: Millbrook Press, 1996. ISBN 1-56294-182-8. This book is included for the amazing three-dimensional watercolor illustrations of Brickman. The birds fly off the page in this story of how two swallows raise their young in a bird house built by two children. The back of the book has suggestions for building a swallow box and deciding where to put it. There are also some interesting facts about tree swallows.

Temple, Lannis, ed. *Dear World: How Children Around the World Feel About Our Environment.* New York: Random House, 1993. ISBN 0-679-84403-1. Temple traveled all over the world asking children to write letters and draw pictures expressing how they felt about the environment. The results are beautiful. Children can write their own letters and feel a connection with children all over the world. Some of the letters talk about global problems and others about favorite spots and secret places. It is hard not to be moved by these letters.

Tibo, Gilles. *Simon and His Boxes*. Montreal: Tundra Books, 1992. ISBN 0-88776-345-6. Simon explains that whenever he finds a box, he makes it into a house for himself and for his animal friends. The problem is that they never stay in the houses. The birds fly away, and the fish jump out. Finally, a jack-in-the-box suggests that he do something else, and he does. Simon uses the boxes to clean up the woods. Charming illustrations make this a wonderful story.

Van Allsburg, Chris. *Just a Dream*. Boston: Houghton Mifflin, 1990. ISBN 0-395-53308-2. Walter is not the least bit concerned about the environment. One night, he has a strange dream. Surreal illustrations take us with Walter and his bed as he goes into the future. What he sees changes what he does when he wakes up. The ending has a nice idea for a birthday party.

Activities

Cooperative Physical Challenges

This activity can be used to teach environmental issues and promote group cooperation and problem-solving. Each of the challenges can be combined with a story that teaches. Feel free to adapt the story to your place. This is one story set in the place where I teach.

"You are part of an environmental protection team that is helping survey osprey nests on Long Island. While taking a boat to Gardiner's Island, the boat sinks. The group must climb onto a nearby island."

Challenge: (Materials: Large cardboard box. Cut up a box and lay it flat on the ground.) "You must all get onto the island. The box is the island. No feet can be on the ground for more than ten seconds."

If it is easy the first time, cut off part of the island and have them try again. Make it more and more of a challenge by cutting off more and more of the island. After each challenge, take time to discuss how the group is functioning. Talk with the children about how they solved the problem and the group dynamics.

"Once on the island, your group becomes tangled in a web of cat briars."

Challenge: Divide the team into groups of about seven. "Stand in a circle, shoulder-to-shoulder. Reach across and grab the hand of another child. With your other hand, grab someone else's hand. There should be a tangle of hands in the middle. No one should have a free hand. Untangle yourselves and form a circle without letting go of each other's hands."

"Now that you are untangled, it is time to move on. The only way to get to the osprey nest is to cross a muddy salt marsh. If you end up touching the mud, you could get sucked in."

Challenge: (Materials: Two large cardboard boxes.) "You are crossing a salt marsh. Without special equipment, you will sink. All you can use is this box. The group must cross the marsh from here to there (set up a 30-foot distance to cover). Your feet must stay on the cardboard. If anyone touches the ground, the group must start over." (Hint: the children can rip apart the box.)

"Finally, you make it to the nest. Ospreys are shy, and your group has to be able to work in silence."

Challenge: "You must line up shoulder-to-shoulder by birthdays from January to December. The catch is that you must do this without speaking."

"To help the osprey, your group is studying their eggs. There is a nest up in the tree, and someone in the group has to reach the nest and carefully put the egg back." (For added challenge, the group could carry an egg through the entire set of adventures without breaking it.)

Challenge: Tie some string to a cup and throw the cup over a branch in a tree. Tie off the string so the cup is about nine feet off the ground. "You have to boost one member of the team up while the others spot him or her. While the student is being held up, put the egg (a tennis ball) in the cup."

If there are no trees that fit the bill, the children can stick a piece of tape as high as possible on a wall.

"You have saved the osprey. The only way to get to a safe place for a boat rescue is to cross a river. There are only a few rocks on which the group can step. The rocks are loose. If too many people stand on them, they will wash away in the current."

Challenge: "The group has to walk 15 yards. The total number of hands or legs that can touch the ground is determined by the number of people in the group. Divide the total number of legs in the group by two and subtract one. For example, if there are ten people in the group, only four limbs can touch the ground. You all have to hold onto each other and move across as a group. It is dark and you don't want to lose contact with each other."

These adventures are adapted from the Project Adventure program (Rhonke, 1984). Contact them for more information at (508) 468-7981. They are a wonderful resource for adventure education and can provide you with a large variety of physically challenging, cooperative problem-solving activities. Even without the environmental education benefits, these activities help children with learning cooperation skills, problem-solving, and trust, plus they are fun.

Enough Space

The main reason for the extinction of animals and plants both worldwide and locally is the loss of habitat. Habitat is lost to flooding, development, homes, shopping malls, erosion, and deforestation. Look for examples in your community. Discuss the situation. What are the pros and cons of the recent development in your area?

Living things need space in which to live and to find the resources they need to survive. To demonstrate this concept, compare the growth rate of beans grown one seed to a cup to beans grown 15 seeds to a cup.

Another way to demonstrate this concept is to lay a big piece of cardboard on the floor. Ask the children to stand on it. The cardboard symbolizes a forest or any other local habitat. Explain to them a shopping mall is being built. Rip off a piece of cardboard to symbolize the loss of the habitat. Can the children fit on the cardboard now? When new homes are being built means ripping off even more cardboard. How many children can fit on the cardboard now?

The following tag game makes the same point. You will need eight to 10 pieces of rope of varying lengths. Tie them into loops and spread them on the playing area. The children begin to play tag. Inside any loop is safe. If you play this as a version of freeze tag, everybody has the chance to stay in the game. As the children play, take away one loop at a time, crowding the children into a smaller and smaller area.

River Game

Children "develop" their section of a river and then discuss the consequences of the development on their neighbors. Each child is given a section of river outlined on a sheet of paper. This is their piece of the river. They can do whatever they want and build whatever they want on the land and river. Give the children time to draw their plans on the papers. Collect all the sections of river and lay them out end to end to make a complete river. This is a good chance to introduce watersheds and related landforms. (A watershed is the area of land that drains into a given body of water.) Ask each child to briefly explain what they plan to do on their section. After everyone is finished, ask the group if any one has a problem with what anyone else is doing.

An interesting discussion should evolve about the fact that what happens in one place affects what happens in another. We all live in a watershed and need to remember to share its resources, but there can be a variety of opinions about what to do with the land and water. This activity works best when it is not presented as a lesson on environmental protection. The children's developments are more honest. Relate the activity more directly to the community by studying a map of the watershed where the children live. Show them that no matter where they live, they are connected to a major river or a large body of water. Trace their watershed from one place to another.

Put It Back Together

This is a simple activity with a strong message. Give each child a chocolate chip cookie. Tell them to take out the chips. After the children have taken out all the chips, ask them put the cookie back together. It is impossible. The cookie symbolizes the Earth, and the chocolate chips symbolize the resources we take from the Earth. They can use a spoon, fork, tweezers, or whatever else is available. It should be interesting to watch which children try to take the cookie apart carefully and which dive right in. The point is very clear; we can't always fix things and put them back together. Another even simpler way to send them the same message is to have each child break a stick and try to put it back together.

Resource Game

This is an extremely powerful game. If you are doing only one activity from this chapter, this is the one to do. Split the group into two teams. They will watch each other play the game and ideally learn from one another.

The only material you need is a large amount of beans or some other small object. The beans represent the Earth's resources. The object of the game is to get 10 beans. The children can trade the 10 beans, thereby using the resources, for something of value. Try using a coupon for a night free of homework.

The rules of the game are simple. Play with about 10 children at a time. The children sit in a circle around the beans. Start with 25 beans in the center. Each round will be 30 seconds long. At the end of each round, you will double the amount of beans that are left behind. If two beans are left, add two. If there are 10 left, add 10. If there are no beans left, the game is over. As soon as a child has 10 beans, he or she can turn the beans in for the prize.

The first group will just dive on the beans as soon as you say "go." Maybe one person will get 10. There probably will be no beans left after 30 seconds, so there are no beans to double. The game is over for that team. The second team may repeat the first team's mistake or the may figure out what to do. If they are patient and leave some beans out until the end of each round, you will keep adding more beans. There will plenty of resources for everyone. Even when the children figure out what to do, it is amazing how hard it is for them to remain patient without grabbing. The level of trust will make for a good discussion. The ones that truly understand will leave some beans behind for the next generation. Discuss how the children reacted to the game and how they should have managed the resources.

Environmental Impact Statement

This activity can be conducted in a single lesson or extended into a longer project. Create a scenario in which there will be some development of a local natural area. It could be as simple as a parking lot expansion into a grove of trees or a new shopping mall on a wetland. When a major development is planned, the federal government requires an Environmental Impact Statement(EIS) to help people decide if the development is a good idea. The EIS describes the land as it currently exists, explains what will happen to a place when the development is complete, describes what will happen to the animals and plants, and details the costs and benefits of the plan to the environment and to the community.

If the children have already been studying a particular place, use the information to answer some of the questions in an EIS. If not, take a trip to a natural area that will be part of the role play. Depending on the amount of time, the children can identify some of the plants, look for animal signs, make maps, and make a list of resources in the area. Use some of the activities in chapters 5 and 6. The children can be broken into groups to survey various aspects and present their findings to the rest of the group in a written report or orally.

Town Meeting

After the EIS is complete, hold a town meeting to decide on the development. The town meeting is best done with one or two other adults (it can be done with just one as long as he or she can play different roles). This activity can be conducted completely separate if the children are not involved in the EIS activity.

The Story

Mrs. Smith has donated a large area of land to the town. Now the town has to decide what they want to do with the land. One proposal to consider is being made by a developer who plans to build an amusement park.

The Mayor

The mayor acts as the moderator, explaining the issues and keeping the meeting under control.

The Developer

The developer has plans to build an amusement park or some other project on the land, depending on the story you are using.

Part One

Explain what role-playing means. The children will be role-playing adults in the community making a decision about the land left by Mrs. Smith. It is important that they keep to their roles so the leaders can keep to theirs. After explaining the situation, the mayor introduces the developer. The more realistic the setting, the better. Props and displays help everyone play the roles more realistically.

The developer explains the plans for the development. It is very helpful to have some kind of picture displaying the area before development and after the amusement park is in place. The explanation should include an account of what the land will be used for and how it will be used. The developer emphasizes the benefits of more jobs and increased taxes that can be used for improving the community. This introduction to the development lasts about 5-10 minutes. Explain all the amazing rides in the new park.

Part Two

The citizens are divided into groups to brainstorm a list of questions. This is a time for questions only, no comments. There will be time for that later. The questions will range from what will happen to the animals to how much does it cost to go on a ride?

Part Three

The children select one spokesperson to read the questions to the developer. Each group will read the entire list of questions while the developer takes notes. After all the questions have been asked, the developer answers each one. In answering the questions, dismiss much of the concern for pollution, animals, and plants. Focus on the benefits. Depending on how you play the role, the meeting can get a little feisty.

This part often turns into a give-and-take discussion. Many of the children will point out that the developer only cares about money. I counter with the fact that their concern for animals means someone may not have a job. As I answer questions, I also ask questions and make comments to draw out their knowledge and show them how complicated some of these issues are. This activity can be used as an evaluation tool by noting what knowledge the children use to make their argument.

Part Four

The mayor explains that it is time to vote on the proposal. Each child has the opportunity to make a comment in favor or against the plan. After the comment session, hold a blind vote.

In the final discussion, talk about what they would like to see the land used for. It is also good to discuss the fact that there are pluses and minuses. It is hard to decide. People do need jobs; they need to be able to support their families. As members of a democracy, we have a responsibility to educate ourselves and to make informed decisions. We also may have to sacrifice something to help the environment.

A variation of this role-play for older children is to assign roles of various interest groups. There could be a local environmental group, business group, parent group, teenagers, and construction workers' union. Feel free to develop you own scenarios.

Local Action

The motto "Think globally, act locally" applies to children and environmental action. Find a local issue that children can understand and one in which they can make a difference. Some of the aspects to consider are the interests of the students, how much information they can gather on the issue, and what effect the students can have. Focus on one issue so the work has the most impact.

This is a place where you can get involved with current events. Survey the local newspaper for stories on local issues. Use these as examples and as sources of ideas for projects. Try to follow one story for a period of time to see how it develops. Another way to look for an issue to work on is to take a walk through the neighborhood. Survey the community or simply ask the children. If they express concern about global problems, such as rain forest deforestation or something like the Greenhouse Effect, focus the efforts on local aspects of the issue, such as reducing local traffic. Concern for the rain forest could inspire a project on local migratory birds.

Allow the children to make their own decisions. Guide them instead of lead them. If they feel it is not their project, the long-term effects are lessened. Sometimes this means the progress can be slow as they work things out themselves. One has to remember that aside from trying to solve the immediate problem, you are helping the children become lifelong participants in our democracy.

Once a topic has been chosen, work can begin. First, the children try to learn as much as possible about the issue from all sides. The students should be able to speak as experts. Knowledge will help them plan an effective campaign. Part of this stage is to document the problems with photographs, interviews, research, or some other means. Start by making a list on chart paper of "What We Know" and "What We Need to Know." This list will provide the basis for the plan.

Plan how to find the answers to the "What We Need to Know" list. Use the newspaper, the Internet, letter writing, television, guest speakers, lessons from you, interviews, books, and other reference materials. Local issues mean the children can do first-hand research, such as surveys; mapping; population estimates; and experiments, observations, and site studies.

Once they have the information, planning the solutions can begin. The exact actions and solutions the group takes depend on a variety of considerations: the class' ability and interests, the causes of the problems, who can solve the problem, and political considerations in the community and the school.

After developing potential solutions, it is time to go to whomever it is who can help put the solution to work. This may be an elected official, a school administrator, a company executive, or a business owner. I am focusing on elected officials, but much of the process is the same no matter who it is.

Students can become involved in lobbying the government to help the environment. Students can learn how laws are made and how government works. Students can contact elected officials through letters, telephone calls, and town meetings. Arrange an appointment and pay a visit. The students should be sure to know their material; be direct; and be prepared to give an explanation of the problem, a solution, and the action you want to be taken. Get a commitment.

Whether the children will do any actual lobbying or not, the skills involved are worth practicing and using. These role-playing lessons will help children gain the confidence and skills needed for effective environmental problem-solving. The activities listed are ways to practice.

Debates

If there is a difference of opinion among the class, the children can debate the issue in front of the rest of the group. In many cases, the children may agree. One child can take on the opposing view and have a debate. It is a challenge to debate effectively in support of an opinion one personally opposes. It is good practice to put oneself in someone else's shoes.

Lobbying Game

Once students are familiar with the issues and the roles of government officials, they can role-play a lobbying situation. A possible scenario: The town council is considering a new law to keep leaf blowers out of the community. The committee is undecided and is holding a hearing. Assign students to one of the following roles: staff members of various environmental organizations, leaf blower manufacturers, landscapers, home owners, and concerned citizens. Give the students time to prepare questions, comments, and speeches for their role. Depending on the student's background, the teacher may have to provide information on how to play the role. Write some of the basic facts and positions taken by each group on a sheet of paper and give one to each group. Establish a format where the students ask questions, make speeches, and debate the issue, concluding with a vote on the bill. Larger classes can be divided into two groups.

A variation on the game would be to role-play individual visits to members of Congress. Divide the class into pairs. One student plays the role of an environmental activist, the other a congressional representative. Using his or her knowledge, the activist can lobby the member of congress.

Persuasive Essay

A persuasive essay is very good practice for anyone trying to understand both sides of an issue. Environmental issues are often controversial. Children love to argue, but they can use help on being effective. The persuasive essay is a chance for the children to practice thinking clearly and making their point effectively.

Make a list of local environmental issues. Some possibilities are littering, housing development, hunting, and tree planting.

All the children pick a topic they feel strongly about and begin to think of as many reasons to support their point of view as possible. The children should organize these reasons into categories and list supporting facts. Children can even do some research to back up their point of view.

Beginning with an attention-grabbing lead, the children write a rough draft. Each reason to support their point of view can be a paragraph. The more reasons to support their point of view, the better. Another technique is to consider some of the positive points of the other side and then take away the argument by referring to it and offering a better solution. For example, in an essay against a housing development, acknowledge the need for new housing but suggest a more environmentally sensitive solution. After revising and editing, share the essays in a public forum.

Letter Writing

Letter writing can be effective. Most politicians believe that one letter represents at least ten other people who feel the same way. Thirty letters on one issue forces local politicians to take notice. It is more important to get many people to write many short, concise letters instead of a few long ones. Many of the same points for lobbying apply to letter writing.

Letters to the Editor

Letters to the editor are also very effective. Elected officials are very aware of the topics in the "Letters to the Editor" section. They know many people read each one.

Petitions

Write a short, simple statement of belief. To be effective, many names are needed. Petitions are a good way to spread the message and to educate people on a particular issue. Contact the press. Local newspapers and television stations are always looking for stories. Contact them well in advance of a planned event. Provide them with all the information they need, especially time and date. Even after the event, write a short article and submit it to the newspapers if no media representatives attended the event. You don't always have to wait for a big event. The news media may be interested in your project as a work in progress.

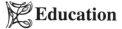Education

One of the most effective ways to create change is for the students to educate others. Students can teach children and adults about their issue and proposed solutions in a variety of ways.

Speeches

Students can learn how to write and give a speech. Consider audiences outside of the typical school community.

Skits

Students can write their own plays and perform them for others.

Posters

Combining art and language, students can present information in a vivid manner.

Audiovisual Equipment

Information can be presented using videos or tape recorders.

Student Teachers

Students can develop interesting lessons to teach other children.

Fairs

Students can organize an event to teach about local environmental issues. The fair could consist of various booths that teach the other students in an active manner about various aspects of the problem.

Guest Speakers

Students can arrange to have speakers from a local environmental organization to come to the school.

Unsung Hero Projects

Children need heroes. The problem is that too often the only heroes children have are sports or entertainment figures. Even though these people can provide inspiration, it is important for children to realize that there are heroes in their own community. The goal of this writing project goes beyond simply teaching children writing and research skills. The goal is to provide the students with models who will inspire them to help themselves and to help others. The students will also learn they have some of the same qualities that make others heroes. By learning about people and the events in their community, the children will feel a closer connection to the place in which they live. Each child or group of children will find, interview, and write a biography of someone who is helping the environment in the community.

The first step is to make a chart defining a hero. You can begin with animals. In the library, ask the children to think of an animal that they consider to have heroic qualities. Give them time to look through books for ideas. After 10 or 15 minutes, gather the class to discuss the results. Some examples: musk oxen, because they work together to protect the young; dogs, because they help people; beavers, because they build homes for animals; and chipmunks, because they plan ahead by storing food.

The children watch the news and collect articles of heroes in the news. Discuss the events and how the people were able to make a difference. These newspaper stories will provide more examples and therefore more qualities for the list. The results of their findings will be a basis for making a list of the qualities of a hero.

Compile a final chart listing the qualities of hero. One hero may not have all the qualities, but each one has some combination. Ask the children for the names of some famous people. From the names they suggest, highlight their heroic qualities. Here are some sample qualities of a hero: doesn't think of him or herself, helps without bragging, acts as a role model, helps the community, does something extra in the job or community, gives up something, takes risks, fails but doesn't give up, motivates others, shares, has a vision of what can be done, and is optimistic.

At this point, tell the students that they will be finding a local hero who has some combination of these qualities and writing a biography of that person. They can ask parents, friends, and relatives for suggestions. You may want to have some names in mind for the children who need a suggestion. Any of the local environmental groups will have suggestions.

Find as many picture book biographies as you can. It is worth your time to just study the biography section of the public library. To introduce the activity, show the students the stack of books. Tell them that writers read books for three reasons: for pleasure, to gain information, and to get ideas. Tell the students to read these books as a way to get ideas for writing their own biographies. Read one of the books to the class. Afterward, ask the class what techniques the author used to convey the information.

Some techniques are time sequence—the book begins at childhood and goes to adult; begins with a major event, then from childhood to adult; or begins with adulthood, goes back to childhood, and ends with a major event. Use quotations from the subject or other people, photographs, illustrations with captions, maps, timelines, charts, personal viewpoint (author's opinion), variation in narrator (for example, the subject's pet or first person), background information on the issues involved, descriptions of the setting of the hero's work or life, examples of the subject's work, and newspaper clippings related to the person and his or her work.

Once the students have the idea, give them time to read the books in class. At the end of each session, ask the children what techniques they discovered. Record the ideas on a chart.

Now that the students are familiar with biographies, they will have a good idea of the kind of information needed to write their own biographies. The only step remaining is to gather the information.

Interviewing a Local Hero

Now that the students have selected a subject for their biography, they can find the information needed to write the biography. The primary source of information will be gained from interviews with the subject and someone familiar with the subject. Before going out to interview anyone, the children will need to learn how to conduct an interview.

Modeling a bad interview is a good way to teach children how to conduct a good interview. In front of the students, interview another teacher. During the interview, make several interviewing mistakes:

Come unprepared and late.

Ask yes or no questions only.

Ask questions that are personal or irrelevant.

Begin talking about yourself.

Act bored, as if you are not listening.

Ask questions to which you already know the answers.

Interrupt the answers.

After you have modeled the interview, ask the students what mistakes you made. This will lead to a discussion of the characteristics of a good interview.

Here are some qualities of a good interview: Prepare some questions ahead of time. Be sure not to overemphasize the prepared questions. Wonderful bits of information can be gained by following up on a comment made by the subject. Do not stick to a script so much that important and new information is not followed up on. Pay attention to more than just the spoken answers. Observe the actions of the subject. What were the surroundings of the interview? How does that reflect on the subject's personality? Avoid yes or no questions. Ask questions that prompt thought and provide information. Be on time. Bring whatever materials are needed. Ask permission if using a recording device. Do not go into long stories about yourself. Pay attention and listen. Don't interrupt. No one wants to share a story with someone who is not listening. A silence after a question probably means a good question. Be polite and respectful. Take notes. Check the notes before leaving in case there are any more questions. Find out if there is any other information, such as books, articles, or pictures, that would help. Another important thing to do is to go over the notes and add any information before it is forgotten. This would include the observations the children made.

Make an appointment before the interview. Explain to the subject why he or she is being interviewed. Prepare some questions ahead of time. Some possible questions are: What kind of work are you doing to help others or the environment? What is your educational background? Does your work send a message to others? Tell me about your childhood and the effect it has had on your work. What are your hobbies, interests, and fun activities? Do you have any regrets? Of what accomplishment are you most proud? Who or what inspired you? What goals do you have?

The students should be sure not to limit themselves to these questions. Depending on who the student interviews, the questions will need to be modified. If possible, the children should do some background reading in order to understand the issues being worked on. This will help the students understand about what their hero is talking. It will also help the students to ask more meaningful questions. After the interviews, the students should write the subject a thank you note.

To practice interviewing skills, interview someone in front of the students. Model the techniques discussed earlier. On chart paper, model how to take notes. You can pick a topic and let the students interview you. The students can interview each other. One way is to put the students in pairs and give them each four minutes to find out as much as possible. They can even write biographies of each other as a way to practice and get to know each other. The class can practice by interviewing another teacher. Each student can interview someone at home for more practice.

After practicing and discussing the art of interviewing, the students are ready to interview their hero. To gain more information, the children can also interview someone who knows the hero.

After all the biographies are finished, the students can discuss a culminating activity. Some suggestions are: creating a class library; sending copies to the hero; making reports to the local newspapers, radio stations, and television stations; holding a "Hero Day Party," and designing and presenting awards at a special event. The last step is for the students to begin their work to becomes heroes themselves.

School Ground Projects

Adopt a Street

Your group can pick an outdoor place that needs to be cleaned up. The children can clean it up and keep it clean. Enlisting the support of your local government can bring the children some recognition. Many towns have official "Adopt a Highway" programs, which may also include parks, schoolyards, and city streets.

Tree Planting

The act of planting a tree is one of the simplest but most satisfying acts one can do to help the environment. Children are involved in a concrete action that makes a difference. Students have a real responsibility to care for the tree. Planting a tree is an act that students will look back upon with a sense of accomplishment because they will see the results year after year.

There are many places to obtain seeds or seedlings. Local nurseries may be interested in donating trees. The State Department of Environmental Protections may have programs to supply trees for free. The following organizations have seeds and seedlings for a small donation. The trees come with education packets.

Trees for Life, 1103 Jefferson Street, Wichita, KS 67203

National Arbor Day Foundation, 100 Arbor Avenue, Nebraska City, NE 68410

Jewish National Fund, 114 East 32nd Street, New York, NY 10021

Trees can be planted almost anytime, but there are tree planting holidays that can be tied into a tree planting day.

In 1870, J. Sterling Morton called for a campaign for tree planting. By 1894, the idea of a tree planting day, known as Arbor Day, spread to every state.

Tu Bi'shevat (The New Year of Trees)

This Jewish holiday celebrates tree planting both in Israel and the United States. The holiday originates from the practice of counting the age of trees before they could be harvested. Today, the holiday is celebrated with food from trees and tree plantings in Israel. The holiday is celebrated on the 15th day of Shevat, which is usually in February.

Wilderness Areas

Find an area on the school grounds and create a nature preserve no matter how small. By setting aside an area of lawn and letting it grow wild, children can create mini-wilderness areas. A variety of plants will grow that animals will enjoy. To make the habitat even more beneficial, add some brush piles. Brush piles are simply piles of old branches, logs, and brush. It provides small mammals and birds a crucial part of their habitat: shelter. Old Christmas trees work great too.

A telephone call to a local nursery can help you find some native plants that grow well in your area, which may provide food for birds. By planting native plants adapted to the local environment, children conserve water, create wildlife habitat, and have a chance to grow a garden.

Compost Pile

Leaves and vegetable scraps can be easily composted and used to improve soil. A compost bin is easy to make with chicken wire and wood. Throw in a few leaves to get things started. Then simply add food waste, grass clippings, and other vegetable matter. Turn the pile on occasion and keep moist. The compost will decay into soil that can be used for planting flowers, vegetables, or simply returned to the earth.

Bird Houses

Bird houses can be made from scrap wood or purchased at any garden store. Providing shelter will help increase song bird populations and give your child a chance to watch a bird's life cycle. Even one bird house makes a difference. It is even better to build a bird house trail, then place them around the schoolyard, park, or nearby natural area. The bird house trail can be done in conjunction with other habitat improvement projects.

Inside the School

There are many possible projects within the walls of the school. Children can look into energy conservation issues, food waste, and paper use. Like other local issues, the children should first document the problem, develop a solution, and go the to an administrator or whoever else has the power to make things happen.

Personal Contract

Make a list of personal actions people can take to improve the environment. From the list, each child can pick one action and sign a personal contract promising to take that action. You can create a contract by making a certificate:

I _____ promise to

_____

in order to help preserve the local habitat of _____

_____.

signed _____

witness _____

I make two copies of each contract. The child gets one to take home; the other one is put in an envelope and addressed by each child to their current home. Collect the letters and save them to be sent later as a reminder.

Field Guides for Children

Golden Nature Guides series. New York: Golden Press. This series includes guides on birds, flowers, trees, spiders, and mammals. The Golden guides feature pictures, range maps, and simple text of common plants and animals.

Peterson First Guides. Boston: Houghton Mifflin, 1987. These are great guides and easily used by children and adults. Most of the species readers are likely to find can be identified in these books. The simple arrangement and keys will help guide the user to a correct identification.

Stokes, Donald W., and Lillian Stokes. *Stokes Nature Guides* series. Boston: Little, Brown. This series includes books on insects, birds, animal tracking, reptiles, and amphibians, and wildflowers, and are a good source of information on common animals and plants. The books provide interesting natural history information on the kinds of wildlife and plant life most often seen.

Acorn Naturalists are a great source for buying field guides. They also have many other environmental education tools that will help you in developing a program. Call (800) 422-8886 for a catalog.

Braus, Judy A., and David Wood. *Environmental Education in the Schools: Creating a Program That Works.* Peace Corps Information and Collection, 1993.

Bromley, Karen. *Journaling: Engagements in Reading, Writing, and Thinking.* New York: Scholastic, 1993. ISBN 0-590-49478-3.

Cerullo, Mary M. *Reading the Environment, Children's Literature in the Science Classroom.* Portsmouth, NH: Heinemann, 1997. ISBN 0-435-08383-X.

Cohen, Dorothy H. *The Learning Child.* New York: Schocken Books, 1972. ISBN 0-8052-0856-9.

Criswell, Susie Gwen. *Nature with Art: Classroom and Outdoor Art Activities with Natural History.* Englewood Cliffs, NJ: Prentice-Hall, 1986. ISBN 0-13-610304-9.

Hay, John. *A Beginner's Faith in Things Unseen.* Boston: Beacon Press, 1995. ISBN 0-80708532-4.

Horning, Kathleen. *From Cover to Cover: Evaluating Books for Children.* New York: HarperCollins, 1997. ISBN 0-06-024519-0.

Louv, Richard. *Childhood's Future.* Boston: Houghton Mifflin, 1990. ISBN 0-395-464

Murray, John A. *The Sierra Club Nature Writing Handbook.* San Francisco: Sierra Club, 1995. ISBN 0-87156-436-X.

Oppenheim, Joanne, Barbara Brenner, and Betty D. Boegehold. *Choosing Books for Kids.* New York: Ballantine Books, 1986. ISBN 0-345-3268-3.

Orion Society. *An Annotated Bibliography of Children's Picture Books with Nature Themes.* New York: The Orion Society, 1993.

Sinclair, Patti K. *E for Environment: An Annotated Bibliography of Children's Books with Environmental Themes.* New Providence, NJ: R. R. Bowker, 1992. ISBN 0-8352-3028-7.

Snyder, Gary. *A Place in Space, Ethics, Aesthetics, and Watersheds.* Washington, DC: Counterpoint, 1995. ISBN 1-887178-02-3.

Tall, Deborah. *From Where We Stand: Recovering a Sense of Place.* Baltimore, MD: The Johns Hopkins University Press, 1996. ISBN 0-8018-5422-9.

Thoreau, Henry David. "Walking." In *Civil Disobedience, and Other Essays.* New York: Dover, 1993. ISBN 0-486-27563-9.

Trelesase, Jim. *The New Read-Aloud Handbook.* New York: Penguin Books, 1989. ISBN 0-14-046-881-1.

Wilson, Edward. *Biophilia: The Human Bond with Other Species.* Cambridge, MA: Harvard University Press, 1984. ISBN 0-674-07441-6.

About the Author

Dan Kriesberg's interest in the outdoors began when he was a child, exploring the woods around his home. He has worked as a naturalist, an elementary science teacher, and is currently teaching fourth grade at the Locust Valley Intermediate School in Locust Valley, New York. His community-based environmental education program is now in its fourth year. He has written articles for numerous educational magazines.

Dan and his wife, Karen, a second grade teacher, have two children, Zachary and Scott Walden. Dan spends much of his time hiking in the woods and writing.

from **Teacher Ideas Press**

CLOSE ENCOUNTERS WITH DEADLY DANGERS: Riveting Reads and Classroom Ideas
Kendall Haven

Predators and prey of the animal kingdom hunt, fight, and survive in these spine-tingling accounts that will enthrall your students. Fifteen action-packed tales are filled with accurate scientific information on many of the world's ecosystems and their inhabitants, including lions, anacondas, and sharks. Suggestions for activities and research follow each story. **Grades 4–8.**
xv, 149p. 6x9 paper ISBN 1-56308-653-0

CULTIVATING A CHILD'S IMAGINATION THROUGH GARDENING
Nancy Allen Jurenka and Rosanne J. Blass

Each of these 45 lessons focuses on a specific book about gardening and offers related activities such as reading, writing, poetry, word play, music, dancing, dramatics, and other activities to enhance creativity and build literacy skills. A great companion to *Beyond the Bean Seed.* **Grades K–6.**
xiv, 143p. 8½x11 paper ISBN 1-56308-452-X

NATURE AT YOUR DOORSTEP: Real World Investigations for Primary Students
Carole G. Basile, Fred Collins, Jennifer Gillespie-Malone

Share the wonder of nature with young learners while building their scientific knowledge and skills! Engaging activities guide learning about birds, habitats, biodiversity, and other topics into the study of all major areas of ecology. Students can perform the simple projects right in their own backyards (or school yard)! **Grades K–3.**
xxvi, 161p. 8½x11 paper ISBN 1-56308-455-4

LEARNING FROM THE LAND: Teaching Ecology Through Stories and Activities
Brian "Fox" Ellis

Breathe life into the dry bones of geologic history! An integrative approach of hands-on science and creative writing lesson plans helps students explore ideas and reflect the depth with which they understand them. Step-by-step lesson plans give you the confidence and skills to take your classes outdoors. **All levels.**
xxviii, 145p. 8½x11 paper ISBN 1-56308-563-1

EXPLORATIONS IN BACKYARD BIOLOGY: Drawing on Nature in the Classroom, Grades 4–6
R. Gary Raham

Discover life science adventures in your own backyard (or school yard)! Exciting classroom and field activities give students the opportunity for hands-on exploration. Using drawing and writing skills, they record their experiences in a Naturalist's Notebook, which encourages further discoveries. **Grades 4–6.**
xix, 204p. 8½x11 paper ISBN 1-56308-254-3

For a FREE catalog or to place an order, please contact:

Teacher Ideas Press
Dept. B993 · P.O. Box 6633 · Englewood, CO 80155-6633
1-800-237-6124, ext. 1 · Fax: 303-220-8843 · E-mail: lu-books@lu.com

 Check out the TIP Web site!
www.lu.com/tip

DATE DUE

OCT 8			
JUN 0 9 2001 IL#82/1687MEA			
OCT 2 4 2001			
MAY 0 7 2006			
APR 1 6 2007			
GAYLORD			PRINTED IN U.S.A.